Buying a Home in *South Africa*

A Survival Handbook

by

Graeme Chesters

SURVIVAL BOOKS • LONDON • ENGLAND

First Edition 2005

Survival Books Limited, 1st Floor,
60 St James's Street, London SW1A 1ZN, United Kingdom
☎ +44 (0)20-7493 4244, ▤ +44 (0)20-7491 0605
✉ info@survivalbooks.net
💻 www.survivalbooks.net
To order books, please refer to page 327.

British Library Cataloguing in Publication Data.
A CIP record for this book is available
from the British Library.
ISBN 1 901130 02 9

Printed and bound in Finland by WS Bookwell Ltd

ACKNOWLEDGEMENTS

My thanks to all those who contributed to the successful publication of this book, in particular the many people who provided information and took the time and trouble to read and comment on the draft versions. I would especially like to thank Joe and Kerry Laredo (editing, proofreading and desktop publishing). I would also like to thank my wife Louise for accompanying me on research trips within South Africa and the many South Africans who offered help and hospitality, particularly Arief in Cape Town and Stefan in Stellenbosch. Finally, thank you to Jim Watson for the cover design, illustrations, cartoons and maps.

Order forms are on page 327.

What Readers & Reviewers

When you buy a model plane for your child, a video recorder, or some new computer gizmo, you get with it a leaflet or booklet pleading 'Read Me First', or bearing large friendly letters or bold type saying 'IMPORTANT - follow the instructions carefully'. This book should be similarly supplied to all those entering France with anything more durable than a 5-day return ticket. It is worth reading even if you are just visiting briefly, or if you have lived here for years and feel totally knowledgeable and secure. But if you need to find out how France works then it is indispensable. Native French people probably have a less thorough understanding of how their country functions. - Where it is most essential, the book is most up to the minute.

Living France

Rarely has a 'survival guide' contained such useful advice. This book dispels doubts for first-time travellers, yet is also useful for seasoned globetrotters - In a word, if you're planning to move to the USA or go there for a long-term stay, then buy this book both for general reading and as a ready-reference.

American Citizens Abroad

It is everything you always wanted to ask but didn't for fear of the contemptuous put down - The best English-language guide - Its pages are stuffed with practical information on everyday subjects and are designed to complement the traditional guidebook.

Swiss News

A complete revelation to me - I found it both enlightening and interesting, not to mention amusing.

Carole Clark

Let's say it at once. David Hampshire's ***Living and Working in France*** is the best handbook ever produced for visitors and foreign residents in this country; indeed, my discussion with locals showed that it has much to teach even those born and bred in l'Hexagone. - It is Hampshire's meticulous detail which lifts his work way beyond the range of other books with similar titles. Often you think of a supplementary question and search for the answer in vain. With Hampshire this is rarely the case. - He writes with great clarity (and gives French equivalents of all key terms), a touch of humour and a ready eye for the odd (and often illuminating) fact. - This book is absolutely indispensable.

The Riviera Reporter

A mine of information - I may have avoided some embarrassments and frights if I had read it prior to my first Swiss encounters - Deserves an honoured place on any newcomer's bookshelf.

English Teachers Association, Switzerland

Have Said About Survival Books

What a great work, wealth of useful information, well-balanced wording and accuracy in details. My compliments!

Thomas Müller

This handbook has all the practical information one needs to set up home in the UK – The sheer volume of information is almost daunting – Highly recommended for anyone moving to the UK.

American Citizens Abroad

A very good book which has answered so many questions and even some I hadn't thought of – I would certainly recommend it.

Brian Fairman

We would like to congratulate you on this work: it is really super! We hand it out to our expatriates and they read it with great interest and pleasure.

ICI (Switzerland) AG

Covers just about all the things you want to know on the subject – In answer to the desert island question about the one how-to book on France, this book would be it – Almost 500 pages of solid accurate reading – This book is about enjoyment as much as survival.

The Recorder

It's so funny – I love it and definitely need a copy of my own – Thanks very much for having written such a humorous and helpful book.

Heidi Guiliani

A must for all foreigners coming to Switzerland.

Antoinette O'Donoghue

A comprehensive guide to all things French, written in a highly readable and amusing style, for anyone planning to live, work or retire in France.

The Times

A concise, thorough account of the DOs and DON'Ts for a foreigner in Switzerland – Crammed with useful information and lightened with humorous quips which make the facts more readable.

American Citizens Abroad

Covers every conceivable question that may be asked concerning everyday life – I know of no other book that could take the place of this one.

France in Print

Hats off to ***Living and Working in Switzerland***!

Ronnie Almeida

General Map

The map below shows the major towns and cities and the principal geographical features of South Africa. Maps of the nine provinces, the road network and the four climatic regions can be found in **Appendix E**.

Contents

THE AUTHOR

Graeme Chesters was born in Cheshire in 1963, finished his education at Bristol University and worked in the City of London for ten years before turning to writing full time. He has written for several newspapers and magazines, as well as producing eight books, including ***How to Avoid Holiday & Travel Disasters***, ***Living & Working in the Gulf States & Saudi Arabia*** and ***The Wines of Spain***. Graeme was based in Spain for several years and writes about subjects ranging from wine to football and travel to television. He is married to Louise, is child-free and lives on the border of Kent and London.

IMPORTANT NOTE

Readers should note that the laws and regulations for buying property in South Africa aren't the same as in other countries and are also liable to change periodically. **I cannot recommend too strongly that you check with an official and reliable source (not always the same) and take expert legal advice before paying any money or signing any legal documents. Don't, however, believe everything you're told or read – even (dare I say it?) herein!**

To help you obtain further information and verify data with official sources, useful addresses and references to other sources of information have been included in most chapters and in **Appendices A**, **B** and **C**. Important points have been emphasised throughout the book in **bold** print, some of which it would be expensive or foolish to disregard. **Ignore them at your peril or cost!** Unless specifically stated, the reference to any company, organisation, product or publication in this book doesn't constitute an endorsement or recommendation.

AUTHOR'S NOTES

- All prices are shown in rand (R), unless otherwise stated, with the equivalent in pounds sterling (at an exchange rate of £1 = R11.5) in brackets. To convert rand to US$, divide by 6 (the exchange rate in November 2004 was US$1 = R6.02). Most prices shown in South Africa are inclusive of VAT at 14 per cent, which is the method used in this book unless otherwise stated. Prices quoted should be taken as estimates only, although they were mostly correct at the time of publication and fortunately don't usually change overnight.
- Times are shown using am for before noon and pm for after noon. All times are local, so you should check the time difference when making international calls.
- His/he/him also means her/she/her (please forgive me ladies). This is done to make life easier for both the reader and (in particular) the author and **isn't** intended to be sexist.
- Warnings and important points are shown in **bold** type.
- The following symbols are used in this book: ☎ (telephone), 📠 (fax), 💻 (Internet) and ✉ (email).
- Lists of **Useful Addresses**, **Further Reading** and **Useful Websites** are contained in **Appendices A, B** and **C** respectively.
- For those unfamiliar with the metric system of weights and measures, imperial conversion tables are included in **Appendix D**.
- Maps of South Africa showing the provinces, major roads and climatic regions are included in **Appendix E**, and a map showing the major cities and geographical features is on page 6.

INTRODUCTION

If you're planning to buy a home in South Africa or even just thinking about it, this is **THE BOOK** for you! Whether you want a farmhouse, cottage or beachside apartment, a holiday or permanent home, this book will help make your dreams come true. The aim of ***Buying a Home in South Africa*** is to provide you with the information necessary to help you choose the most favourable location and the most appropriate home **to satisfy your requirements.** Most importantly, it will help you avoid the pitfalls and risks associated with buying a home in South Africa.

You may already own a home in another country; however, buying a home in South Africa (or in any 'foreign' country) is a different matter altogether. One of the most common mistakes many people make when buying a home abroad is to assume that the laws and purchase procedures are the same as in their home country. **This is almost certainly not true!** Buying property in South Africa is generally safe, particularly when compared with some other countries. However, if you don't follow the rules provided for your protection, a purchase can result in disastrous financial loss, as many people have discovered to their cost.

For many people, buying a home in South Africa has previously been a case of pot luck. However, with a copy of ***Buying a Home in South Africa*** to hand you will have a wealth of priceless information at your fingertips – information derived from a variety of sources, both official and unofficial, not least the experiences of the author, his friends, colleagues and acquaintances. This book doesn't contain all the answers; what it **will** do is reduce the risk of making an expensive mistake that you may bitterly regret later, and help you make informed decisions and calculated judgements, instead of costly mistakes and uneducated guesses – forewarned is forearmed! ***Buying a Home in South Africa* will help you save money and will repay your investment many times over.**

Before buying a home in South Africa you need to ask yourself why you want to buy a home there? Is your primary concern a good investment or do you wish to work or retire there? Where and what can you afford to buy? Do you plan to let your home to offset the running costs? What about property, capital gains and inheritance taxes? ***Buying a Home in South Africa*** will provide answers to these and many other questions. It won't, however, tell you where to live and what to buy, nor, once you've made your decision, whether you will be happy – that part is up to you!

Buying a home in South Africa is a wonderful way to make new friends, broaden your horizons and revitalise your life – and South Africa provides a welcome bolt-hole to recuperate from the stresses and strains of modern life. I trust that this book will help you to avoid the pitfalls and smooth your way to many happy years in your new home in South Africa, secure in the knowledge that you've made the right decision.

Good luck!

Graeme Chesters
November 2004

1.

MAJOR CONSIDERATIONS

Buying a home abroad is not only a major financial commitment but also a decision that can have a huge influence on other aspects of your life, including your health, security and safety, your family relationships and friendships, your lifestyle, your opinions and your outlook. When buying property in South Africa, you aren't simply buying a home, but a lifestyle. You also need to take into consideration any restrictions that might affect your choice of location and type of property, such as whether you will need (or be able) to learn another language, whether you will be able (or permitted) to find work, whether you can adapt to and enjoy the climate, whether you will be able to take your pets with you, and not least, whether you will be able to afford the kind of home (and lifestyle) that you want. In order to ensure that you're making the right move, it's as well to face these and other major considerations before making any irrevocable decisions.

WHY SOUTH AFRICA?

South Africa is one of the most beautiful and diverse countries in the world, with far more than its fair share of ravishing landscapes. It's a country of huge variety, offering something for everyone: magnificent beaches for sun-worshippers, beautiful unspoiled countryside and an abundance of stunning wildlife, for nature-lovers, one of the world's most popular cities (Cape Town), an abundance of mountains and countless miles of coastline for sportspeople, vibrant nightlife for the jet set, fine wines for oenophiles, a range of cuisines for gourmets, rock art stretching back to the dawn of *homo sapiens sapiens* for culture vultures, and tranquillity for the stressed. Few other countries in the world offer such an exhilarating mixture of beauty, culture, history, nature and friendliness, and as a location for a holiday, retirement or permanent home, South Africa has few rivals. South Africans of all racial and cultural backgrounds tend to be open and welcoming, keen to introduce foreigners to their country and share its attractions but also refreshingly realistic and honest about the challenges their country is facing. In addition to offering a wide choice of properties and generally good value, South Africa enjoys a pleasant climate for most of the year, particularly along the coasts.

Despite the many excellent reasons for buying a home in South Africa, it's important not to be under any illusions about what you can expect from a home there. The first and most important question you need to ask yourself is what you want a home in South Africa for? For example, are you seeking a holiday or a retirement home? If you're seeking a second home, will it be used mainly for short or for long stays?

Do you plan to let it to offset some of the mortgage and running costs? How important is the property income? Are you primarily looking for a sound investment? Do you plan to work or start a business in South Africa? Often buyers have a variety of reasons for buying a home in South Africa; for example, many people buy a holiday home with a view to living there permanently or semi-permanently when they retire. If this is the case, there are many more factors to take into account than if you're 'simply' buying a holiday home that you will occupy for only a few weeks per year, when it may be wiser not to buy at all! If, on the other hand, you plan to work or start a business in South Africa, you will be faced with a whole different set of criteria.

Can you really afford to buy a home in South Africa? What of the future? Is your income secure and protected against inflation and currency fluctuations? In the '80s, many foreigners purchased holiday homes abroad by taking out second mortgages on their family homes and stretching their financial resources to the limit. Not surprisingly, when the recession struck in the '90s, many people had their homes repossessed or were forced to sell at a huge loss when they were unable to maintain the mortgage payments.

The property market in South Africa has been buoyant in the early 21st century and property prices have increased annually by the following rates: 2000, 18.9 per cent; 2001, 14.5 per cent; 2002, 14.2 per cent; 2003, 14.5 per cent (compared with average annual inflation of around 5 per cent) and in some cities, fashionable resorts and regions prices have risen much faster than average (see **Cost Of Property** on page 29). Nevertheless, there's no guarantee that this trend will continue.

You shouldn't rely on making a quick profit when buying property in South Africa, as you need to recover the costs associated with buying a home when you sell. You should look upon a property purchase as an investment in your family's future happiness, rather than merely in financial terms.

Unless you know exactly what you're looking for and where, **it's sensible to rent a property for a period until you're more familiar with an area**. As when making any major financial decision, it isn't wise to be in too much of a hurry. Many people make expensive (even catastrophic) errors when buying homes in South Africa, usually because they don't do sufficient research and are too hasty, often setting themselves ridiculous deadlines (such as buying a home during a week's holiday). Not surprisingly, most people wouldn't dream of acting so rashly when buying a property in their home country! It isn't uncommon for buyers to regret their decision after some time and wish they'd purchased a different type of property in a different region - or even in a different country!

> **SURVIVAL TIP**
> **Before deciding to buy a home in South Africa, it's wise to do extensive research (see page 113), study the possible pitfalls (see page 114) and be prepared to rent for a period (see page 120).**

Advantages & Disadvantages

There are both advantages and disadvantages to buying a home in South Africa, although for most people the benefits far outweigh the drawbacks. Among the many advantages are:

- Guaranteed summer sunshine in most areas and a pleasant climate for much of the year in many parts of the country;
- Good value (provided you avoid the most fashionable areas), particularly if you want a country house with a large plot or an urban property in an upcoming part of town;
- The solidity and spaciousness of rural homes;
- Impressive design and a huge variety of architectural styles;
- A buoyant property market;
- Safe purchase procedures (provided you aren't reckless);
- The integrity of (most) licensed estate agents;
- The availability of good food and excellent wines at reasonable prices;
- Good rental possibilities (in many areas);
- Reliable, inexpensive local tradesmen and services;
- Sophisticated transport and telecommunications systems;
- A relaxed, slow pace of life in rural areas;
- The natural splendour of the countryside.

Naturally, there are also a few disadvantages, including:

- The high purchase costs associated with buying property in comparison with some other countries;
- High inflation (currently almost 10 per cent per annum);

- A high crime rate in some urban areas;
- Traffic congestion and pollution in some towns and cities and a high road death rate in the country as a whole;
- Cool, wet, windy winter weather in some regions;
- Overcrowding in popular tourist areas;
- The duration and cost of flights to South Africa from Europe or North America, although prices are coming down.

You should also bear in mind the following pitfalls that await anyone purchasing property abroad:

- Unexpected renovation and restoration costs (if you don't do your homework);
- The risk of overpaying for a home and being unable to sell it and recoup your investment;
- The possibility of over-stretching your finances (e.g. by taking on too large a mortgage);
- The heavy workload associated with owning a large home and garden (although hiring staff is inexpensive in South Africa).

Finally, it is instructive to consider the views of South Africans, particularly those who left the country in the early post-apartheid years (a phenomenon sometimes disparagingly called the 'chicken run'), fearing a breakdown of law and order and a Zimbabwe-style persecution of whites. According to the website Homecoming Revolution (💻 www.homecomingrevolution.co.za), which is a non-government site started by two young South African businesswomen, an increasing number of the South Africans who emigrated during the last decade – many to Australia, Canada, New Zealand, the UK and the US – are returning, disappointed with the weather, the high cost of living, poor public services and a stressful lifestyle in their adopted countries and attracted by a belief in South Africa's bright future.

Some commentators maintain that there was a 'conspiracy' in the '90s to lure South Africa's brightest people abroad, with the country portrayed only in terms of growing crime, AIDS infection and political instability, an impression which some South African expatriates were happy to endorse because it reinforced their decision to leave the country. Rarely did you read about the positives of post-apartheid South Africa: the houses and shopping centres being built in the townships, the fact that one of DaimlerChrysler's most efficient plants is in South Africa, multinationals making higher profits in Africa than in any other continent, and falling interest and inflation rates. But that has changed and in the 21st century South Africa is increasingly being portrayed in a realistic, positive light, with the emphasis firmly on sun, space, bush, beaches, surf, wildlife, clear skies and barbecues (*braais*).

BUYING FOR INVESTMENT

In recent years, South African property has been an excellent investment, particularly in the most sought-after coastal regions, where prices have risen fastest. There are various kinds of property investment. Your home is an investment in that it provides you with rent-free accommodation. It may also yield a return in terms of increased value (a capital gain), although that gain may be difficult to realise unless you trade down or move to another region or country where property is cheaper. Of course, if you buy property other than for your own regular use, e.g. a holiday home, you will be in a position to benefit from a more tangible return on your investment. There are four main categories of investment property:

- A holiday home, which can provide your family and friends with rent-free accommodation while (hopefully) maintaining or increasing its value; you may be able to let it to generate supplementary income.
- A home for your children or relatives, which may increase in value and could also be let when not in use to provide an income.
- A business property, which could be anything from a private home with bed and breakfast (see page 241) or guest accommodation to a shop or office.
- A property purchased purely for investment, which could be a capital investment or provide a regular income, or both. In recent years, many people have invested in property rather than shares or savings to provide an income on their retirement.

A property investment should be considered over the medium to long term, i.e. a minimum of five and preferably 10 to 15 years. Bear in mind that property isn't always 'as safe as houses' and investments can be risky in the short to medium term. You must also take into account income tax if a property is let (see page 213) and property taxes (see page 217). Capital gains tax is charged at normal income tax rates in South Africa and you may be liable for tax on any profit made if the property isn't your main residence (see page 215). You also need to recoup purchase costs of 10 to 12 per cent when you sell (see **Fees** on page 138).

When buying to let, you must ensure that the rent will cover the mortgage (if applicable), running costs and void periods (when the property isn't let). Bear in mind that rental rates and letting seasons vary with the region and town, and an area with high rents and occupancy rates today may not be so fruitful in the future. Gross rental yields (the annual rent as a percentage of a property's value) are from around 5 to 10 per cent per year in most areas (although gross yields of 15 per cent or more are possible) and net yields (after expenses have been deducted) 2 to 3 per cent lower. Yields vary considerably with the region or city and the type of property.

Before deciding to invest in a property, you should ask yourself the following questions:

- Can I afford to tie up capital in the medium to long term, i.e. at least five years?
- How likely is the value of the property to rise during this period and by how much?
- Can I rely on a regular income from my investment? If so, how easy will it be to generate that income, e.g. to find tenants? Will I be able to pay the mortgage if the property is empty and, if so, for how long?
- Am I aware of all the risks involved and how comfortable am I with taking those risks?
- Do I have enough information to make an objective decision?

See also **Mortgages** on page 184, **Property Taxes** on page 217, **Location** on page 92 and **Chapter 9** (Letting).

CLIMATE

South Africa's seasons are the reverse of those of a northern hemisphere country, with summer from November to March and winter from June to August. South Africa is a large country (around 2,000km/1,243mi from north to south and around 1,500km/932mi from west to east), lying between latitude 22° south (a small area of the country lies north of the Tropic of Capricorn) and 35° south (a Mediterranean-type climate latitude). As a result, South Africa has a range of climates, its mountains and the surrounding oceans being important influences on its weather patterns. Johannesburg, for example, lies 1,500km (932mi) north of Cape Town (and therefore closer to the equator), but its higher altitude means that average temperatures are only marginally higher. And because the cold Benguela current flows along the west coast and the warm Agulhas current runs along the east, Durban on the east coast is an average 6°C warmer and receives a massive 16 times more rain than Port Nolloth, which lies at the same latitude on the west coast.

South Africa's tourist authorities like to project an image of a country which enjoys perpetual blue skies, sunshine, fresh air and warmth, but this isn't always the case. For example, Cape Town can be cool, wet and blustery in the winter; Johannesburg, despite being close to the Tropic of Capricorn, lies at 1,752m (5,748ft) above sea-level, and winter days can be distinctly chilly, with frosts at night; Durban, which sells itself as a sub-tropical paradise, can be stiflingly humid and uncomfortable during the summer. Much of South Africa lies at a relatively high altitude (the majority of the inland area is at least 1,000m/3,300ft above sea-level) and, because temperature falls by around 0.5°C/0.9°F for every 100m (330ft) in height, the weather in much of the country is often cooler than its latitude suggests. South Africa broadly has four climatic regions, described below and shown on a map in **Appendix E**.

South-West (Cape Region)

This small south-western region encompasses the area within around 300km (185mi) of Cape Town and has a broadly Mediterranean climate, with warm or hot, dry summers and mild or cool, wet winters. The city of Cape Town receives an annual average of 508mm (20in) of rain spread over 62 days, with 322mm (12.5in) falling on 38 days during the winter months. The warmest months, November to March, have 65mm (2.5in) of rain, falling on 12 days. (By comparison, Los Angeles has 300mm, London 530mm, New York 1,200mm, and Sydney 1,222mm). Cape Town is a sunny city, with nearly six hours per day in the cloudiest month (July) and over 11 in the sunniest (December).

Nevertheless, temperatures in Cape Town are lower than might be expected for its latitude (because of the cold current off South Africa's west coast), rarely rising above the upper twenties Celsius (low- to mid-eighties Fahrenheit) in the summer, and sometimes falling as low as 5°C (41°F) in the winter (although they can also rise to a pleasant 17°C/63°F or more in the coldest months) when winds blow from the frigid South Atlantic. Although summers are usually warm and dry, the weather can be unpredictable, especially when the wind blows, which it sometimes does for days. Winds are common at any time of year but mostly during the summer, when the so-called Cape Doctor blows from the south-east, laying Table Mountain's famous 'tablecloth' – a thick cloud bank that lies along the top of the mountain, particularly in the afternoons. In the early 21st century, the Cape Doctor has been less frequent and powerful than it used to be, possibly a sign of global climate change or a result of the recurring El Niño weather cycle, and periods of warm, sunny winter weather (referred to as the 'secret season') have become increasingly common. Locals and visitors tend to think that the Cape is at its best in spring (September and October) and autumn (April and May), when the weather is pleasantly warm and there's little wind.

North-West

The north-western part of the country has semi-desert and desert climatic patterns. Rainfall is usually low, varying between around 63mm (2.5in) at Port Nolloth on the Atlantic coast (not far south of the Namibian border) and around 357mm (14.1in) at Upington in the north of the region (towards the border with Botswana) and at Oudtshoorn in the south, near the coast. Annual rainfall can be concentrated into short periods: in some years, a quarter or a third of the year's rainfall falls in a few days or even a single day.

Temperature variations (over a 24-hour period) of 16°C (29°F) are a feature of the region, much of which is well away from a moderating maritime influence and with little cloud cover. Night frosts are common, for example at Oudtshoorn between May and August, and at Upington between May and October. Summer daytime temperatures average 30°C to 35°C (86°F to 95°) in inland parts of the region, regularly soaring over 40°C (104°F). Nights are mild or cool. Winter daytime temperatures can rise to the mid-teens Celsius (mid-sixties Fahrenheit), but nights can be very cold.

The north-west coast of South Africa is famous for its mists, which form in the morning, when wet winds blow over the cool Benguela current, and burn off as the sun increases in strength later in the day.

East Coast

Whereas the west coast's temperatures and rainfall are modest because of the cold current flowing along the coast, the climate of the east and part of the south coast is influenced by warm water, with higher temperatures and rainfall. Rainfall decreases from north to south in this region: Durban has annual rainfall of 1,003mm (39.5in), on 89 days, East London has 860mm (33.75in), on 81 days, and Port Elizabeth has 641mm (25.25in), on 74 days. Rainfall intensity is constant throughout the year in the south of the region, whereas Durban in the north sometimes experiences damagingly heavy summer rain. Humidity is high during the summer, especially in the north of the region, where it regularly exceeds 80 per cent.

The south has more sunshine than the north: Port Elizabeth has 2,818 hours per year, East London 2,710 and Durban 2,352. Temperatures fall from north to south, notably at night, but the entire region is frost-free.

The coast of Kwazulu-Natal, lives up to its claim to be the 'tropical province', with warm winters, bath-like seawater and even coral, although the region is actually a fair way south of the Tropic of Capricorn (Durban is at latitude 29.53° south). Summer temperatures are usually only slightly above Cape Town's, but winters are warmer (by around 10°F) and this is many people's favourite season. It's the part of coastal South Africa with the best climate for buyers in search of warm weather throughout the year, although the summer humidity can be draining and unpleasant.

Centre & North-East (Eastern Highveld)

This large region includes the cities of Johannesburg, Bloemfontein, Kimberley, Pretoria and Pietersburg. It has considerably less rainfall than the east coast but much more than the north-western climatic region. Within the Eastern Highveld, rainfall decreases towards the west, where there's an increasingly desert-like climate. Most of the rain falls in the summer, often in the form of violent thunderstorms. The region is unusually sunny, particularly in the winter, which is one its attractions: Johannesburg, for example, receives around nine hours of sunshine per day from May to August. Low humidity is another feature of the region.

Altitude has an important bearing on temperature throughout the region, and lower areas are generally warmer than higher ones. Even at latitudes approaching the Tropic of Capricorn, high altitude can mean low winter temperatures and cool or cold nights for much of the year. There are wide diurnal temperature ranges. Summer temperatures average in the upper twenties to lower thirties Celsius (upper seventies to mid-eighties Fahrenheit), but they can soar much higher (without the draining humidity of the east coast). Daytime winter temperatures are in the mid-to-upper teens Celsius (upper fifties to mid-sixties Fahrenheit), but nights are cold and frosts common, for example in Johannesburg between April and September, and in Bloemfontein between April and October.

Temperatures

The table below gives a summary of average maximum daytime temperatures each month in five major cities (temperatures in Pretoria are similar to those in Johannesburg).

Average Maximum Temperatures (°C)	J	F	M	A	M	J	J	A	S	O	N	D
Cape Town	27	27	26	23	20	19	17	18	19	22	24	26
Durban	27	28	27	26	24	23	22	22	23	24	25	26
Johannesburg	26	26	24	22	19	16	16	20	23	25	25	26
Kimberley	33	31	28	25	21	19	19	22	25	28	30	32
Port Elizabeth	25	26	25	23	22	20	20	20	20	21	22	24

ECONOMY & INFRASTRUCTURE

When you're contemplating buying a property abroad, the financial implications of the purchase are usually one of your main considerations. These include not only the state of the South African economy but also that of your home country (or the country where you earn your income). The state of the economy in your home country (and your assets and job security there) may dictate how much you can afford to spend on the purchase, whether you can maintain your mortgage payments and the upkeep of a property, and how often you can afford to visit South Africa each year. Your home country's economy is also important if you plan to retire to South Africa and will be primarily living on a pension. If you intend to live and work in South Africa, or more importantly plan to run a business, the state of the South African economy will be a major consideration.

South Africa's economy is the major force in all of Africa south of the equator. The agricultural sector is of prime importance and, as well as being almost self-sufficient in food production, South Africa is a major exporter of certain foodstuffs, notably fruit and wine. Sugar, maize, livestock and cereals are other important agricultural products. Mining continues to be the backbone of the industrial sector. South Africa has extensive deposits of many important commodities, including chromium, coal, diamonds, gold, manganese, platinum and vanadium. South Africa is the world's leading producer and exporter of diamonds and gold, and the latter makes up around a third of South Africa's total export income. Oil is the only major mineral that the country lacks. The US, the UK, Germany and Japan are currently South Africa's main trading partners.

Although agriculture and mining continue to be crucial to South Africa's economy, manufacturing and service industries have become increasingly important since the mid-20th century. Manufacturing currently comprises around 20 per cent of the country's economic output and is dominated by metal-based industries, particularly steel and heavy engineering. Financial services and tourism are the principal parts of the service sector, which is set to become a major contributor to South Africa's economy.

After the end of apartheid in the mid-'90s, South African economic development was less than spectacular, as there was a policy of fiscal restraint. Recent government initiatives – including the transfer of economic assets to 'black empowerment entities' – might speed things up, but the economy is currently still sluggish, although expected to pick up from 2004, as the government is looking to increase investment, provide more low-cost services and market the country more imaginatively.

A government report released in late 2003 (*Towards a Ten Year Review*) concluded that South Africa has achieved levels of economic stability 'not seen in the country for 40 years' and that these have lain a solid base for future improvements. A good example of this was the reduction of the budget deficit from 9.5 per cent of gross domestic product (GDP) in 1993 to just over 1 per cent in 2002/03. Similar improvement is now being felt in the level of inflation, which was at almost 10 per cent in 2003 but has fallen significantly in 2004 and is expected to be around 5 per cent in 2005. Since 1994, the economy has grown at an average rate of 2.8 per cent per annum, but lower inflation has slowed growth somewhat (it was just over 2 per cent in 2003).

Unemployment continues to be a major problem (currently over 26 per cent), but at the same time a shortage of skilled workers hinders economic expansion. Some commentators argue that the greatest long-term threat to the workforce is the high level of HIV/AIDS infection in South Africa (see page 45).

On the plus side, South Africa has a sophisticated infrastructure, including modern, efficient transport, with a system of highways, trains and airways which make travel within the country easy and comfortable. Energy is widely available and inexpensive (South Africa supplies half of Africa's electricity and is one of the world's four cheapest producers of electricity, Eskom being one of the world's top five utility companies, by size and sales). The country also has a state-of-the-art telecommunications infrastructure (it's ranked 23rd in telecommunications development in the world, with almost 40 per cent of the telephone lines in the whole of Africa). The costs of transport and telecommunications, however, are high, while the horrendous level of road deaths on South Africa's roads is a major cause of concern (government figures put the annual death toll at around 10,000, but a survey by the Medical Research Council estimated that around 18,000 people were killed in road accidents in 2000). To put this in context, the

UK, with a population a third larger than South Africa's, has around 3,400 road deaths per year.

COST OF PROPERTY

One of the major considerations for anyone contemplating buying a home in South Africa is whether they can afford to buy there and, if so, what kind of home can they afford and where? Foreign buyers have traditionally been attracted by the relatively low cost of property compared with that in many European countries. However, prices have risen considerably in the last few years, particularly in the cities and coastal regions, and property in the most popular areas is no longer as much of a bargain it once was, which can come as a surprise to newcomers. In fact, there are few bargains left, except in remote areas.

Nevertheless, property in South Africa remains good value compared with that in many other countries (sometimes very good value), particularly rural properties with a large plot. A slice of South African sunshine style needn't cost the earth, with the average house price at the end of 2003 estimated by the *Cape Argus* newspaper to be R418,000 (£36,350), although the average price in the desirable areas of the cities and coastal stretches favoured by foreign buyers was considerably higher.

According to the same report, the average price in Cape Town was put at R451,000 (£39,000) and much higher in the best areas of the city. Whereas a modest, detached property in a quiet coastal area two hours' drive north of Cape Town can cost as little as R240,000 (£21,000), you will have to pay a minimum of around R2,170,000 (£190,000) for a similar property in a trendy marina area of the city. And for those with the financial resources the sky's the limit, with large, luxury apartments and houses in the best areas of South Africa costing many millions of rand. For more details of property prices, see **Where To Buy** on page 80 and **Property Prices** 131.

If you're seeking a holiday home and cannot afford to buy one outright, you may wish to investigate a scheme that provides sole occupancy of a property for a number of weeks each year rather than buying a property. Schemes available include part-ownership, leaseback and timesharing (see **Timeshare & Part-Ownership Schemes** on page 152).

Don't rush into any of these schemes without fully researching the market and before you're absolutely clear what you want and what you can realistically expect to get for your money.

COST OF LIVING

No doubt you would like to try to estimate how far your rand will stretch and how much money (if any) you will have left after paying your bills. Anyone planning to live in South Africa, particularly retirees, should take care not to underestimate the cost of living, which has increased considerably in the last decade. South Africa isn't a cheap destination any more, particularly following property price increases in the 21st century and the strengthening of the rand, although there's a huge disparity between the cost and standard of living in the prosperous regions and those in the poor areas: the former is First World, the latter Third World (or, to use the politically-correct terms, the former is Developed World, the latter Developing World). Inflation was currently running at almost 10 per cent in 2003 but it has been significantly reduced and a rate of 5 per cent is expected for 2005.

The cost of living in the popular (with expatriates) parts of South Africa's major cities is much the same as in cities in Australia, France, Germany, the UK and the US. Luxury and quality products are expensive, but wine and spirits are relatively inexpensive, as is dining out, although there are fears that the steep price rises seen in some restaurants and hotels over the last couple of years will deter tourists from visiting South Africa. (An investigation by the Congress of South African Trade Unions, fearful of job losses among its members if visitor numbers decline, identified 40 per cent price increases in 2004 among some businesses in the tourist sector, but these are the exception.)

Food costs slightly less in South Africa than it does in the UK but prices are similar overall to those in most other western European countries, although you may need to modify your diet. A budget of R2,000 to R3,000 (£175 to £260) feeds two adults well for a month, excluding fillet steak, caviar and alcohol (other than a moderate amount of inexpensive beer or wine). On the other hand, it's possible to live frugally in South Africa if you're willing to forego luxuries and 'live off the land'. Shopping for selected 'luxury' items (such as stereo equipment, electrical and electronic goods, computers and photographic equipment) abroad can also yield savings.

Overall, it's difficult to calculate an average cost of living in South Africa, as it depends on an individual's circumstances and lifestyle. A list of the approximate **minimum** monthly major expenses for an average single person, couple and family of four is shown in the table below. If you work in South Africa, you need to deduct the appropriate percentage of your salary for income tax and social security contributions (see **Chapter 7**). The numbers in brackets refer to the notes following the table.

ITEM	MONTHLY COSTS (R)		
	Single	**Couple**	**Family Of Four**
Housing (1)	3,500	4,500	6,000
Food (2)	1,750	2,500	4,000
Utilities (3)	300	400	700
Leisure (4)	800	1,250	2,000
Transport (5)	700	800	1,100
Insurance (6)	400	600	1,000
Clothing	300	600	1,200
Totals	**7,750 (£675)**	**10,650 (£925)**	**16,000 (£1,390)**

1. Rent or mortgage payments for a modern or modernised apartment or house in an average suburb, excluding major cities and other high-cost areas. The properties envisaged are a studio or one-bedroom apartment for a single person, a two-bedroom property for a couple and a three-bedroom property for a family of four.
2. Doesn't include luxuries or expensive alcoholic drinks.
3. Includes electricity, gas, water, telephone, pay (e.g. satellite) TV and heating costs.
4. Includes all entertainment, restaurant meals, sports and holiday expenses, plus newspapers and magazines.
5. Includes running costs for an average family car, plus third party insurance, annual taxes, petrol, servicing and repairs, but excludes depreciation or credit purchase costs.
6. Includes 'voluntary' insurance such as supplementary health insurance, household, third party liability, travel, car breakdown and life insurance.

VISAS

Before making any plans to buy a home in South Africa, you must ensure that you will be permitted to use the property when you wish and for whatever purpose you have in mind. This includes ensuring that you have the required permits and visas. While foreigners are freely permitted to buy property in South Africa, most aren't allowed to remain in the country longer than one or three months per year without an appropriate permit or visa (see below), which may limit your enjoyment of a holiday home.

If there's a possibility that you or a family member will wish to work or live permanently in South Africa, you should ensure that this will be possible before making any plans to buy a home there (see also **Working** on page 41).

The following categories of people **don't** require a visa to travel to South Africa for tourist, business or transit purposes:

- Holders of South African passports (or official travel documents issued in place of a passport);
- Holders of passports from the following countries: Australia, the Republic of Ireland and the United Kingdom, including the British Islands Bailiwick of Guernsey and Jersey, Isle of Man and Virgin Islands, as well as British Overseas Territories, but **not** nationals of British Dependent Territories (Anguilla, Bermuda, British Antarctic Territory, British Indian Ocean Territory, Cayman Islands, Falkland Islands, Gibraltar, Montserrat, Pitcairn, Henderson, Cucie and Oeno Islands, the Sovereign Base of Akrotiri and Dhekelia, and the Turks and Caicos Islands), who **do require a visa**.

Holders of passports from the following countries can visit South Africa for a holiday or business trip (or for transits) of **up to 30 days without a visa**: Antigua and Barbuda, Barbados, Belize, Benin, Bolivia, Cape Verde, Costa Rica, Cyprus (diplomatic and official passport holders can stay up to 90 days for holiday visits), Egypt (only diplomatic and official passport holders for holiday visits), Gabon, Guyana, Hong Kong (only holders of Hong Kong British National Overseas passports or Hong Kong Special Administrative Region passports), Hungary (diplomatic and official passport holders can stay up to 120 days for holiday visits), Jordan, Lesotho, Macau (only holders of Macau Special Administrative Region passports), Malaysia, the Maldives, Mauritius, Morocco (only diplomatic and official passport holders for holiday visits), Namibia, Peru, Poland (diplomatic and official passport holders can stay for holiday visits of up to 90 days), the Seychelles, the Slovak Republic, South Korea, Swaziland, Thailand, Tunisia, (only diplomatic and official passport holders for holiday visits), Turkey, Zambia and Zimbabwe (only government officials, including police officers on cross-border investigations).

Holders of passports from the following countries can visit South Africa for a holiday or business trip (or for transits) of **up to 90 days without a visa**: Andorra, Argentina, Austria, Belgium, Botswana, Brazil, Canada, Chile, the Czech Republic, Denmark, Ecuador, Finland, France,

Germany, Greece, Iceland, Israel, Italy, Jamaica, Japan, Liechtenstein, Luxembourg, Malta, Mexico, Monaco, the Netherlands, New Zealand, Norway, Paraguay, Portugal, Romania (only diplomatic and official passport holders for holiday visits), San Marino, Singapore, Spain, St Vincent & the Grenadines, St Helena, Swaziland, Sweden, Switzerland, Taiwan, Uruguay, the US and Venezuela.

You require a visa if **any** of the following applies:

- You aren't a national of one of the above-mentioned countries;
- You intend to stay in South Africa longer than the permitted exemption period;
- You intend to work or study in South Africa;
- You intend to take part in a sports event;
- Your visit is related to the pursuit of your career;
- You intend to take up permanent residence in South Africa.

The possession of a visa doesn't guarantee you entry into South Africa. It entitles you only to proceed to a South African port of entry, where an immigration officer will check that you satisfy the basic requirements for entry into the country.

Whether or not you need a visa, you require the following in order to be granted entry into South Africa:

- A passport valid long enough to cover the intended period of stay.
- A 'clear and sound mind and body' (whatever that means!) and no criminal record.
- Enough money to support yourself during your stay and to pay for return passage if you don't have a return or onward ticket.

If you come from, journeyed through or disembarked at a country in the yellow fever belt of Africa or South America, you must also have proof of inoculation against the disease. The inoculation only becomes valid ten days after the inoculation and remains valid for ten years.

Visas aren't issued at South African ports of entry and airline officials are obliged to insist on seeing visas before allowing passengers to board aircraft. **If you arrive in South Africa without a visa, the law requires immigration officers to refuse you entry and to put you on a return flight.**

You must therefore apply for a visa at your nearest South African Consulate, Embassy or High Commission (see below). If you cannot go in person, you can post the application, but it must be accompanied by your passport in order to endorse it. If South Africa isn't represented in your home country or a neighbouring country, you may send your application directly to the Department of Home Affairs, Sub-directorate: Visas, Private Bag X114, Pretoria 0001, South Africa (☎ 012-314 8911, 💻 www.home-affairs.gov.za).

You should apply for a visa a minimum of four weeks before your date of departure for South Africa. It takes a minimum of ten days on average to process a visa application but can take much longer. South African visas currently cost R425 (or US$63 or €54), but this is subject to change and you should check the South African Department of Home Affairs website for the current price (💻 www.home-affairs.gov.za/visa_detail.asp).

A visa application form must be completed and signed by each applicant over the age of 18 and by each applicant under the age of 18 who has a valid passport. The form must also be accompanied by the following:

- Your original passport, valid for long enough to cover your stay and with at least one free page;
- Two passport photographs;
- The fee (see above);
- Full details of your intended travel arrangements, including air tickets, accommodation details and documentation indicating your financial resources for the stay.

People under the age of 18 travelling independently of their family must accompany their visa application with certified consent from both parents or guardians, signed before a public notary.

People over 60 must provide proof of medical insurance when applying for visas and this may also be required in other cases.

For further information about visas, contact your nearest South Africa office abroad (Consulate, Embassy or High Commission). There's a selected list in **Appendix A** and a full list on the South African Department of Foreign Affairs website (💻 www.dfa.gov.za/foreign/sa_abroad). You can also make enquiries directly to the authorities in South Africa, at the Department of Home Affairs, Sub-directorate: Visas, Private Bag X114, Pretoria 0001, South Africa (☎ 012-314 8911).

There are various types of visa for South Africa, according to your status, as detailed below.

Visitor's Visas

Visitor's visas are issued to the following people, among others:

- Those visiting for holiday and family visits, on organised study or tourism packages and for sporting activities;
- Spouses or dependent children accompanying visa or temporary residence permit holders (see page 36);
- People who intend to apply for permanent residence.

Additional visa application requirements for the above are:

- Documentation supporting the purpose of the visit;
- Proof of funding for the visit (either a bank statement or a letter from the relevant institution agreeing to provide funding for you).

If you're married to a South African and want to accompany or join your spouse in the country, apply for a visitor's visa and accompany the application with an affidavit 'to join spouse' completed and signed by your spouse. When you arrive in South Africa, you will be issued with a temporary residence permit (see page 36).

If you're engaged to be married to a South African and want to accompany or join your fiancé(e) in the country, apply for a visitor's visa and accompany the application with an affidavit completed and signed by your fiancé(e) that you're to be married within three months. When you arrive in South Africa, your visa will be replaced by a temporary residence permit (see page 36).

Business Visas

Business visas are issued to people visiting South Africa to hold business discussions, attend business meetings, explore investment opportunities, promote commerce, trade or industry, or visit a business enterprise as a shareholder or director. Business visas are also issued to professional photographers and foreign media representatives who intend to cover current events in South Africa for a foreign market. Additional visa application requirements for the above are:

- A letter or letters confirming the business trip from the company or companies being represented, which will meet travel and accommodation expenses;
- A letter or letters confirming the business trip from the South African company or companies being visited. If this cannot be supplied,

supply the names, residential addresses and telephone numbers of the South African companies to be contacted during the visit.

- An itinerary and proof of accommodation booking;
- Proof of funds, e.g. a bank statement.

WORK PERMITS

Owing to the high unemployment rate, permits to work in South Africa are issued to foreigners only when a particular job or type of job cannot be filled by a South African national. There are three types of permit: for employees; for those setting up a business on their own; and for those setting up a partnership. Applications for work permits can be made in your home country or in South Africa; they're initially granted for a maximum of a year but can be extended and they're regarded as a kind of temporary residence permit. More information can be found on the Public Services website (💻 www.southafrica.info/public_services/foreigners/work_seekers/workpermits.htm).

RESIDENCE

South Africa's immigration requirements are subject to change and each application is treated individually, so the following information should be treated only as a guide. The best sources of up-to-date information about South African immigration are your nearest South African Consulate, Embassy or High Commission if you're abroad (see **Appendix A**) or your nearest Department of Home Affairs office if you're in South Africa, or the Department of Home Affairs, Sub-directorate: Permanent Residence, Private Bag X114, Pretoria 0001, South Africa (☎ 012-314 8536).

South African immigration law recognises the need to protect the health, security and employment prospects of South African citizens. The country has a vast supply of unskilled and semi-skilled workers, so that unskilled and semi-skilled workers are rarely accepted as immigrant workers to South Africa. As a general rule, a prospective South African immigrant shouldn't apply for a job for which there are already sufficient potential applicants in South Africa to meet the country's needs.

On the other hand, immigrants who will contribute to South Africa's economy are welcomed, particularly skilled workers of a type for which there's a shortage in South Africa. Entrepreneurs and industrialists who wish to establish businesses in the country are likely to be welcomed with open arms. **In view of the need to create jobs for South Africans,**

prospective immigrants are recommended to demonstrate a serious commitment to devoting their experience, skills and assets to the betterment of themselves and the people of South Africa.

Applications for residence are considered individually on merit by an autonomous statutory body, the Immigrants Selection Board, and its basic criteria are that you should be of good character, be a desirable inhabitant, not be likely to be harmful to the welfare of the country and not engage in an occupation which is already sufficiently practised in the country.

If you comply with these criteria, you can proceed to apply for residence, which is generally done in your country of origin, at your nearest South Africa office (Consulate, Embassy or High Commission) and you must wait for the outcome of the application before going to South Africa. You can apply for some types of residence while in South Africa, at your nearest Home Affairs office, provided that you fulfil at least **one** of the following criteria:

- You're in the country on a valid work permit (see page 36);
- You're married to, or the child of, a South African citizen or permanent resident and have a valid temporary residence permit (see below);
- You're being sponsored for immigration purposes by a blood family member who is permanently and lawfully resident in South Africa, and are in South Africa on a valid temporary residence permit (see below);
- You've been exempted from the requirement to hold a temporary residence permit (see below).

Temporary Residence Permit

Certain categories of person are issued with a temporary residence permit, valid for a year, during which time they must apply for a permanent residence permit. (The temporary permit may be extended if your application isn't processed in time.) There are currently around a dozen categories, some of which are (deliberately?) ill-defined, and applications are treated individually in many cases, although the system is under review. However, the three main categories are:

- Spouses of South African residents who want to join their spouse in the country (see **Spouses & Children** on page 39).
- Fiancé(e)s of South African residents who want to join their fiancé(e) in the country (see **Fiancé(e)s** on page 39).
- Sponsored people (see below).

Permanent Residence

There are various categories of resident (or immigrant), as detailed below. The relevant category is decided by officials of the Department of Home Affairs, which aims to process residence applications within 12 months, although complex applications sometimes take up to 18 months to deal with. Part of the application process is attending an interview with a member of the Department of Home Affairs (if you're applying within South Africa) or the Department of Foreign Affairs (if you're applying outside South Africa). If your application is rejected, the reasons will be supplied in writing, as well as details of your right to appeal against the decision and the time-frame and procedures of an appeal.

Once your residence (or immigration) permit has been granted, you have six months in which to take up permanent residence. Otherwise, your permit will lapse and may be withdrawn. Residence permits can be withdrawn for various reasons, including the following:

- Any information supplied in your application is found to be incorrect.
- You change your occupation within three years of being granted permanent residence without being granted permission to do so by the Department of Home Affairs.
- You obtained your permit on the basis of a marriage undertaken less than two years before the date of issue of the permit, and the marriage is terminated less than two years after this date, unless you can persuade the Department that the marriage wasn't entered into for the purpose of securing permanent residence.

Workers

To qualify for residence as a worker, you must normally meet the following criteria:

- Be aged between 18 and 51;
- Have a permanent offer of employment made by a South African registered company;
- Have been offered a position commensurate with your qualifications and experience.
- Have a statement from your prospective employer stating why a South African citizen or permanent resident cannot fill or be trained to fill the position. Your prospective employer must submit proof (e.g. press clippings of advertisements placed over a period of at least

a month in national newspapers) that the job has been advertised and that no suitable South African has applied, unless it's obvious that no South African would be suited to the post.

- Have registered with the appropriate South African bodies if you're professionally qualified;
- Have paid a non-refundable application fee (R1,520 or US$225 or €190) and have applied for residence abroad

Spouses & Children

Marriage to a South African citizen or permanent resident doesn't automatically guarantee that you will be granted permanent resident status. You will first be considered as a prospective immigrant in your own right, particularly if you have professional qualifications. Only if you don't qualify under another category will you be considered under the category of spouse.

If that's the case, you must submit proof of marriage and your spouse's ability to support you and any dependent children. You can apply from abroad or within South Africa and there's no fee. If you apply within South Africa, you must enter the country on a visitor's visa, with an affidavit 'to join spouse' completed and signed by your husband or wife. When you arrive in South Africa, the visa will be replaced by a temporary residence permit valid for one year. You must apply for permanent residence before this expires or for an extension to your temporary residence permit if your permanent residence isn't finalised in time.

Fiancé(e)s

If you're engaged to a South African citizen or permanent resident and wish to apply for immigration to South Africa, you're first considered as a prospective immigrant in your own right, especially if you have professional qualifications. Only if you don't qualify for immigration under another category will you be considered under the category of fiancé(e).

You must apply for this category abroad and if you choose not to join your South African fiancé(e) and await the outcome of the application abroad, you must deposit a refundable immigration fee. If you choose to join your fiancé(e) and to await the outcome of the application in South Africa, you must deposit a refundable repatriation fee. In both cases, the fee will be refunded on presentation (at a South African Consulate, Embassy or High Commission abroad or a Home Affairs office in South Africa) of a marriage certificate and the original receipt.

If you choose to join your fiancé(e) in South Africa to await the outcome of your application, you must enter South Africa on a visitor's visa. To apply, you will need an affidavit completed and signed by you fiancé(e) that you're to be married within three months. On arrival in South Africa, your visa will be replaced by a temporary residence permit valid for one year. You must apply for permanent residence before this expires or extend your temporary residence permit if your permanent residence isn't finalised in time.

Retired People

If you're retired and financially self-supporting and want to apply for residence in South Africa, you must submit documentary proof of financial assets which are readily transferable to South Africa. When considering your application, the extent of the transferable amount and/or the confirmation of a sufficient ongoing income from abroad (e.g. a pension) will be taken into account when considering your application. You must apply abroad and a non-refundable fee (R1,520 or US$225 or €190) is required.

Financially Independent People

If you wish to apply for residence under this category, you must transfer an amount of at least R1,500,000 (£130,435) to South Africa, of which R700,000 (£60,870) must be invested in the South African economy for a period of three years. After three years, you must prove that this requirement has been met, failing which your immigration permit can be withdrawn. You must also refrain from engaging in employment or starting your own business without the approval of the Department of Home Affairs, and notify the Department of any change of address during the three-year period. You must apply abroad and a non-refundable fee (R1,520 or US$225 or €190) is payable.

Own Business

If you wish to establish a business in South Africa, you must provide evidence that you have sufficient funds to support yourself and your family during the set-up period (which can be three years or more) and must transfer a minimum amount of money (determined by the Immigrants Selection Board) in order to set up the business. A year after establishing it, you must submit the following to the Department of Home Affairs:

- Audited financial statements in order for the viability of the business to be determined;
- Evidence that at least two South African citizens or permanent residents, excluding members of your family, have been and still are employed;
- Evidence that the amount determined by the Immigrants Selection Board has been used for the intended purpose;

Own Business In Partnership Or Co-Operation

If you go into business with others, you must submit evidence to the Department of Home Affairs, a year after entering the venture, that your involvement has resulted in a substantial contribution to the South African economy or the full-time employment of at least two South African citizens or permanent residents, excluding members of your family.

WORKING

Before moving to South Africa to work, you should dispassionately examine your motives and credentials and ask yourself the following questions:

- What kind of work can I realistically expect to find in South Africa?
- Are my qualifications and experience recognised in South Africa?
- Are there any jobs in my profession or trade in the area where I wish to live?
- How good is my English? Unless your English is fluent, you won't be competing on equal terms with many South Africans – you won't anyway, but that's a different matter! Most South African employers aren't interested in employing anyone without, at the very least, an adequate working knowledge of English.

The answers to these questions can be disheartening, but it's better to ask them **before** moving to South Africa than afterwards. While hoping for the best, you should plan for the worst and have a contingency plan and sufficient funds to last until you're established. Many people turn to self-employment or start a business to make a living, although this path is strewn with pitfalls for the newcomer. **Many foreigners don't do sufficient homework before moving to South Africa.** See also **Economy & Infrastructure** on page 27.

LANGUAGE

South Africa has no fewer than 11 official languages, all equal under the law. English ranks only fifth in terms of the number of people who speak it as a first language, but it's the usual language of administration, commerce, the media and politics and is widely spoken in all of South Africa's cities and most towns. The most commonly spoken language is Zulu, followed by Xhosa, Afrikaans, Pedi, English, Tswana, Sotho, Tsonga, Swati, Venda and Ndebele.

It's usual for the black inhabitants of South Africa's cities to speak as many as six languages, while white inhabitants often speak two: English and Afrikaans. Most documentation in South Africa is printed in both these languages, although the vast majority of Afrikaans-speakers also speak good English.

Around 40 per cent of white South Africans are mother-tongue English speakers, but, as is the case with the various 'styles' of English spoken throughout the world, South African English has developed its own accent and characteristics, some due to the influence of Afrikaans. Grammar, spelling and vocabulary usually follow British rather than North American English, as does usage. For example, South Africans invariably refer to a 'lift' rather than an 'elevator', and when refilling the car, ask for 'petrol' not 'gas'. Repetition is sometimes used to emphasise a point. For example, a crowded bar or restaurant is referred to as 'full, full', and a freezing winter day might be 'cold, cold'. South African English also borrows words from Afrikaans and native African tongues, making for an interesting and varied vocabulary. Those wanting to know more are recommended to consult the *Oxford Dictionary of South African English* or visit the Afrikaans Language Museum (☎ 021-872 3441) in Paarl (a town in the Cape Wine Region).

It's still widely believed that Afrikaans is spoken exclusively by descendants of the Dutch settlers in South Africa (members of the Afrikaner tribe), but in fact it's spoken by as many non-white as white South Africans - roughly 3 million of each. Afrikaans developed out of Dutch from the 17th century, when the first settlers arrived, gradually dispensing with the Dutch language's complex grammar and acquiring words from English, French, indigenous African languages and even the languages spoken by East Asian slaves. It was recognised as a descrete language in 1925, having previously been regarded as a dialect of Dutch. Afrikaans is the dominant language in the Western and Northern Cape, while in the Free State it's the language of the media.

With a little 'acclimatisation', Dutch-speakers should be able to understand and communicate with Afrikaans-speakers. For those who wish to learn it, Afrikaans is a phonetic language, words usually being pronounced the way they're spelled (unlike English), and it uses the guttural consonantal sounds of Germanic tongues. The letter 'g' is pronounced 'kh', 'oe' is pronounced 'oo' and 'v' is pronounced 'f'. The numbers from one to ten – *een, twee, drie, vier, vyf, ses, sewe, agt, nege, tien* – and the following words and phrases provide a starting point for people wanting to learn Afrikaans; and you should receive a positive reaction to your efforts, however faltering.

English	**Afrikaans**
Hello	*Hallo*
Good morning	*Goeiemôre*
Good afternoon	*Goeiemiddag*
Good evening	*Goeienaand*
Good night	*Goeienag*
Please	*Asseblief*
Thank you	*Dankie*
Pardon	*Ekskuus*
Yes	*Ja*
No	*Nee*
Do you speak English?	*Praat u Engels?*
I only understand a little Afrikaans	*Ek verstaan net 'n bietjie Afrikaans*

Road signs in South Africa are sometimes only in Afrikaans and the following are among the most common words used:

Afrikaans	**English**
Eerste	First
Geen ingang	No entry
Gevaar	Danger
Ingang	Entry
Links	Left
Lughawe	Airport
Ompad	Detour
Pad	Road
Padwerke voor	Roadworks ahead

Regs	Right
Stadig	Slow
Tweede	Second
Verbode	Forbidden
Versigtig	Carefully

HEALTH

One of the most important aspects of living in South Africa (or anywhere for that matter) is maintaining good health. Although South Africa has what medical authorities regard as one of the healthiest climates in the world, a tradition of playing sports and enjoying an active, outdoor lifestyle, access to plenty of fresh fruit and vegetables, and some of the planet's cleanest air, its people aren't as healthy as might be imagined. South Africa's major public health concerns are HIV/AIDS, smoking-related diseases and tuberculosis (see below), all of which affect the non-white population more than the white; apart from these, the country is relatively free of major health problems, which is a surprise to some people, given Africa's reputation as a continent riven by diseases and other health hazards. Although South Africa's life expectancy statistics can come as a shock to Westerners (in 2003, life expectancy at birth was 46.56 years for the total population), life expectancy for white South Africans is similar to that of most Europeans, Australasians and North Americans thanks to better access to health information, contraception and healthcare, as well as a much lower death rate from murder (the majority of South Africa's many murders are of non-whites by other non-whites, mainly in the townships).

Immunisations aren't currently required or even recommended for those visiting South Africa's major cities and coastal resort areas (although some doctors recommend you to check that your polio and tetanus jabs are up-to-date), unless you've come from an area where yellow fever is endemic (for example, Kenya, Tanzania and the northern half of South America), in which case you need to carry documentary proof that you've been vaccinated. This situation, however, could change and **you're recommended to consult your doctor at least six weeks before travelling to the country to check the current situation**. For those travelling off the beaten track in South Africa for any length of time, some doctors recommend shots against typhoid and a Havrix injection against hepatitis A. Vaccinations against hepatitis B are needed only by those who will be working in healthcare, while a cholera vaccination is both unpleasant and generally ineffective.

HIV/AIDS

South Africa's most pressing health issue (seen as a crisis by many) is the HIV/AIDS epidemic, which has seen a steadily declining life expectancy in the country in recent years. In 2004, it was estimated that 20.1 per cent of the population aged between 15 and 49 was infected, although infection levels among whites are similar to those in Europe and North America. Part of the reason for the severity of the country's HIV/AIDS crisis has been the South African government's slowness even to recognise the problem, let alone try to educate the populace and combat it. HIV/AIDS didn't even become a notifiable disease until 1999, making it impossible to compile infection rates or coordinate treatment policies. Some commentators argue that the best hope for the country seems to be the sterling work of some of the private sector, non-governmental organisations, which are trying to educate the public and help victims.

Perhaps stung by such remarks, the South African government seems at last to be waking up to the situation. At the end of 2003, the government agreed to provide anti-retroviral treatment in the public health sector, and this is now reckoned to be the world's largest AIDS treatment programme. It's likely to cost R12 billion (more than £1 billion) to treat 1.2 million South Africans by 2008 but is expected to save 1.7 million lives between 2003 and 2010. The government also intends to boost the prevention campaign, so that the 40 million South Africans not infected with HIV/AIDS don't join the 4 million plus who are.

Smoking

South Africa also suffers from a fairly high incidence of smoking-related health problems. According to figures released by the World Health Organisation (WHO) 26.5 per cent of adults smoke (the same percentage as the UK), but there's a sharp dichotomy between men and women (42 per cent and 11 per cent respectively). Cigarettes are cheap (around R13/£1.15 for a packet of 20) and discouragement isn't yet widespread, although some bars and restaurants advertise a 'quitline' (☎ 011-720 3145) and an increasing number are becoming entirely non-smoking, as are other public areas, such as shopping centres.

Tuberculosis

In view of the healthy climate, the rate of tuberculosis (TB) in South Africa is much higher than it should be. The country has one of the world's highest rates of infection, more than double that found in other developing countries, and up to 60 times higher than in Western Europe and the US. The explanation is probably a lack of knowledge of the symptoms among the populace, a failure to complete courses of treatment properly and the cramped conditions in the townships where the disease is most common. The early 21st century has seen an increased awareness of the problem and tentative moves to stem the rate of infection.

Malaria

Malaria isn't a risk in most of South Africa and is mainly restricted to parts of the east, particularly the north of Kwazulu-Natal, Limpopo (Northern Province), Mpumalanga and Swaziland; parts of North West province are also at risk. **Consult your doctor about the anti-malarial medication appropriate for the part of South Africa you're visiting and be sure to take the full course.** The highest risk is during the hot, wet months from November to April. No anti-malarial medication is infallible, but it significantly reduces the risk of contracting malaria.

It's also important to take precautions not to be bitten in the first place. Mosquitoes are most active between dusk and dawn, and during those hours you should wear light-coloured clothing (ideally long trousers and a long-sleeved top) and use a mosquito repellent containing DEET; you shouldn't wear aftershave or perfume, because these are thought to attract mosquitoes, and you should sleep under a mosquito net impregnated with permethrin, a mosquito repellent.

Bilharzia

Bilharzia (or bilharziasis or schistosomiasis) is carried by tiny worms in fresh water. The worms enter the body through the skin, eventually burrowing to the bladder or intestines and lodging there to produce a large amount of eggs. Some weeks after the worms enter the system, patients start to run a fever, feel unwell and sometimes experience abdominal pain and blood in the urine. The best way to avoid bilharzia is to stay out of fresh water in regions where it's found (there's no danger in seawater or chlorinated swimming pools), which is most of South Africa. If caught early, the disease is easy to medicate with praziquantel.

Natural Hazards

Africa is famous for the variety and magnificence of its wildlife, and South Africa is no exception. Indeed, flora and (especially) fauna are two of the country's leading tourist attractions. Some of the wildlife is dangerous, however, and certain precautions should be taken to minimise your (already small) chance of becoming a victim.

Sharks

To listen to some people, you'd think that you risk life and limb every time you dip your toe into the ocean off South Africa, while others will tell you that there's no risk at all. Both are wrong. South Africa's oceans host many of the world's shark species, including most of those considered dangerous to humans, but the risk of being attacked is low (provided that you're sensible). The statistics below from the International Shark Attack File (ISAF) show the number of unprovoked shark attacks recorded between 1905 and 2003. (Between 1990 and 2003, there were 63 recorded attacks, of which eight were fatal.)

Territory	Total Attacks	Fatalities	Last Fatality
Natal	89	27	1999
Eastern Cape	77	6	1998
Western Cape	30	7	2003
Other	3	0	Never
Total	**199**	**40**	**2003**

These figures rank South Africa third in the world in the number of shark attacks, behind the US and Australia, although the South African figures should almost certainly be higher because there are thought to have been a lot of unrecorded attacks (usually on non-whites off beaches unprotected by shark nets). They would be higher again were it not for the effective shark nets now found off many of South Africa's most popular bathing beaches (particularly in Kwazulu-Natal, whose warm waters are attractive to bathers, unlike the frigid ocean off the Western Cape). Nevertheless, compared to the number of people entering the water, the number of attacks is tiny.

The best way to avoid becoming a victim is not to swim off un-netted beaches; if you do so, you should avoid swimming at dawn and dusk (when sharks are especially active), avoid dirty water (you will be unable to see sharks approaching) and keep out of the water if you have a bleeding cut or graze (sharks can detect miniscule amounts of blood from several hundred metres).

Snakes

South Africa is home to around 170 species of snake, of which 16 are potentially lethal to humans. These are split into three groups: cobras and mambas, which are front-fanged snakes; adders, boomslangs and vine snakes, which are back-fanged snakes; and spitting snakes, which propel venom at their targets, with great accuracy and over distances of up to several metres.

The likelihood of coming across any snake is small – if the snake detects you first, as it often does, it will do its best to avoid contact – but if you do encounter a snake, slowly move away from it. If you're unsure whether a snake is poisonous or not, play safe and assume that it is. Leave all snakes alone and reduce your risk of being bitten when stepping on one unwittingly by wearing stout shoes or boots and long trousers in areas where snakes might be. Don't poke around under rocks and logs, as these are favourite hiding places. Poisonous sea snakes are sometimes found in South African oceans. You're very unlikely to encounter one in the water, but they're sometimes washed up on the beaches after storms, so never pick up a snake you find on the sand (some species of sea snake are highly venomous).

If you're bitten or sprayed with venom, move slowly and deliberately and seek medical help as soon as possible.

Spiders & Scorpions

There are plenty of spiders and scorpions in South Africa but, like snakes, they do their best to avoid you, and your only real chance of being bitten is to delve under rocks and logs, where they like to hide. If you're unlucky enough to be bitten by a spider or a scorpion, seek immediate medical help.

South Africa's most dangerous spider is the button spider, the region's equivalent of the North American black widow. They have shiny brown or black, spherical bodies (don't most spiders?) and live among rocks or long grass, particularly in dry, semi-desert areas, i.e. away from most day-to-day human activity.

There are also 175 species and sub-species of scorpion in South Africa. The dangerous ones tend to have thin pincers and thick tails, but you should avoid them all: some have venom powerful enough to kill a child or vulnerable adult.

Other Animals

Put aside thoughts that in South Africa you run the risk of being attacked by lions, leopards, cheetahs and other dangerous beasts. You might see them on safari (if you're lucky and visiting at the right time of year) but never in cities, towns or coastal resorts.

Baboons and ostriches can be dangerous and should be treated with caution (the former have canines as long as a lion's, the latter can deliver a fatal kick), while hippos kill more people in Africa than any other animal (except the mosquito). Crocodiles are also a hazard and stay well away from rivers and lakes in areas where they live.

The largest 'animal risk' in South Africa is rabies, which is endemic in the Northern Cape, Limpopo (Northern Province) and Kwazulu-Natal; there have also been outbreaks in other provinces, except the Western Cape. The virus is carried by a number of animals, particularly dogs, and the best way to avoid it is not to approach or pet animals.

Other Health Hazards

The most common health problems for newcomers to South Africa are probably too much sunshine (leading to sunburn and sometimes heat stroke or heat exhaustion) and diarrhoea. The sun is strong in South Africa all year (none of the country is more than around 35° from the equator), even when it's relatively cloudy, and sunscreen (SPF25 to 30 for the first week or two, thereafter nothing lower than SPF15) and a broad-brimmed hat are strongly recommended, as are good-quality sunglasses which protect against UVR as well as UVB.

Most cases of diarrhoea in South Africa are mild and don't last long but are simply the body's reaction to a change in climate, food and water. If, however, the diarrhoea is severe and lasts for longer than 48 hours, consult a doctor as a matter of urgency; you might have contracted a type of dysentery and require antibiotics.

Mention should also be made here of South Africa's horrendous road accident statistics (see page 27): between 10,000 and 18,000 people are killed every year on South Africa's roads and many more are injured, so you should take particular care when using the country's roads, whether as a motorist or as a pedestrian.

Healthcare

Healthcare in South Africa reflects the country's position as a blend of the First and Third Worlds: some public healthcare facilities in rural areas are very basic indeed, while some private facilities (and medical research) are cutting-edge, placing South Africa firmly at the forefront of medical advances. Generally, public facilities tend to be underfunded, bureaucratic, inefficient and hopelessly over-subscribed, whereas many private facilities are excellent - as good as any found in Australasia, Europe and the US.

To find a general practitioner (GP) - i.e. a family doctor - in your area, contact the Health Professions Council of South Africa (☎ 012-338 9300 or 6680, 💻 www.hpcsa.co.za), with which all medical practitioners must be registered.

Public Healthcare

Public hospitals and clinics in South Africa are usually reasonably well equipped and staffed (although not always) but are often very overcrowded with patients and you need to wait for a long time to be seen (by staff who are usually overworked and sometimes indifferent); and you must often pay for treatment. Although the state contributes around 40 per cent of all healthcare expenditure, the public health system has to serve just over 80 per cent of the population. Public health uses around 11 per cent of the government's budget, which is allocated to the nine provinces. The amount of funds they receive and the efficiency of their use varies considerably, and poorer provinces, such as the Eastern Cape, offer a much lower standard of healthcare than richer provinces like Gauteng and the Western Cape.

The South African public sector health system is trying to improve its service. It's now split into 42 health regions and 162 health districts, and a new administrative structure is being developed. Since 1994, over 700 clinics have been built or upgraded, almost 2,300 clinics given new equipment and 125 mobile clinics introduced. There are now over 3,500 clinics in the public sector, offering free healthcare to children under six and to pregnant and breastfeeding women. To alleviate a long-standing shortage of doctors, 450 foreign doctors have been employed, many of them from Cuba. The government has also made it easier for other foreign doctors to practise in South Africa, and newly-qualified South African doctors and chemists now undertake a year of compulsory community service in understaffed hospitals and clinics. Unfortunately, the country still suffers from a medical 'brain drain', with countries like the UK and Canada keen to recruit South African doctors who have a good reputation.

If you're treated at a state hospital in South Africa and are a non-resident, you must pay and South Africa has no reciprocal health agreements with other countries; even citizens and residents often have to pay, the amount depending on your salary and how many dependants you have (hospitals have rating scales to calculate the amount to charge you). Charges are often low (by Western standards), however: for example, pensioners pay only around R13 (£1.13) for a consultation, medicine and in some cases tests. The maximum charge (for top income earners) is R55 (£4.78) for a consultation, although you must pay extra for medicine and tests. Top-earning patients pay R484.90 (£42.15) per day for hospital stays, excluding medicine and theatre costs. Specialist treatment is available at state hospitals, but waiting lists can be very long and it's recommended to opt for private treatment if you can afford it (see below).

Private Healthcare

Despite these attempts to improve the public system, it's still inadequate, and **all visitors, temporary residents and permanent residents in South Africa are strongly recommended to have comprehensive medical insurance to pay for private healthcare**. Private hospitals and clinics are a much better choice for those who can afford them, and the costs are rather lower than in many western countries, particularly the US. Around 18 per cent of South Africa's population are members of medical schemes that give them access to private healthcare, and the number of private hospitals is growing quickly: in 1997 there were 161, by 2004 there were 200.

Two of the largest private healthcare providers are Netcare (💻 www.netcare.co.za), with around 43 hospitals and 18 day clinics throughout South Africa, and Medi-clinic (💻 www.mediclinic.co.za), which has around 35 hospitals.

Your insurance should include cover for private 'rapid response' emergency services, the private equivalent of ambulances. The state ambulance system is severely stretched, partly because of South Africa's high rate of road accidents. The largest private rapid response company is Netcare 911, which has the biggest fleet of response vehicles (cars, ambulances, helicopters and fixed wing aircraft) and paramedics in the country. For more information go to the Netcare website (💻 www.netcare911.co.za).

In the medium to long term, the government intends to introduce a social insurance policy, which will require all employees to have health insurance. The insurers, however, fear that they will be forced to insure large numbers of low-income earners and are lobbying for a subsidised national health scheme.

Homeopathic & Traditional Medicine

People in search of alternative healthcare are well served in South Africa, where there are plenty of homeopaths, acupuncturists, sound healers, iridologists and other practitioners. Health food shops are often a useful source of information about practitioners in your area. For more information about homeopaths, contact the Homeopathic Association of South Africa (☎ 012-333 1828/4920).

South Africa also has an estimated 200,000 traditional healers (*sangomas*), who use a combination of plant and animal remedies in their potions, known as *moti*. They also incorporate a spiritual element into the treatment and use divination, employing bones to communicate with the ancestors about cures. Although this might seem like mumbo-jumbo to some, there are attempts in South Africa to integrate elements of western and traditional medicine, and research is being undertaken into the efficacy of some traditional medicines to cure malaria and tuberculosis (and it shouldn't be forgotten that plenty of western medicines are derived from animals and plants). In September 2004, legislation was introduced to license traditional healers.

PETS

If you plan to take a pet to South Africa, it's important to check the latest regulations. Make sure you have the correct papers, not only for South Africa but also for any countries you stop in to reach South Africa. Particular consideration must be given before exporting a pet from a country with strict quarantine regulations, such as the UK. If you need to return prematurely with a pet to a country with strict quarantine laws, even after a few hours in South Africa, your pet must go into quarantine, e.g. for six months in the UK.

Dogs from the following countries aren't currently required to be quarantined: Australia, Belgium, Canada, Denmark, Finland, France, Germany, Ireland, Italy, the Netherlands, New Zealand, Norway, Spain, Sweden, the UK and the US. Dogs from most other countries must spend 30 days in quarantine on arrival in South Africa; there's currently no quarantine requirement for cats. The import of cattle, goats, horses, sheep and other animals requires a 'Livestock Improvement Permit', which must be obtained from The Directorate Veterinary Services, Sub-directorate Import Export Control in Pretoria (☎ 012-319 7438/7640).

In order to import animals and animal products into South Africa, you must complete an application form, obtainable from the Permit Office, Room G52, Delpen Building, c/o Annie Botha and Union Street, Pretoria, South Africa (☎ 12-319 7414/5 or 12-319 7514), and post or fax it to The Director, Animal Health, Import Export Control, Private Bag X138, Pretoria 0001, South Africa (🖷 012-329 8292). A Veterinary Import Permit will be issued and sent to you after payment of a fee (currently R90/£7.82 but the amount increases frequently, so you should check the latest figure), which must be deposited in the following bank account:

Name of Bank:	Standard Bank of South Africa
Branch No:	010845
Name of Branch:	Arcadia
Account No:	011219556
Name of Account Holder:	National Department of Agriculture

Enter your full name under 'Reference'. Note that you're responsible for any bank charges, whether in South Africa or elsewhere.

A Veterinary Health Certificate is sent to you along with the Veterinary Import Permit. The former needs to be completed, in English, by a veterinarian authorised to do so by the Veterinary Administration of the exporting country, within ten days of departure of the animal to South Africa. When quarantine is required (see above), you must contact the Quarantine Officer at the port of entry: Cape Town (☎ 021-551 2050); Durban (☎ 031-368 6011); Johannesburg (☎ 011-973 2827).

Dogs and cats imported into South Africa should be booked as 'manifested cargo' not as 'excess baggage, and they must be older than eight weeks. The following must be presented to the South African Veterinary Import Control Officer at the port of entry:

- The original Veterinary Import Permit;
- The original Veterinary Health Certificate;
- Any other documentation specified, e.g. an indemnity declaration or a rabies vaccination certificate (currently not required for dogs coming from Australia, New Zealand or the UK).

For further information, contact The Directorate Veterinary Services, Sub-directorate Import Export Control in Pretoria (☎ 012-319 7514).

There are a number of diseases and dangers for pets in South Africa that aren't found in most European countries, including the fatal leishmaniasis (also called Mediterranean or sandfly disease), which can be prevented by using sprays or collars.

Obtain advice about this and other diseases from a veterinary surgeon on arrival in South Africa. In areas where there are poisonous snakes, some owners keep anti-venom in their refrigerator (which must be changed annually). Note, however, that this shouldn't be used on humans. Health insurance for pets is available from a number of insurance companies and it's wise to have third party insurance in case your pet bites someone or causes an accident.

Further information about pet-related matters can be obtained from *Animal Talk,* which describes itself as South Africa's favourite family pet magazine (💻 www.animaltalk.co.za) and the SPCA of South Africa, the national council for the prevention of cruelty to animals (💻 http://home.global.co.za/~spca).

NUDIST BEACH
PENGUINS ONLY

2.

THE BEST PLACE TO LIVE

Having decided to buy a home in South Africa, you must choose the region and what sort of home to buy. You may be fortunate and buy the first property you see without doing any homework and live happily ever after. However, a successful purchase is much more likely if you thoroughly investigate the towns and communities in your chosen area, and compare the types and prices of properties and their relative values. It's a lucky person who gets his choice absolutely right first time; there's a much better chance if you do your homework thoroughly.

SURVIVAL TIP
If you're unsure about where and what to buy, the best decision is usually to rent for a period (see page 120).

When assessing a location, take into account its popularity, which will greatly affect prices. Instead of Cape Town, for example, where prices have been soaring, you might consider the coastal Western Cape to the north of the city, the Winelands, the Garden Route, the Eastern Cape (near the cities of Port Elizabeth and East London) or the Hyacinth coast to the south of Durban - all beautiful regions, but mainly without Cape Town's inflated prices. If you're buying a holiday home, consider also the accessibility of a region or area from your home country, as well as local transport networks.

The 'best' place to live in South Africa obviously depends on your preferences and it's impossible to specify a best location for everyone. The aim of this chapter is to identify the positive and possible negative aspects of each region in order to help you to choose the part of South Africa that suits you and your family best.

GEOGRAPHY

South Africa occupies the stubby 'foot' of Africa and most of the country lies to the south of the Topic of Capricorn. It stretches from the Limpopo River in the north to Cape Agulhas in the south, and covers 1,223,410km^2 (472,236mi^2), including the Prince Edward Islands, which lie 1,920km (1,193mi) south-east of Cape Town. South Africa is around five times the size of the UK (with only two-thirds of its population), or larger than the US states of California and Texas combined, but it covers less than 5 per cent of the vast continent of Africa. To the north, it borders Namibia, Botswana, Zimbabwe, Mozambique and Swaziland, the small kingdom of Lesotho is surrounded by South African territory, and to the south of South Africa lies ocean stretching to Antarctica.

The country is dominated by an inland plateau, averaging 1,200m (3,937ft) above sea-level and covering over 60 per cent of South Africa; the country's highest peak is Injasuti, rising to 3,400m (11,155ft) above sea level. A coastal plain runs along much of the Atlantic and Indian ocean coasts, varying in width from 60km (37mi) in the west to around 200km (124mi) in the east. The coastline runs for 2,954km (1,835mi), with the west coast bordered by the Atlantic Ocean, the east coast by the Indian Ocean. The west is washed by the cold Benguela current, while the east is washed by the warm Mozambique-Agulhas current. The South African coastline has few natural bays and the only significant natural harbour is at Saldanha Bay in the south-west Cape.

South Africa has a wide variety of terrain, including the desert sands of the Kalahari in the west, the semi-desert Karoo and grasslands in the centre, the sub-tropical valleys and coastal plains of the east, the thornscrub of the north, the gentle hills and fertile valleys of the wine region near Cape Town, and the often-snowy peaks of the Drakensburg range in the east.

The region around Cape Town is famous for its *fynbos* ('fine bush') habitat, consisting of over 8,000 species of often low-lying, evergreen plants, around three-quarters of which are found nowhere else on the planet. The Cape Peninsular, including the rich habitat of the emblematic Table Mountain, is estimated to have more plant species than the whole of the UK. One of the country's symbols is the protea – a family of succulent plants, some with distinctive and impressive flowers, of which there are 82 species in South Africa; 69 of these are found in the coastal region of the Western Cape. Floral glories are also a feature of the more northerly regions of the Western Cape coast and the Namaqualand area of the Northern Cape. After spring rains, both become carpeted with displays of dazzling beauty, stretching as far as the eye can see – one of the country's most arresting sights.

Another distinctive feature of the South African landscape is the Great Karoo (Karoo means 'hard and dry'), an arid area which spreads across parts of the Western Cape and Northern Cape. It covers around a quarter of South Africa and is home to many of the country's sheep. The Little Karoo (or Klein Karoo) is a smaller region of a similar type, lying between the Swartberg and Langeberg ranges.

South Africa is generally a dry country (its average rainfall is half the world average), with permanent rivers confined mainly to parts of the Cape and the slopes of the eastern plateau; even here, some rivers are only seasonal and their size varies with the rainfall. The Orange River is the country's major water course, rising in Lesotho and emptying into the Atlantic after a journey of 1,400km (870mi) and including an impressive waterfall, the Augrabies Falls.

South Africa has the second-highest waterfall in the world, the Tugela Falls in the Drakensburg, which fall 948m (3,110ft), making them a only slightly smaller than the Angel Falls in Venezuela, at 979m (3,212ft). South Africa has no natural lakes of any significance and its aridity partly explains the country's tiny amount of tree cover (the other cause is deforestation, mainly by humans): a mere 1 per cent of its land is covered by indigenous trees, and another 1 per cent by imported ones, mainly pines from Europe and North America and eucalyptus trees from Australia.

PROVINCES

South Africa has nine provinces (see map on page 312), which vary greatly in size, terrain, population and climate (see page 23).

Eastern Cape

The Eastern Cape occupies the south-east of South Africa, covering 169,580km^2 (65,475mi^2), which is 13.9 per cent of the total, and has a population of just over 6 million. It's sandwiched between two glamorous neighbours, the Western Cape and Kwazulu-Natal, and has sometimes been unfairly ignored as a result. But this is a province with a wide range of attractions, including long stretches of unspoiled coastline, immense dunes, an interesting history and culture, varied wildlife and some attractive towns.

The north-west of the province is occupied by part of the Karoo, a beautiful, stark region of semi-desert that covers a lot of central South Africa. A visit to the Karoo's Mountain Zebra National Park is a great way to combine wildlife-watching with an appreciation of the region's arid plains and stark, flat-topped hills. The undoubted highlight of the Karoo Nature Reserve is the deep Valley of Desolation, with stunning rock towers rising from the valley floor.

Around an hour inland from Port Elizabeth are two of the province's better game reserves, Addo Elephant Park and the Shamwari Game Reserve (the latter boasting of being the only one of South Africa's game reserves that's free of malaria all year).

In the north-east of the province is a section of the Drakensberg mountain range (called the 'barrier of spears' by Zulus), marking the transition from 'highveld' (high altitude grassland) to 'lowveld' (low altitude grassland), with spectacular scenery, lakes and waterfalls, offering great walking and fishing country. There are also examples of San rock art, and one of South Africa's prettiest and most complete Victorian villages, Rhodes, is to be found here. Near Rhodes is Tiffendell,

South Africa's only ski resort, but skiing is usually on artificial snow because the real thing tends to melt soon after it has fallen.

North-east of East London is the Wild Coast (formerly Transkei), the poorest part of the province but with a wild, hilly coast that's both very beautiful and a great hazard for shipping, as the number of shipwrecks confirms. The Wild Coast's largest town is Umtata, an impressively ugly place, offering little of interest. But the 60km (37mi) drive from Umtata to Port St Johns on the coast offers spectacular scenery.

Port Elizabeth

Port Elizabeth (also known as PE and the 'Friendly City'), on the far south coast on elegant Algoa Bay and at one end of the Garden Route, is the province's commercial and transport centre. It's South Africa's sixth-largest city, with a population of around 780,000. The town is undergoing extensive development: 20 minutes away is the Coega Project, a massive new harbour complex that will create thousands of jobs and be a catalyst for a great deal of investment in the region. It also has some attractive beaches and a historical centre to compensate for the smokestacks and oil tankers.

Other Towns & Resorts

To the east of Port Elizabeth, on the so-called 'Sunshine Coast', are some resorts with stunning locations, including Kenton-on-Sea (see page 90). The Karoo (see above) is home to Graaff-Reinet, arguably the Eastern Cape's most beautiful town and one of the oldest in South Africa, founded in 1786. The east of the Eastern Cape is its least developed part, with East London the only city and the second-largest in the province (with a population of 425,000, it's South Africa's tenth-largest). It has good connections with the rest of South Africa and some excellent beaches, but not a great deal else of interest.

Inland from East London lies Bisho, the provincial capital, but a place of little interest. Important towns in the province include Aliwah North, which is famous for its hot sulphur springs; Cradock, which is the hub of the Central Karoo; Grahamstown, the so-called City of Saints, with over 40 churches; King William's Town, famous for early settlers and military history; Stutterheim, the centre of the province's forestry industry; and Uitenhage, a centre of vehicle-manufacturing.

Population

The Eastern Cape has a population of 6.3 million (15.5 per cent of the country's total).

Economy

The Eastern Cape contributes 7.6 per cent of the nation's gross domestic product (GDP), but this should increase because the province has been earmarked as a priority for economic development. It isn't mineral rich but has agriculture and forestry. The Langkloof in the south-west is a fertile valley with vast deciduous fruit orchards, while the Karoo is important for sheep farming. The Alexandria-Grahamstown area produces pineapples, chicory and dairy products; tea and coffee are grown at Magua; and cattle, maize and sorghum are important in the former Transkei area. Port Elizabeth's and East London's economies are based on manufacturing, mainly automotive.

Communications

Port Elizabeth and East London are the transport hubs of the province. Not surprisingly, there's a port at Port Elizabeth and a harbour at East London, and the Eastern Cape is served by four airports: at Port Elizabeth, East London, Umtata and Bulembu.

The N2 road runs along the south-west coast past Port Elizabeth, before heading inland and running the length of the central southern part of the province and into Kwazulu-Natal. The R72 runs along the coast from past Port Elizabeth to East London, the N9 serves the far west of the province, the N10 runs from south to north in the western third and the N6 runs from the coast at East London to the north. A series of R roads serves most of the rest of the province.

Two mainline trains, the Amatola from East London and the Algoa from Port Elizabeth, connect the province with Johannesburg and Pretoria. Other services run to Bloemfontein and Cape Town, and the province has an extensive bus service, particularly along the N10 and N6.

Property

The coast of the Eastern Cape - particularly along the so-called Garden Route - is one of the most popular areas for foreign buyers (see **South Coast** on page 87). Figures released by ABSA bank ranked the Eastern Cape fifth out of the nine provinces during the period 2000 to 2003 in terms of average house price, at R278,820 (£24,245).

Free State

The Free State is a landlocked province and the heartland of the Afrikaner tribe - descendants of the original Dutch settlers. (The Free State was formerly known as the Orange Free State but, after the ANC landslide win in the 1994 election, the 'Orange' was dropped because of its associations with Dutch Calvinism and apartheid.) It covers an area of 129,480km² (49,992mi²), which is 10.6 per cent of the country's total.

The Free State consists mainly of a plateau, averaging 1,370m (4,500ft) above sea level, its western third marking the geographical centre of South Africa. The plateau is a rolling prairie, chequered with farmlands and dotted with windmills. Agriculture is important, with seemingly endless fields of maize and sunflowers covering much of the province. The eastern border overlooks the mountain kingdom of Lesotho and contains the Free State's most interesting landscapes and one of its visitor highlights in the Golden Gate Highlands National Park (another part of the Drakensberg range), with beautiful sandstone mountains. The park is noted for its visual splendours, including some of South Africa's best ancient rock art, rather than its wildlife.

Bloemfontein

The capital, Bloemfontein (the 'City of Roses'), which is roughly in the middle of both the province and the country, is South Africa's judicial capital and the province's only large town, although its population is only 333,000. It has a reputation as South Africa's hick capital, but this is undeserved and it's an attractive blend of British, Mediterranean and classical buildings. It was also the birthplace of J.R.R. Tolkein, although there are few reminders of the fact.

Other Towns

Other important towns in the province include Bethlehem, which is the gateway to the Eastern Highlands; Kroonstad, an agricultural, administrative and educational centre; Odendaalsrus, a gold-mining town; Sasolburg, which has a petrol-from-coal industry; and Welkom, the heart of the goldfields.

Population

The Free State has a population of 2.6 million (6.5 per cent of South Africa's total)

Economy

The Free State contributes 6.2 per cent of the country's GDP. Field crops and animal products are important and the province also produces 90 per cent of South Africa's cherry crop, in the Ficksburg district. Soya, sorghum, sunflowers and wheat are grown in the east of the province, while its high-lying areas produce 40 per cent of the country's potatoes. The mining industry is the Free State's biggest employer: 30 per cent of the country's gold comes from the province, and silver and uranium are important. Manufacturing is the second-largest sector, including chemical products (particularly from coal) and agricultural products.

Communications

The Free State has a high-density road network, the main national highway, the N1, passing through the heart of the province. In addition, the N6 and N8 serve the south of the Free State, the N5 and N3 the north-east, and the R59, R34 and R30 the north-west. Bloemfontein airport offers flights to destinations around the country, and trains run from Bloemfontein to Cape Town, Durban, East London, Johannesburg, Port Elizabeth and Pretoria.

Property

According to figures released by ABSA bank, the Free State's average house price during the period 2000 to 2003 was the second lowest of the nine provinces, at R243,865 (£21,200).

Gauteng

Gauteng (meaning 'place of gold') is by far the smallest of the nine provinces, covering a mere 1.4 per cent of the country (17,010km^2/ 6,568mi^2), but it's home to over 18 per cent of the population and is the most densely-populated province in South Africa - colourful, vibrant and polluted.

Gauteng's major attraction is its main cities, Johannesburg and nearby Pretoria (see below), which make it the administrative, commercial and industrial centre of South Africa, accounting for almost 40 per cent of the GDP.

Gauteng lacks spectacular natural attractions but its areas of grassland are broken by impressive rock outcrops called *kopkies*, which have a certain charm; and a small area of the Magaliesberg Mountains is found in the province.

Johannesburg

Johannesburg (sometimes, not always, called Jo'burg by locals) is South Africa's third-largest city, with a population of around 2 million. It owes its origin to gold mining but now displays extremes of wealth and poverty. It's an intriguing city, with an alarming crime rate but reputedly the best infrastructure in Africa. Many visitors escape the city as quickly as possible (often immediately after arriving at the airport), which is a pity, because it has attractions, including an impressive cultural life and some of South Africa's buzziest townships, notably famous Soweto (short for South West Townships), a city in its own right (with a population of 1.5 million it ranks as South Africa's fifth-largest city) and Johannesburg's premier tourist attraction. The home of two Nobel Peace Prize winners (Nelson Mandela and Desmond Tutu), it's South Africa's most extreme township, with wealth and poverty existing side by side and some of the world's worst murder and rape rates. (Foreigners should visit Soweto only on an organised tour, when they're normally safe.)

Pretoria

Around 50km (31mi) north of Johannesburg, and virtually joined to it by building development, lies Pretoria, the country's fourth-largest city, with a population of just over 1.5 million. The capital of South Africa and its administrative centre, Pretoria is a much more traditional, sedate city, with a background as a Boer farming centre. Pretoria is still seen as a stronghold of Afrikaner culture, language and identity, although that reputation is changing and it's becoming more cosmopolitan. The city is famous for its jacaranda trees, which have impressive canopies of purple blossom in the spring; there are said to be 75,000 of them in and around Pretoria.

Other Towns

Other important towns in Gauteng include Benoni (South-Africa's seventh-largest city, with a population of 490,000, and the distribution centre for the surrounding gold-mining area), Boksburg, Brakpan, Germiston, Kempton Park, Krugersdorp and Roodepoort. Vanderbijlpark and Vereeniging (South Africa's eighth-largest city, with a population of around 465,000) are major industrial centres, while Bronkhorstspruit, Heidelberg and Nigel are important agricultural areas.

Population

Tiny Gauteng is home to 18.1 per cent of the population, 7.35 million people, which makes it the country's most densely-populated province.

Economy

The name 'Gauteng' comes from the Sotho word meaning 'place of gold', which is appropriate because much of the province's wealth derives from that metal (it's more accurate to say 'the region's wealth', because the province of Gauteng was created only in 1994), but manufacturing industry is now a far greater income generator, as the price of gold has been low for some time. The finance industry is also significant. Gauteng's agriculture is geared towards providing fresh produce for the province's many cities and towns, particularly dairy produce, fruit, vegetables, meat, eggs and flowers. Maize, groundnuts, sunflowers, cotton and sorghum are also produced.

Communications

Johannesburg has the country's major airport, served by domestic and international flights to and from numerous destinations, and Gauteng has an extensive network of roads, including important national roads converging on Johannesburg and Pretoria. The N1 runs from the south-west corner of the province to Johannesburg in the centre and on to and past Pretoria in the north; the N14 enters from the west, the N4 from the east and the N3 from the south-east. There are also numerous provincial roads (those beginning with the prefix R) serving Gauteng. Trains connect Johannesburg and Pretoria with cities throughout South Africa, as does an extensive bus service.

Property

Wealthy Gauteng has the second highest house prices in South Africa, mainly because of the luxury developments in and around Johannesburg. According to ABSA bank figures, during the period 2000 to 2003, the average house price in Gauteng was the second-highest in the country at R373,720 (£32,500), just under R20,000 (£1,750) lower than in the Western Cape but considerably higher than anywhere else in South Africa.

Kwazulu-Natal

Kwazulu-Natal (sometimes called South Africa's garden province) covers 92,100km^2 (35,560mi^2), which is only 7.6 per cent of the country, but houses over 20 per cent of its population. It offers a variety of attractions (probably more than any of South Africa's other provinces), including Zulu culture (architecture, art, music and dance), big cities, beaches, mountains and wildlife. It's also more politically unstable than any other province, the primarily Zulu political party Inkatha having a history of discord with the ruling ANC party, although there's rarely any public manifestation of unrest and foreign visitors and homebuyers are largely unaffected. The coast has warm water and a pleasant, sub-tropical winter climate (although humidity can be high in summer), and this has been exploited with a 250km (15mi) strip of holiday and retirement homes at Margate, Port Shepstone and Umhlanga Rocks.

Along the northern coast of the province, the Maputaland region borders Mozambique. Maputaland is an intriguing mix of wilderness, wetland and lakes and is one of South Africa's most isolated regions. Coral reefs lie off the coast at Sodwana Bay and the region has the country's best scuba diving and snorkelling.

Kwazulu-Natal's excellent game parks are concentrated in the north of the province, west of Maputaland. Some of them are almost the equal of Kruger (although not in size) and the most famous is probably the Hluhluwe-Umfolozi Park.

The middle of the province, around the Tugela River, was once designated the most English area of South Africa. It's a pretty rather than impressive region, with sugar plantations and polo clubs.

The south-west of the province is occupied by part of the Drakensberg range. As well as being stunningly beautiful, it's a hikers' and fly-fishers' paradise, as well as home to over 600 San rock art sites, comprising over 22,000 individual drawings and paintings, dating back between 8,000 and over 20,000 years.

Durban

The city of Durban, South Africa's second-largest city, with a population of just over 2.7 million, lies in the southern half of this strip and is the province's industrial centre and main harbour. It's the largest port in Africa, one of the world's ten largest harbours and one of the fastest-growing urban areas in the world. Cape Town is by far South Africa's most inviting city for the visitor, but Durban comes a respectable second, offering an interesting blend of Zulu, Indian and white influences, sights, sounds and cuisines. It's also known for its rampant, oversized vegetation.

Other Towns & Resorts

Around 80km (50mi) north-west of Durban lies Pietermaritzburg, the provincial capital and South Africa's ninth-largest city, with a population of around 460,000. It's a multicultural city with a high student population, a good art gallery and some attractive Victorian buildings. Another important town is Richards Bay, a significant coal export harbour, and there are several coastal resorts, including Margate, Port Shepstone and Umhlanga Rocks. In the interior, Eshowe is the centre of the sugar cane and forestry industries, Estcourt of meat processing, Newcastle of steel production and coal mining, and Ladysmith and Richmond of mixed agriculture.

Population

Kwazulu-Natal (sometimes called South Africa's garden province) covers 92,100km^2 (35,560mi^2), which is 7.6 per cent of the country, has a population of 8.4 million (20.7 per cent of the total).

Economy

The province contributes almost 15 per cent of South Africa's GDP. Apart from coal in the north and some heavy minerals around Richards Bay, Kwazulu-Natal lacks mineral resources, but the sugar cane plantations on the Indian Ocean coast are a mainstay of the economy and subtropical fruit and forestry are important. Manufacturing also provides a lot of jobs.

Communications

Kwazulu-Natal has an extensive communications network. International visitors usually arrive at either Durban International Airport or Durban harbour, while the province is also served by local airports, notably at Margate, Pietermaritzburg and Richards Bay.

The major N2 road enters the province in the south and runs two-thirds the length of the coast before veering inland and into Mpumalanga. The N3 runs from Durban to Pietermaritzburg and then to Ladysmith. The R56 and R33 are also important highways through the middle of the province. There are plenty of bus services, but trains are less common.

Property

The coast of Kwazulu-Natal north and south of Durban is one of the most popular areas for foreign property buyers (see **East Coast** on page 91). During the period 2000 to 2003, ABSA bank figures place Kwazulu-Natal as the third most expensive province, with an average house price of R295,060 (£25,650), well behind second placed Gauteng at R373,720 (£32,500).

Limpopo (Northern Province)

Northern Province was officially renamed Limpopo in 2002 but is still commonly referred to by its previous name; in this book it's therefore referred to as Limpopo (Northern Province). The new name derives from the Limpopo River, which separates the province (and South Africa) from Zimbabwe. Limpopo (Northern Province) covers 123,910km² (47,842mi²), which is 10.2 per cent of the country, and is a hot, thorny region bordering Botswana, Zimbabwe and Mozambique. It has been unflatteringly described as South Africa's no-man's-land but in fact is a land of contrasts, including 'bushveld' (rolling grassland with some bush cover), impressive mountains, indigenous forests and modern plantations. Limpopo (Northern Province) also offers Stone Age and Iron Age sites, hot springs and plenty of space. A more positive way of describing the province is as a fine example of untamed Africa. This is best seen in the lowveld to the east, rich in game and home to the famous Kruger National Park, which Limpopo (Northern Province) shares with Mpumalanga (see above).

Limpopo (Northern Province) boasts, among other attractions, three impressive mountain escarpments. The best known is the north-south Drakensberg escarpment (described elsewhere), and in the north (halfway between Pietersburg and the border with Zimbabwe) are the Soutpansberg Mountains, which reach around 1,700m (5,578ft). These mountains attract enough rain for agriculture to flourish in the area, with stands of avocados, bananas, macadamia nuts and mangoes, while to the north are plains that are home to distinctive, statuesque baobab trees. In the south-west of Limpopo (Northern Province) lies the Waterberg, one of South Africa's least known mountain ranges. Its name derives from the fact that it used to harbour lakes and swamps, but these days it's drier, although there are still streams, springs and some wetlands, which attract numerous bird species. For those in search of wildlife the Waterberg is a tranquil alternative to Kruger, although its animal life isn't quite as rich.

East of Pietersburg lies the Letaba, an area of forested mountains and lakes, providing a welcome relief from the veld surrounding it, and the beginning of the Drakensberg escarpment, which runs south into Mpumalanga. It's also an agricultural region, growing avocados, macadamia nuts and tea.

The northern part of Limpopo (Northern Province) is hot, green and rural, resembling Zimbabwe more than South Africa. The major geographical feature is the attractive Soutpansberg Mountains (see above). The pretty town of Louis Trichardt lies in the foothills, in one of South Africa's most picturesque areas.

Pietersburg

Pietersburg, the capital city (population 91,500), lies in the centre of theprovince. It's an administrative and industrial city and the most important place on the N1 road.

Other Towns

Other important provincial towns include Ellisras, Louis Trichardt (see above), Messina (famous for its baobab trees), Nylstroom (known for grape production), Phalaborwa and Thabazimbi (both mining centres), Potgietersrus, Thoyoyandou, Tzaneen (producing tea, forestry products and tropical fruits) and Warmbaths (which has a popular mineral spa).

Population

Limpopo (Northern Province) has a population of 4.9 million (12.2 per cent of the country's total).

Economy

Limpopo (Northern Province) contributes only 3.7 per cent of the nation's GDP, with agriculture an important part of the local economy. Cattle production is significant and, as well as the crops mentioned above, the following are important: coffee, cotton, grapes, maize, peanuts, sunflowers and tomatoes. The province is also rich in minerals, including asbestos, chrome, coal, copper, diamonds, iron ore, phosphates and platinum.

Communications

The Gateway International Airport at Pietersburg, which was opened in 1996, has been developed as a major economic growth project to justify its name and become a gateway to the rest of Africa (which is what the province sees itself as). Similarly, the N1 (sometimes called the Great North Road), which cuts through Limpopo (Northern Province) from south-west to north-east, is South Africa's link with much of the rest of the continent and, in fits and starts, joins Cape Town and Cairo. The other major road is the N11, which runs through the western centre of the province, roughly from north to south. The rest of Limpopo (Northern Province) is served by a fairly extensive network of R roads.

There's a reasonable bus service in the province, but trains are thinner on the ground. There are two main trains from Johannesburg, one calling at Louis Trichardt, the other at Messina, Potgietersrus and Warmbaths.

Property

Limpopo (Northern Province) had the seventh-lowest average house price of the nine provinces during the period 2000 to 2003, according to figures from ABSA bank: R246,490 (£21,435).

Mpumalanga

Mpumalanga (pronounced 'umpumulangu') means 'the land of the rising sun' in Siswati and Zulu, and the province extends east of Gauteng to the borders of Mozambique and Swaziland. It covers 79,490km^2 (30,683mi^2), which is 6.5 per cent of the country, and has a similar percentage of South Africa's population. The province is dominated by the Kruger National Park, which it shares with Limpopo (Northern Province). The Kruger, which occupies most of the eastern area of Mpumalanga, bordering Mozambique, and in total covers an area around the size of Wales or the state of Massachusetts, is one of Africa's best game parks. It's arguably the jewel in the crown of South Africa's tourist industry, with its abundant game: around 150 species of mammals and over 500 of birds. The former include buffalo, cheetah, wild dog, elephant, giraffe, hippo, hyena, impala, leopard, lion, black and white rhino, warthog, wildebeest, zebra and numerous types of antelope. In addition, there are many species of insect, amphibian and reptile.

The province has other interesting geographical features, including an impressive mountain area called the Escarpment (part of the Drakensberg range), which lies to the west of Kruger and offers terrific views, particularly at Blyde River Canyon (the third largest canyon in the world) – justifiably regarded as one of the world's best vistas and a favourite in South African tourist brochures. (The Escarpment is around a four-hour drive east of Johannesburg Airport and a favourite destination for city dwellers wanting to escape the stress of urban life.)

The middle of the province, which skirts the N4 road, is an uninspiring industrial region, surrounding the capital city Nelspruit.

Nelspruit

Nelspruit (population 94,000), which is in the centre of the eastern border area of Mpumalanga, is a traditional Afrikaner town but rapidly becoming more relaxed and racially mixed. It attracts a lot of visitors, both as a business centre and as a southern entry point to the Kruger park. It also boasts the second-largest botanical gardens in South Africa.

Other Towns

Other important towns in the province include Barberton, a gold-mining town; Ermelo, which produces wool; Piet-Retief, known for tropical fruit and sugar; Standerton, which has a large dairy industry; and Witbank, a centre of local coal-mining. Sabie, the centre of the country's agro-forestry industry, lies in the middle of South Africa's largest artificial forest: its rows of pines look odd and dull when set against the surrounding areas of indigenous woodland. North of Sabie is Pilgrim's Rest, a restored gold mining settlement and a reminder of the area's original main industry.

Population

Mpumalanga has a population of around 2.8 million (7 per cent of the country's total).

Economy

Mpumalanga contributes 8.15 per cent of the nation's GDP. The main agricultural products are citrus and tropical fruits, nuts and a variety of vegetables. The province is rich in coal and has the three largest power stations in the southern hemisphere which, unfortunately, have given it the worst air pollution in South Africa. Ngodwana has one of South Africa's largest paper mills, and Middelburg produces steel and vanadium.

Communications

This small province has a reasonable network of roads, good railway connections (particularly from Nelspruit to Johannesburg, Maputo and Pretoria) and several small airports, notably at Hoedspruit, Nelspruit, Phalaborwa and Shukuza. The N2 road enters the province from the south-east and the N17 from the west, and they converge at Ermelo. The N11 runs from north to south, almost through the centre of Mpumalanga. The N4 is the major road in the northern half of the province, running from west to east.

Property

According to figures from ABSA bank, during the period 2000 to 2003, Mpumalanga's average house price was R250,790 (£21,800), placing it sixth out of the nine provinces.

North West

The North West province covers 116,320km^2 (44,911mi^2), which is 9.5 per cent of the total, and stretches west from Gauteng to the Botswana border and the Kalahari. It's one South Africa's most visited provinces on account of its two major attractions: the excellent game viewing in the numerous game reserves and parks (particularly the Pilanesberg National Park and Madikwe Game Reserve) and, in complete contrast, the glitzy entertainment centre of Sun City (see below). Apart from Sun City and the game parks, however, there's little of interest to visitors in the province.

The North West province is known for agriculture, particularly the endless yellow and green fields of sunflowers and maize that cover much of the land; it also has the richest platinum deposits in the world.

The Magaliesberg Mountains lie along its eastern side, home to small resorts and timeshares for nature-seeking inhabitants of Johannesburg, and a welcome relief from the unbroken flatness of most of the province.

In the north-east of the province is Hartbeespoort Dam, known as the 'jewel of the North West province' – a semi-tropical area offering watersports, a floating restaurant and the province's largest outdoor market. Nearby is the Sterkfontein Caves World Heritage Site, home to some of the oldest and richest hominid deposits in the world, giving the region its nickname 'the cradle of mankind'.

Sun City

In the north of the province is the above-mentioned resort of Sun City, a weird – even surreal – development of four hotels, golf courses, parks, casinos, entertainment centres and glitz sitting in the bushveld of northern South Africa. A blend of Las Vegas and Disneyland, Sun City is a gambling and entertainment heaven for some people, a vulgar hell for others. When it was built, around 25 years ago, by famous South African entrepreneur Sol Kerzner, Sun City was one of the few places in the country where gambling was legal and it built its name on that, but gambling has since been legalised throughout the country, and the resort is said to be struggling.

Other Towns & Resorts

The twin towns of Mafikeng and Mmabatho are the capital of the province, often lumped together and called just Mafikeng and with a combined population of 44,000. The city is best-known for the Boer War siege, when Robert Baden-Powell (founder of the scouts) defended the town for 217 days before being relieved by forces from Rhodesia and the south. Today, Mafikeng has a few interesting attractions, particularly its striking collection of contemporary African buildings, incorporating Tswana designs and colours.

The far east of the province is home to the Afrikaner town of Potchefstroom (which, fortunately, is often shortened to 'Potch'), supposedly the most beautiful town in North West, as well as one of the largest - in a province with few large settlements. As well as attractive botanical gardens, it has a university and 14 museums and national monuments. Other important towns in the province include Klerksdorp, Orkney and Stilfontein, which are centres of gold and uranium production.

Population

The North West province has a population of around 3.4 million (8.3 per cent of South Africa's total).

Economy

The North West province contributes just over 5 per cent of the nation's GDP. Mining is crucial to the economy, employing around a quarter of the labour force. Diamonds and gold are significant (the area around Rustenburg and Brits is the largest platinum production area in the world), and there are marble and fluorspar mines. Agriculture is also important, especially maize, sunflowers and groundnuts, while the area around Vryburg has some of the world's largest cattle herds. Other crops include tobacco, citrus fruits, paprika, peppers and cotton.

Communications

The province doesn't have a major airport, but Mafikeng and Sun City have small airstrips offering flights to and from Johannesburg. The province is well served by roads, however. Its major highway is the N12, which runs along the south-east border and on to Johannesburg in neighbouring Gauteng. The R47, R378 and R27 serve the western interior of the province, and the R505, R53 and R30 serve the east. The N4 is the major thoroughfare in the north, the R565 branching off it to Sun City. Trains serve Bloemhof, Klerksdorp and Potchefstroom, with services to Cape Town and Johannesburg.

Property

According to figures released by ABSA bank, during the period 2000 to 2003 the average house price in the North West province was R282,421 (£24,558), the fourth most expensive of the nine provinces.

Northern Cape

The Northern Cape is South Africa's largest province, covering 361,830km^2 (139,702mi^2), which is around a third of the country's area (making it slightly bigger than Germany), yet is has the smallest population – a mere 2.1 per cent of the total. It offers sanctuary from the fast pace and stresses of modern life, being known for its silence, solitude, stunning landscapes and wildlife.

The Northern Cape is home to the Orange River, South Africa's largest waterway and one of the province's major geographical features, assets and attractions; in fact, it has been called the province's lifeblood. The river marks South Africa's border with Namibia to the north and the region around the river is the greenest and most fertile in a province that's dominated by hot, arid land; the river also boasts the world's sixth highest waterfall.

The Northern Cape also boasts fine examples of ancient San rock art, attractive national parks, including Augrabies Falls, Richtersveld and Vaalbos, and, for the environmentally-unfriendly, extensive terrain suitable for 4x4 safaris (in the interior of the province). A ground-breaking development (in 1999) was the establishment of the Kgalagadi ('land of thirst') Transfrontier Park, which joins South Africa's Kalahari Gemsbok National Park with Botswana's Gemsbok National Park to make South Africa's first cross-border reserve. It covers around 38,000km^2 (14,672mi^2) – nearly twice the size of the world-famous Kruger National Park – and is home to a wide variety of wildlife.

Namaqualand is a 48,000km^2 (18,750mi^2) area in the west of the province, its terrain consisting of a scrubby, thorn-bush interior and windy Atlantic coastal sand dunes. The display of flowers in the region, particularly in August and September, is one of South Africa's great natural wonders.

The north of the province contains part of the Kalahari desert, which is oblivious to international boundaries and also stretches across parts of Botswana and Namibia. Its name derives from the native word *kgalagadi* ('place without water'), which sums up its bleached, arid landscapes. It's a starkly beautiful semi-desert region of orange and red sand dunes, dry riverbeds and saltpans.

Kimberley

Kimberley is the provincial capital (population 170,000), a small, plain city in the far east of the province, near the border with the Free State. The city grew on account of local diamond reserves and was at one time the diamond capital of the world, boasting the first electric street lighting in the southern hemisphere and the second in the world (behind New York). Diamonds are still produced in the region but in much smaller quantities than formerly. A visit to the 500-metre-wide, 240-metre-deep 'Big Hole' (now a water-filled excavation), where tens of thousands of workers used to dig for diamonds, is a reminder of the previous scale of the industry.

Other Towns

Other important towns in the province include Upington, which is a centre for the sheep-farming and dried-fruit industries and is surrounded by the most northerly of South Africa's wine-producing regions; Springbok, which is in the middle of Namaqualand flower country; De Aar, the hub of South Africa's railway network; Sutherland, which has the distinction of being the coldest town in the country; and the sheep-farming towns of Carnarvon, Colesberg, Kenhardt and Prieska.

Population

Despite being South Africa's largest province, the Northern Cape has the smallest population - a mere 850,000, which is just 2.1 per cent of the country's total.

Economy

The Northern Cape is one of the poorest provinces, although there are attempts to alleviate its poverty by increasing tourist income. The province contributes just 2 per cent of the nation's GDP, with sheep farming crucial to its economy. Fishing is also being developed, as the Northern Cape shares with the Western Cape the plankton-rich Benguela current off its coast, providing rich fishing grounds which the province has yet to exploit fully. Agriculture is important in parts of the province: the Orange River valley is intensively planted with fruit, while the Vaalharts Irrigation Scheme near Warrenton allows the production of wheat, fruit, peanuts, maize and cotton.

The Northern Cape is also rich in minerals, e.g. diamonds in the area around Kimberley and the largest iron ore deposit in South Africa near Kathu. Copper, asbestos, manganese, fluorspar, semi-precious stones and marble are also mined in the province.

Communications

The Northern Cape has good air connections: there are major airports at Kimberley and Upington, and a smaller airport at Springbok. The province also has a reasonable road network, meaning that even the interior of this vast region is easily accessible from South Africa's major cities, harbours and airports. The N7 runs up the western strip of the province, through Springbok to the border with Namibia; the N14 runs from Springbok in the west to Upington in the north and on to the province's north-east border; the N1 and N12 serve the south-east, the latter running to Kimberley; the N8 and N10 serve the eastern centre, the former linking Kimberley and Upington; and the R27 joins the south-west of the province with Upington. Trains link Kimberley with Bloemfontein, Cape Town, Durban, Johannesburg and Pretoria.

Property

According to figures released by ABSA bank, during the period 2000 to 2003, the Northern Cape had South Africa's lowest average house price, R225,792 (£19,635), around 10 per cent less than the second cheapest province.

Western Cape

The Western Cape (sometimes referred to as the Western Province) occupies the south-west of South Africa, covering an area of 129,386km^2 (49,956mi^2), which is 10.6 per cent of the country, and is sometimes described as South Africa's Mediterranean, with its warm climate, impressive coastline of sandy beaches, rocky promontories and rolling surf, vineyards, rugged inland mountains and green valleys. The Western Cape is the most mountainous province in South Africa and many people find it the most beautiful; its many attractions include the magnificent city of Cape Town, the wine producing region around Stellenbosch, stunning spring flower displays along the west coast, the Winelands (considered to be one of the world's most beautiful wine regions, with Dutch colonial gabled buildings, undulating valleys, craggy mountains and attractive towns, particularly Stellenbosch and Franschoek) and the glories of the Garden Route, which stretches east from the middle of the province's south coast.

Cape Town

Cape Town is the capital of the Western Cape, the largest city in South Africa (population 3.2 million) and the centre of much that is innovative and fashionable in the country. Its central importance to the country is illustrated by its nickname, the 'Mother City', and it's one of South Africa's major tourist draws, offering culture, history, shopping, restaurants, the stunning Table Mountain and other areas of natural beauty, scores of beaches, diverse architecture and vineyards, among many other attractions. Cape Town has become so popular over the last decade, that in global travel industry surveys, it's often bracketed with Barcelona, San Francisco, Sydney and Vancouver as one of the world's most attractive cities to visit and live in.

Other Towns & Resorts

Other important towns in the province include Vredenburg-Saldanha, a significant harbour for iron exports and the fishing industry; Worcester and Stellenbosch in the Winelands; George, which is renowned for timber and vegetables; Oudtshoorn, famous for its ostrich products; and Beaufort West, on the arid, sheep-rearing plains of the Great Karoo.

Cape Peninsula

Cape Town lies at the north of a peninsular around 52km (32mi) from north to south and an average of 10km (6mi) wide, which contains stunning scenery and a wide range of attractions, including, on the west side, the 10km (6mi) Chapman's Peak Drive along a road cut into the coastal mountains and overlooking Chapman's Bay, Hout Bay and the Sentinel; and the Good Hope Nature Reserve at the southern tip.

Little Karoo

Much of the centre of the Western Cape is occupied by the Little Karoo, a vast expanse of semi-desert, which can be surprisingly beautiful. To the south of the Little Karoo is the Overberg (Afrikaans for 'over the mountain'), where the De Hoop Nature Reserve is one of the highlights of the province, boasting a beautiful coastline, statuesque sand dunes, stunning flora and fauna and the chance to spot whales off the coast, particularly between July and September.

Garden Route

East of the Overberg is the famous Garden Route, a narrow strip of coast with beautiful countryside crammed between the mountains and the ocean. It stretches from Slang River near Heidelberg to the Tsitsikamma Forest and Storms River. The best way to enjoy this highlight of the province is by car, but another option is the Outeniqua Choo-Tjoe steam train on the three-hour journey from George to Knysna. The towns of the Garden Route are also attractions, including Mossel Bay (ignore the industrial part seen from the N2) with its watersports, historic buildings and great restaurants; Knysna, with its mountain and lagoon location, and fashionable hotels and shops; and Plettenburg Bay, the so-called 'jewel of the Garden Route', with a stunning coastal position, favourable climate, sports and nature reserves. East of Plettenburg Bay, and stretching into the Eastern Cape, is the Tsitsikamma National Park, a marine and forest reserve with numerous attractions.

North Coast

North of Cape Town stretches remote, windswept Atlantic coast, an area of stark beauty and plenty of outdoor restaurants from which to enjoy the scenery and watch whales. Attractions include the old town of Langebaan, a resort set on a beautiful lagoon, offering bird watching, stunning flora and an intriguing set of human footprints made 120,000 years ago, at the dawn of *homo sapiens sapiens*. A short distance away, Saldanha is the largest natural bay in South Africa, while Paternoster is one of the most beautiful villages on the coast. Inland lies the majestic, beautiful Cederberg mountain range, which provides great views for drivers along the N7, the main road between Cape Town and Namibia. The town of Clanwilliam is an attractive base from which to explore this beautiful region.

Population

The Western Cape's population of around 4 million (9.7 per cent of the country's total) is swelled considerably by numerous holidaymakers from other parts of South Africa and abroad. Culturally, racially and economically it's the least African part of the country, only around 20 per cent of the population being black African; over half of the population is made up of 'coloureds' (people of mixed race). As well as the trendy and prosperous parts of the Western Cape which fill the tourist brochures – the upmarket suburbs of Cape Town, the wine region and the Garden Route – there's plenty of poverty in the province, as the huge squatter camps near Cape Town Airport graphically demonstrate to everybody flying in and out of the city.

Economy

The Western Cape contributes over 14 per cent of the nation's GDP and, although not rich in minerals, the province compensates with agricultural and fishing products. Apples, grapes, olives, peaches and oranges are important crops, while vegetables dominate agriculture in the east of the province. Wheat, ostrich products, sheep, chickens and the breeding of racehorses are significant. Fishing is important too and the province is fortunate that its west coast is washed by the plankton-rich Benguela current, providing one of the world's richest fishing grounds.

Tourism (centred on Cape Town) is an important part of the province's economy and other significant industries include retail, textiles (one of the largest employers in the Western Cape) and publishing, while numerous important petroleum and insurance companies have their national head offices in Cape Town.

Communications

Cape Town's unchallenged status as South Africa's tourism centre has led to the growth of an excellent transport network throughout the Western Cape. Visitors can disembark at Cape Town International Airport or at the Port of Cape Town, in the shadow of Table Mountain. An extensive web of roads connects the city with the rest of the province: the N7 runs out to the west and north-west of the province; the N1 runs through the middle and north-east of the province; and the N2 runs due east of Cape Town.

Intercity express buses connect Cape Town with major centres throughout the country, services being run by various companies, e.g. Greyhound (☎ 418 4312), Intercape (☎ 386 4400) and Translux (☎ 449 3333). The Metro Rail suburban train service connects Cape Town with Stellenbosch and Paarl. Mainline trains, which can be slow, connect Cape Town with Bloemfontein, Durban, Johannesburg, Kimberley, Pietermaritzburg, Port Elizabeth and Pretoria.

Property

The Western Cape - particularly Cape Town and the peninsula to the south - is a major draw for foreigners looking to buy property in South Africa (see below) and consequently has some of the country's highest prices. Until 1995, Gauteng had the most expensive property in South Africa, but over the past decade it has been eclipsed by the Western Cape, where it's estimated that 10 to 15 per cent of property sales - 15,000 to 22,500 per year - are to foreigners.

According to figures released by ABSA bank, during the period 2000 to 2003, the average house price in the Western Cape was R392,500 (£34,130), the highest of the nine provinces.

WHERE TO BUY

Foreigners buy property in all parts of South Africa. For example, people wanting to get away from it all and commune with nature might opt for an isolated farmhouse in the semi-desert Karoo area in the middle of the country or a cottage near one of South Africa's many wildlife parks. However, the great majority of foreigners buy property in the three areas detailed below.

Potential buyers should note that South Africa's planning regulations, although strict in theory (see **Regulations** on page 161), aren't properly enforced in many areas and some property developers, in their eagerness to cash in on the country's booming property market, ignore the rules, banking on the fact that many small municipalities don't have enough staff to police building in their area. It's proving difficult for the government to remedy this situation centrally, as the constitution devolves planning jurisdiction to provinces and municipalities. The result is that a few areas – notably parts of the coast near Cape Town and Durban – are in danger of overdevelopment.

Cape Town

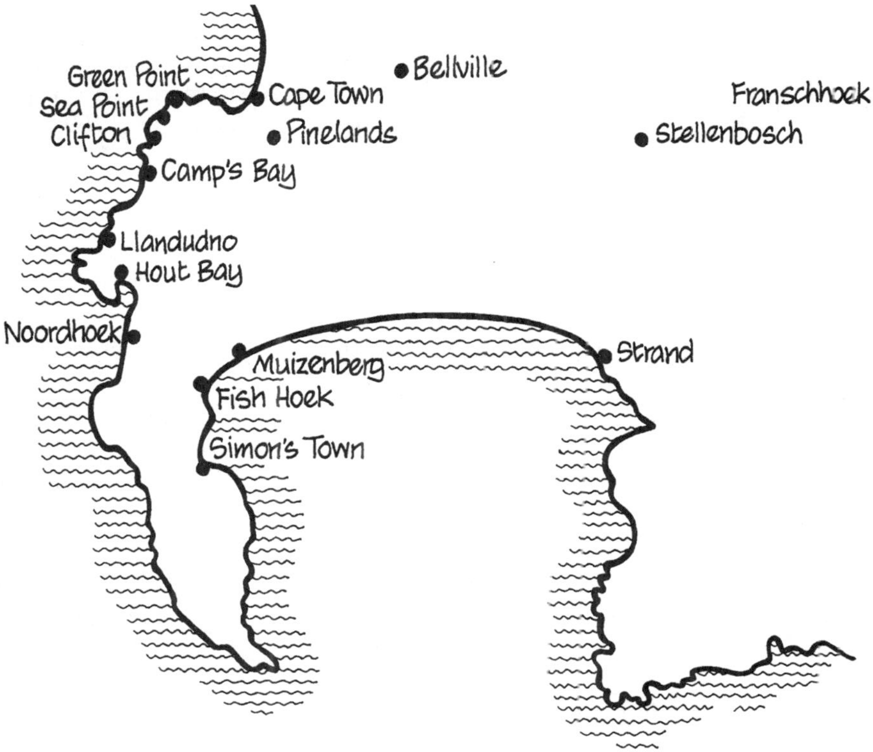

The Cape Town area is the most popular part of South Africa with foreign buyers, despite recent price increases. It offers a wide choice of property type and suburb, from rambling mansions in leafy, rural Constantia, to cottages overlooking deserted beaches on the Cape Peninsula or penthouse apartments in central Cape Town's vibrant V & A Waterfront.

City Bowl

The centre of Cape Town is called the City Bowl, and it has some attractive residential areas, including increasingly trendy Bo-Kaap, with its distinctive, colourful Cape Malay properties and Muslim community. Only a decade ago you could buy a small house or apartment in Bo-Kaap for as little as R40,000 (£3,500), but gentrification of the area and an influx of 'yuppie' buyers have seen the value of such properties skyrocket to around R1 million (£87,000).

Gardens Suburb

South of the City Bowl lies the Gardens suburb, close to Long Street and Kloof Street, with some of the city's best restaurants and the location of the world-famous Mount Nelson Hotel, at which taking Sunday tea is a Cape Town institution (if you can find a table). Apartments and small houses cost in the range of R745,000 (£64,780) to R1.95 million (£169,565).

Waterfront

The V & A Waterfront (invariably known simply as 'the Waterfront') lies just north of the centre of Cape Town. Once a run-down harbour area, it has been transformed into a tourist magnet, with shops, bars, restaurants, an aquarium and much else and is now one of the most sought-after parts of the city, with plenty of security, making it safe to walk around at night. But you pay a price for the privilege: a modern, spacious, well-appointed, three-bedroom, two-bathroom apartment with three terraces, offering views of the sea and Table Mountain costs from around R4.5 million (£390,000), and you must pay even more if you want a prime spot with a mooring for your boat. Development is continuing at the Waterfront, with more exclusive apartment blocks being built (some on reclaimed land) and plans by the entrepreneur Sol Kerzner to build a 'six-star' hotel next to the impressive Two Oceans Aquarium.

Northern Suburbs

To the north and north-west of Cape Town lie the Northern suburbs, which currently offer some of the region's more affordable property. The Blaauwberg area (incorporating Parklands and Table View) is South

Africa's fastest-growing coastal suburb, only a 15-minute drive north of Cape Town on the Atlantic coastline. It has classic views of Table Mountain (which are much used in postcards) and its Canal Walk shopping centre is one of the best in South Africa. A three-bedroom, two-bathroom apartment in a prime beachfront location costs around R1.75 million (£152,000), and property is much cheaper in less popular locations set back from the coast. Nearby Bellville – a quiet, residential suburb with easy access to Cape Town and the Winelands – is another attractive place to buy, where you can buy a basic, one-bedroom, one-bathroom apartment for R273,000 (£23,750).

Green Point & Sea Point

To the west of Cape Town, on the Atlantic side of the Cape Peninsula, is Green Point, slightly set back from the coast, with a 'backpacker' feel to it. Further on is Sea Point, a large suburb hugging the coast (walking along the promenade is popular with people from all over the Peninsula), with many blocks of high-rise apartments making it one of Cape Town's most densely populated areas. Sea Point has a hint of the British resort Brighton about it and in recent years it has had problems with drugs and prostitution, but these are now being addressed. It's only a few minutes from the centre of Cape Town and, as well as plenty of beachfront apartments, there are large family homes on the slopes of Signal Hill. A three-bedroom, three-bathroom, two-reception room house with a large garden and swimming pool costs from around R1.6 million (£140,000).

Clifton & Camp's Bay

South of Sea Point lie the upmarket Clifton and Camp's Bay areas, offering some of the most sought-after property in South Africa, particularly Camp's Bay. Both are classy seaside towns, with a Mediterranean Riviera feel and impressive beaches, although the sea off the Atlantic coast is cold even at the height of summer. Both resorts enjoy an imposing mountain backdrop of Table Mountain, the Lion's Head and the Twelve Apostles hills, and both specialise in large, luxurious houses, with prices in the region of R6 million (£520,000) to R15 million (£1.3 million) or more. (Clifton boasts the most expensive apartment ever sold on the Atlantic seaboard, at R25 million/over £2 million.)

Llandudno

Further down a stretch of otherwise undeveloped west coast and 20km (12.5mi) from Cape Town is Llandudno (pronounced, unlike the Welsh town, 'lindidno'), a small, exclusive seaside community with some of the area's most expensive property and close to Cape Town's main nudist beach. There's only one access road to Llandudno and plenty of competition when any of its limited number of properties come on the market. Prices vary according to the size and quality of the house, but expect to pay between R5 million (£435,000) and R10 million (£870,000) for a three-bedroom, three-bathroom house, and much more for a well-sited, larger property.

Hout Bay

Beyond Llandudno, Hout Bay is a bigger town and a working harbour, with an impressive setting on a large bay, enjoying spectacular views towards the Chapman's Peak Drive, a 10km (6.25mi) road cut into the mountains. Hout Bay has a laid-back, village feel, with plenty of bistros, guesthouses and art and nautical shops, but is within easy reach of Cape Town. You can buy a one-bedroom, one-bathroom apartment in a new block for R675,000 (£59,000) or a three-bedroom, two-bathroom house for R1.4 million (£120,000); a larger property in a prime location costs around R7 million (£600,000).

Noordhoek

Further down the west coast is Noordhoek, a village with a rural atmosphere and great setting - spread out along a beautiful beach - and also within easy reach of central Cape Town. An impressive family home with five bedrooms, three bathrooms, three reception rooms, two garages, a guest cottage and staff accommodation will cost around R3.25 million (£283,000).

Pinelands

To the east of central Cape Town is Pinelands, a well-established suburb very close to the city but with a park-like feel (the name, unsurprisingly, comes from the area's many pine trees). This is a luxurious suburb, with plenty of impressive properties on large plots, with thatched roofs a local speciality. Despite its convenient location - just off the N2 road between central Cape Town and the airport - and quiet, leafy ambience, property isn't outrageously priced. A three-bedroom, one-bathroom, two-reception room house with a swimming pool costs from around R1.4 million (£120,000). A sprawling property with five bedrooms, three bathrooms, four reception rooms and a large garden costs from around R2.15 million (£187,000).

Southern Suburbs

South of Pinelands lie the exclusive Southern Suburbs of Cape Town, including Claremont, Constantia, Kenilworth, Mowbray, Observatory, Rondebosch and Wynberg – an area whose former residents include Earl Spencer (Princess Diana's brother) and Sir Mark Thatcher (Lady Thatcher's son). At their heart is the upmarket suburb of Newlands, with its many oak trees, spectacular views of Table Mountain, a world-famous sports stadium (for rugby and cricket) and the site of the University of Cape Town. Although only 10 or 15 minutes by car from central Cape Town, the Southern Suburbs are quiet, leafy and almost rural. They're home to the impressive semi-wilderness area of the Kirstenbosch Botanical Gardens (💻 www.kirstenbosch.co.za), with over 5,000 plant species set in gardens spread over Table Mountain's lower slopes.

There are some apartments and townhouses in the area, but many of the properties are large, luxurious villas, with landscaped gardens and top-notch security. A modest, three-bedroom, two-bathroom bungalow costs from around R1.9 million (£165,000), and a four-bedroom house with two bathrooms ranges from R2 million (£174,000) to R5 million (£435,000). Larger, top-range houses can easily cost over R20 million (£1.75 million).

East Cape Coast

Moving to the east coast of the Cape Peninsula (the False Bay side, where the water is several degrees warmer than on the Atlantic side), Strand and Gordon's Bay are popular, with their coastal location and good access to central Cape Town, the airport and the Winelands to the north. The drive to the east from Gordon's Bay to Hermanus is one of South Africa's most scenic. Prices reflect the area's popularity: a luxury, sprawling, three-bedroom beachfront apartment can cost R6.5 million (£565,000), but you can buy a huge, five-bedroom, five-bathroom house away from the most popular streets for under R4 million (£350,000).

Muizenberg

At the north-west corner of False Bay, around 25km (15mi) south of Cape Town, lies Muizenberg. It has a spectacular setting on a massive beach (which is popular with surfers), with great views across the Bay and down the Peninsula mountain chain, although the town is slightly scruffy, which is reflected in property prices: you can buy a one-bedroom apartment for R400,000 (£35,000), a large, two-bedroom, two-bathroom apartment in a reasonable setting costs around R1.25 million

(£110,000), and a spacious three-or four-bedroom house is around R1.75 million (£150,000). There are plans to upgrade and beautify the town, so property prices might increase.

Fish Hoek

South of Muizenberg lies the seaside town of Fish Hoek, nestled at the foot of the mountains, overlooking one of the Peninsula's better beaches. Fish Hoek is attracting plenty of international buyers despite a reputation for dullness. It's a popular spot for whale-watching (between June and December), and there's a rail service to Cape Town, which may be an attraction for commuters, although rail travel isn't always safe in South Africa (see page 104). You can buy a five-bedroom, four-bathroom, three-reception room seaside mansion for around R3.5 million (£300,000), and a similar property in a location set back from the coast costs R1.95 million (£170,000). If you want something more modest, an immaculate, two-bedroom, two-bathroom apartment costs around R1.1 million (£95,000).

Simon's Town

Halfway down the False Bay side of the Peninsula lies Simon's Town (sometimes written as Simonstown), famous as a naval base and the location of Boulders Beach, with its colony of penguins (it's odd to see these 'Antarctic' birds basking in the strong South African sun!). The town has plenty of historical properties and large, exclusive homes and isn't raucous like some naval bases, but a pretty, relaxed place (except for the dockyard itself). A two-bedroom, two-bathroom apartment costs around R750,000 (£65,000), a three-bedroom, two-bathroom townhouse R1.35 million (£117,000) and you will pay between R2.5 million (£217,000) and R5 million (£435,000) for a luxurious four- or-five-bedroom house.

Winelands

To the east and north-east of Cape Town lie the Winelands, containing many of South Africa's oldest and best wineries, most within a 60km (37mi) radius of Cape Town. It's a beautiful region of impressive hills and rolling valleys decked with rows of vines (which are particularly striking in the autumn when the leaves change colour), with some of South Africa's most appealing towns, notably Stellenbosch and Franschhoek. The former is an elegant town full of oak trees and is the site of a university, giving it the feel of an American collegiate town. It's generally safe to walk around at night and enjoy the many bars and eateries. Much smaller Franschhoek enjoys a spectacular setting, dominated by three mountains, and has carved itself a niche as the region's culinary capital. Both are attracting a lot of interest from foreign buyers.

Prices in the Winelands vary with location, and favoured spots in town within walking distance of the facilities are at a premium. For example, you can buy an attractive three- or-four-bedroom house on the outskirts of one of the region's towns or in the countryside for R1.4 million (£120,000) - you pay a lot more for a large, luxury house with gardens, swimming pools, guest quarters etc.), but an upmarket, two-bedroom apartment in the centre of Stellenbosch costs around R1.7 million (£148,000). At the other end of the scale, a large Cape Dutch architectural gem (see **Architectural Styles** on page 126) with plenty of land can cost at least R20 million (£1.75 million).

South Coast

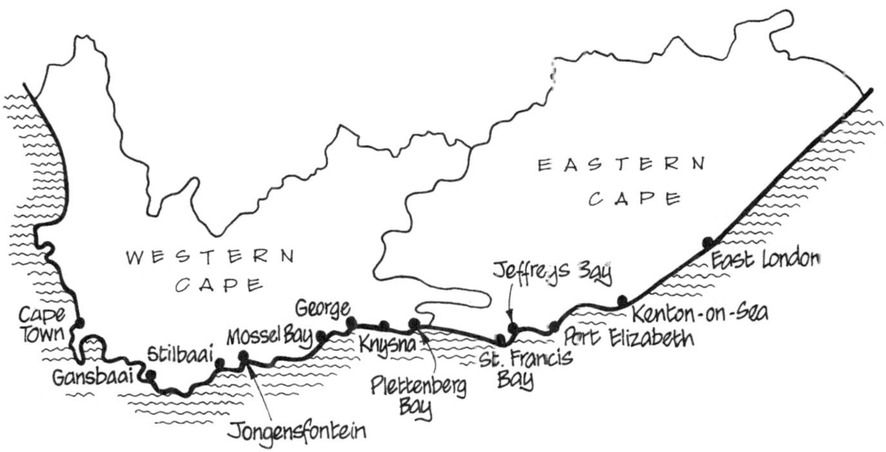

The south coast, i.e. the coasts of the Western Cape and Eastern Cape, is another popular area with foreign buyers - particularly along the so-called Garden Route, which is the stretch of coast between Mossel Bay and Storms River Mouth, running through George, Knysna and Plettenburg Bay in Western Cape and on to Port Elizabeth in Eastern Cape (although definitions of what constitutes the Garden Route vary).

Gansbaai

A two-hour drive east of Cape Town is Gansbaai (Goose Bay), which estate agents reckon to be among the top ten places to invest in property in South Africa. It's a working town, with an active harbour, and boasts spectacular sea and mountain views, whale-watching between June and

December and even cage diving to see great white sharks, which gather off the appropriately-named Danger Point. Prices here are lower than in much of the Cape Town region and you can buy a five-bedroom, four-bathroom house for R1.5 million (£130,000).

Stilbaai & Jongensfontein

Further along the coast are the towns of Stilbaai and Jongensfontein, just off the N2 road and around an hour from George airport. The surrounding area is beautiful and tranquil, with plenty of vacant land ready for development. A two-bedroom, two-bathroom, two-reception room house costs around R850,000 (£74,000), four-bedroom, two-bathroom houses are available for R1.25 million (£110,000) and a sprawling mansion in the best location can be had for under R3 million (£250,000).

Mossel Bay

Mossel Bay is 400km (250mi) east of Cape Town and has gained an unfavourable reputation in South Africa as an ugly industrial place. But this is undeserved because the town also has an attractive historic centre and a good beach. You can buy a three-bedroom, one-bathroom apartment near the beach for around R680,000 (£60,000), while a three-bedroom, two-bathroom apartment in a prime beachfront position costs R900,000 (£78,000). A three-bedroom house in town costs between R1.5 million (£130,000) and R2.5 million (£217,500), but if you move into the surrounding countryside, you can buy an isolated four-bedroom, four-bathroom house in a nature reserve for as little as R500,000 (£43,500).

George

George is a working town, inland of the Garden Route, and even its inhabitants wouldn't describe it as beautiful, but it has an airport and is a good base for exploring the surrounding area, much of which is beautiful. You can buy a one-bedroom apartment in the centre of the business district for R345,000 (£30,000), or a large three-bedroom, two-bathroom house from around R750,000 (£65,000). A stylish, architect-designed house with three bedrooms, three bathrooms, four reception rooms and a swimming pool can be yours for around R1.85 million (£160,000), although the George area also has some very expensive properties (R20 million/£1.75 million and above).

Knysna

Knysna (pronounced 'nize-na') is 100km (62mi) east of Mossel Bay, roughly at the halfway point of the Garden Route. It doesn't have a beach but sits in an attractive hilly setting overlooking a lagoon, close to impressive forests, and has an arty feeling, with some attractive Georgian and Victorian buildings. Three-bedroom, two-bathroom houses in Knysna cost between R900,000 (£78,000) and R2 million (£174,000).

Plettenberg Bay

Plettenberg Bay lies 33km (20mi) east of Knysna and is probably the glitziest of the Garden Route resorts, popular with Johannesburg's wealthier citizens. The town itself is pleasant rather than remarkable but the views across the bay are stunning. A two-bedroom, one-bathroom apartment costs around R675,000 (£59,000), a three-bedroom, three-bathroom apartment around R900,000 (£78,000), and a well appointed four-bedroom house from R2 million (£174,000). Plettenberg Bay also boasts some luxurious mansions, selling at around R22 million (£1.9 million).

St Francis Bay

Just across the border in the Eastern Cape (where increasing numbers of buyers are looking, having decided that the Western Cape is overpriced) is St Francis Bay, a small resort built around a series of canals and waterfront developments. Some people regard it as a heavenly place, others see it as plastic and sterile. A three-bedroom, two-bathroom house away from the water costs around R650,000 (£56,500), and a two-bedroom, one-bathroom house in the port area costs around R800,000 (£70,000). Four- and five-bedroom properties in waterfront positions cost between R2 million (£174,000) and R6 million (£520,000).

Jeffreys Bay

Jeffreys Bay lies 75km (47mi) west of Port Elizabeth and is a small town surrounded by nature reserves, game parks and waterfalls, which compensate for the fact that the town itself is overdeveloped. It's known for surfing and the quantity and quality of the seashells that wash up on its beach, and it attracts many holidaymakers and retirees. A two-bedroom, one-bathroom, two-reception room house costs around R475,000 (£41,000), and a luxurious seafront apartment with five bedrooms and four bathrooms can be bought for around R3.78 million (£330,000).

Port Elizabeth

Port Elizabeth – the 'official' end of the Garden Route – is the largest coastal city in the Eastern Cape (see page 60). You can buy a two-bedroom townhouse for around R380,000 (£33,000), a modest three-bedroom, two-bathroom house for R750,000 (£65,000) and a four-bedroom, three-bathroom house near the beach for R1.6 million (£139,000).

Kenton-On-Sea

East of Port Elizabeth, on the so-called 'Sunshine Coast', lies Kenton-on-Sea, an unspoiled town with a pleasant climate and attractive sea and river views, near to game reserves. A three-bedroom, one-bathroom house costs around R850,000 (£74,000), four-bedroom, two-bathroom houses are around R1.1 million (£95,650), and you can have a five-bedroom property for under R2 million (£173,910).

East London

East London (see page 61) has seen an increase in the number of foreign property buyers, put off the Western Cape by price increases and cool winters, and wanting to avoid the Durban area's summer humidity. Small apartments can be bought for as little as R250,000 (£21,750), while R1 million (£87,000) will buy you a substantial family home.

East Coast

The east coast of South Africa, to the north and south of Durban in Kwazulu-Natal, is the third area popular with foreign property buyers. The coast to the south of Durban is sometimes called the South Coast or the Hibiscus Coast, and the coast to the north the North Coast or the Dolphin Coast.

Amanzimtoti

The attractive seaside town of (Zulu for 'sweet waters'), 25km (15mi) south of Durban, is popular with holidaymakers and commuters and famed for its excellent beaches. A basic three-bedroom house costs around R360,000 (£31,000), an immaculate two-bedroom, two-bathroom apartment is around R590,000 (£51,000), an upmarket, three-bedroom house with a swimming pool R920,000 (£80,000) and an exclusive, beachfront house with four bedrooms, three bathrooms and four reception rooms will set you back R3.5 million (£300,000).

Hibberdene

Hibberdene is a 45-minute drive south of Durban and the airport. It's known as the 'gateway to the Hibiscus Coast' and, as well as a wide range of different types of residential property, it offers retirement complexes and plenty of golf courses. You can buy a smart two-bedroom, two-bathroom house for R400,000 (£35,000) and a five-bedroom house can cost as little as R650,000 (£56,500), but three to five times as much in a prime location.

Port Shepstone

Port Shepstone, the largest town on the South Coast, is the administrative and commercial centre of the area, known for its Norwegian community. Property prices are modest and you can buy a four-bedroom, two-bathroom house for R665,000 (£58,000).

Uvongo

Uvongo is a bustling, year-round holiday town with a magnificent beach and a reef 7km (4.3mi) offshore that's one of the world's premier shark-viewing spots. A one-bedroom apartment costs around R400,000 (£35,000), a three-bedroom, three-bathroom townhouse can be had from around R600,000 (£52,000), R1 million (£87,000) buys a reasonable three-or-four-bedroom house, and R3.5 million (£300,000) will get you a top-of-the-range five-bedroom, four-bathroom, four-reception room house near the beach.

Margate

Just 12km (7.5mi) south of Uvongo is Margate, the South Coast's tourist centre and a popular holiday destination with the citizens of Johannesburg. A basic, one-bedroom apartment costs from around R380,000 (£33,000), three-bedroom houses start at R550,000 (£48,000) and you can buy a luxurious, four-bedroom townhouse for R900,000 (£78,000).

Durban North & Umhlanga Rocks

To the north of Durban, Durban North and Umhlanga Rocks merge to form a premier seaside area, with a 3km (1.85mi) promenade and some of the best homes on the North Coast. This is a tranquil region of coastal forests, game parks, golf courses and beaches. A three-bedroom, two-bathroom, two-reception room house with a garden and swimming pool costs around R1.35 million (£117,500), and a five-bedroom, four-bathroom, four-reception room house costs around R4 million (£350,000).

Ballito

Ballito is 45km (28mi) north of Durban and is known as the 'Pearl of the Dolphin Coast'. It's a friendly resort with a village atmosphere set inland from the coast and surrounded by sugarcane fields. A smart, three-bedroom, two-bathroom apartment costs around R1.1 million (£95,000), and a three-bedroom, two-bathroom house with a double garage and a swimming pool costs R1.65 million (£143,500).

Westville

If you want to escape the holidaymakers and party atmosphere of the coast, Westville is a quite, commuter town, a 15-minute drive inland from Durban. Your money goes a long way there: a luxury property with four bedrooms, three bathrooms and four reception rooms is yours for around R2.2 million (£190,000).

LOCATION

The most important consideration when buying a home is usually its location – or, as the old adage goes, the three most important considerations are location, location and location! A property in a reasonable condition in a popular area is likely to be a better investment than an exceptional property in a remote or unattractive location.

There's no point in buying a dream property if you cannot get to it or it's next door to a power station. South Africa offers almost every type of property imaginable, but location is as important to your enjoyment of a home as whether it's a palace or a hovel.

The wrong decision regarding location is one of the main causes of disenchantment among foreigners who have purchased property in South Africa.

Where you buy a property will depend on a range of factors, including your preferences, your financial resources and whether you plan to work in South Africa. If you already have a job in South Africa, the location of your home will probably be determined by your place of employment. However, if you intend to look for employment or start a business, you must live in an area that allows you the maximum scope. It's unwise to assume that you will find employment in a particular area. If, on the other hand, you're looking for a holiday or retirement home, you can live virtually anywhere, although accessibility and proximity to shops and other services are crucial. When seeking a permanent home, don't be too influenced by where you've spent an enjoyable holiday or two; a town or area that was acceptable for a few weeks' holiday may be far from suitable as a permanent residence.

If you have little idea about where you wish to live, read as much as you can about the different provinces of South Africa (see page 60 and **Appendices B** and **C**) and spend some time looking around your areas of interest. The climate, lifestyle and cost of living vary considerably from region to region and even within a region.

Before looking at properties, it's important to have a good idea of the type of property you're looking for and the price you wish to pay, and to draw up a shortlist of the areas or towns of interest. If you don't do this, you're likely to be overwhelmed by the number of properties to be viewed. Estate agents usually expect serious buyers to know where they want to buy within a 30 to 40km (20 to 25mi) radius and some even expect clients to narrow their choice down to specific towns and villages.

The 'best' place to live depends largely on its proximity to your place of work, schools, country or town, shops, public transport, sports facilities, beaches or other attractions, bars and restaurants. There are beautiful areas to choose from throughout South Africa, but not all are within easy travelling distance of a town or city and the coast. And don't believe the times and distances stated in advertisements and estate agents' brochures; according to some agents' magical mystery maps, everywhere in the north is handy for a local town and dozens of beauty spots, and anywhere in the south is a stone's throw from a beach or airport. South Africa is a BIG country and you shouldn't underestimate distances on a map.

When looking for a home, bear in mind travelling times and costs. If you buy a remote country property, the distance to local amenities and services could become a problem, particularly if you plan to retire to South Africa. If you live in a remote rural area, you will need to be much more self-sufficient than if you live in a town and you will have to use a car for everything, which will add significantly to the cost of living. If you will be working in South Africa, obtain a map of the area and decide the maximum distance you wish to travel to work, e.g. by drawing a circle with your workplace in the middle.

If possible, you should visit an area a number of times over a period of a few weeks, both on weekdays and at weekends, in order to get a feel for the neighbourhood (if possible, walk, don't just drive around!). A property seen on a balmy summer's day after a delicious lunch and a few glasses of wine may not be nearly so attractive on a subsequent visit without sunshine and the warm inner glow. If possible, you should also visit an area at different times of the year, e.g. in both summer and winter, as somewhere that's wonderful in summer can be forbidding and inhospitable in winter (or vice versa). In any case, you should view a property a number of times before making up your mind to buy it.

If you're unfamiliar with an area, most experts recommend that you rent for a period before deciding to buy (see **Renting Before Buying** on page 120). This is particularly important if you're planning to buy a permanent or retirement home in an unfamiliar area. Many people change their minds after a period and it isn't unusual for families to move once or twice before settling down permanently.

Obtain large scale maps of the area where you're looking, which may even show individual buildings, thereby allowing you to mark the places that you've seen. You could do this using a grading system to denote your impressions. If you use an estate agent, he will usually drive you around and you can return later to those that you like most at your leisure, provided you've marked them on your map!

There are many points to consider regarding the location of a home, as detailed below, and you should take into account the present and future needs of **all** members of your family.

Accessibility

Is the proximity to public transport, e.g. an international airport, port or railway station, or access to a main road important? Don't, however, believe all you're told about the distance or travelling times to the nearest main road, airport, railway station, port, beach or town, but check for yourself. If you plan to let a property, it will be more popular if it's within easy reach of an airport with a range of flights, particularly budget flights, from the UK, for example.

Amenities

What local health and social services are provided? How far is the nearest hospital (preferably private) with an emergency department? What shopping facilities are there in the neighbourhood? How far is it to the nearest town with good shopping facilities, e.g. a supermarket? How would you get there if your car was out of action? Note that many rural villages have few shops or facilities, so they aren't necessarily a good choice for a retirement home.

Climate

For most people the climate (see page 23) is one of the most important factors when buying a home in South Africa, particularly a holiday or retirement home. Bear in mind both the winter and summer climate, the average daily sunshine hours, rainfall and wind conditions. You may also wish to check whether the area is noted for fog, which can make driving hazardous, or heavy rain storms. The orientation or aspect of a building is vital; if you want morning or afternoon sun (or both) you must ensure that balconies, terraces and gardens are facing north.

Community

Do you wish to live in an area with many of your fellow countrymen and other expatriates or as far away from them as possible? If you wish to integrate with the local community, avoid foreign 'ghettos' and choose an area or development with mainly local inhabitants. The locals in some villages resent 'outsiders' buying up prime properties, particularly holiday homeowners, although foreigners who take the time and trouble to integrate into the local community are usually warmly welcomed. If you're buying a permanent home, it's important to check your prospective neighbours, particularly when buying an apartment. For example, are they noisy, sociable or absent for long periods? Do you think you will get on with them? **Good neighbours are invaluable, particularly when buying a second home.**

Crime

What is the local crime rate, e.g. burglaries, stolen cars and crimes of violence? In some areas (e.g. major cities and resorts), the incidence of burglary is high and home insurance is higher than in low-crime areas. Is crime increasing or decreasing? Bear in mind that professional crooks like isolated houses, particularly those full of expensive furniture and other belongings, which they can strip bare at their leisure. You're much less likely to be a victim of theft if you live in a village, where strangers stand out like sore thumbs. See also page 254.

Employment

How secure is your job or business and are you likely to move to another area in the near future? Can you find other work in the same area, if necessary? If you may need to move in a few years' time, you should rent rather than buy, or at least buy a property that will be relatively easy to sell without losing (too much) money. What about your partner's and children's jobs or job prospects?

Garden

If you're planning to buy a large country property with an extensive garden, bear in mind the cost and amount of work involved in its upkeep. If it's to be a second home, who will look after the house and garden when you're away? Do you want to spend your holidays mowing the lawn and cutting back undergrowth? Do you want a home with a lot of outbuildings? What are you going to do with them? Can you afford to convert them into extra rooms or guest or self-catering accommodation and, if so, is there a demand for accommodation in the area?

Local Council

Is the local council well run? Unfortunately, some are profligate and simply use any extra income to hire a few more of their cronies or spend it on grandiose schemes, and many local councillors abuse their positions to further their own ends. If the municipality is efficiently run, you can usually rely on good local social and sports services and other facilities.

Natural Phenomena

Check with the local authorities whether an area is particularly susceptible to natural disasters such as floods, storms, forest fires and

▲ *Port Elizabeth, Eastern Cape*

▲ *Abseiling on Table Mountain, Cape Town, Western Cape*

▲ *Rugby Fans, Western Cape*

▲ *Baobab, Limpopo Province*

▼ *Zeven Riveren, Western Cape*

Bo-Kaap Malay Quarter, Cape Town, Western Cape

Beach, Western Cape

Cape Town, Western Cape

Cape Gannets, Western Cape

Wild Coast, Eastern Cape

Victoria & Alfred Waterfront
Cape Town, Western Cape

Cheetah,
KwaZulu-Natal

Tulbagh-Winterhoek
Mountains, Western Cape

Slangriver Homestead,
Western Cape

Durban,
KwaZulu-Natal

Water Skiing, Redhouse, Eastern Cape

Kruger National Park, Mpumalanga Province

Farm Near Paarl, Western Cape

Table Grapes, Hex River Valley, Western Cape

Clifton, Western Cape

landslides. If a property is located near a coast or waterway, it may be expensive to insure against floods, which are a threat in some areas.

Noise

Noise can be a problem in some cities, resorts and developments. Although you cannot choose your neighbours, you can at least ensure that a property isn't located next to a busy road, railway line, airport, industrial plant, commercial area, discotheque, night club, bar or restaurant (where revelries may continue into the early hours). Look out for objectionable properties close to the one you're considering and check whether nearby vacant land has been 'zoned' for commercial activities or tower blocks (which could block your view). In community developments (e.g. apartment blocks) many properties are second homes and are let short term, which means you may have to tolerate boisterous holidaymakers as neighbours throughout the year (or at least during the summer months). In estate agent speak, a 'popular' area may be noisy, while a 'residential' area is usually quiet.

Parking

If you're planning to buy in a town or city, is there adequate private or free on-street parking for you and visitors? Is it safe to park in the street? In some areas it's important to have secure off-street parking if you value your car. Parking is a problem in many towns and most cities, where private garages or parking spaces can be expensive. Bear in mind that an apartment or townhouse in a town or community development may be some distance from the nearest road or car park. How do you feel about carrying heavy shopping hundreds of metres to your home and possibly up several flights of stairs? Traffic congestion is also a problem in many towns and tourist resorts, particularly during the high season.

Property Market

Do houses sell well in the area, e.g. in less than six months? Generally, you should avoid neighbourhoods where desirable houses routinely remain on the market for six months or longer (unless the property market is in a severe slump).

Schools

Consider your children's present and future schooling. What is the quality of local schools? Even if your family has no need or plans to use local schools, the value of a home is often influenced by their quality and location.

Sports & Leisure Facilities

What is the range and quality of local leisure, sports, community and cultural facilities? What is the proximity to sports facilities such as a beach, golf course or waterway?

Tourists

If you live in a popular tourist area, it will be inundated with tourists in summer, and perhaps at other times of the year (South Africa is marketing itself as a year-round destination). They won't only jam the roads and pack the public transport, but may also occupy your favourite table at your local bar or restaurant (heaven forbid!). Although a 'front-line' property on a beach or in a marina development may sound attractive and be ideal for short holidays, it isn't always the best choice for permanent residence.

Many beaches are hopelessly crowded in the high season, streets may be smelly from restaurants and fast food outlets, parking impossible and services stretched to breaking point, and the incessant noise may drive you crazy. Some people prefer to move inland or to higher ground, where it's less humid, more peaceful and you can enjoy panoramic views. On the other hand, getting to and from hillside properties can be difficult and the sometimes poorly maintained roads (usually narrow and unguarded) are for sober, confident drivers only; many country roads in South Africa are suitable only for four-wheel-drive vehicles.

Town or Country?

Do you wish to be in a town or do you prefer the country? Inland or on the coast? Bear in mind that if you buy a property in the country, you will probably have to tolerate poor public transport (or none at all), long travelling distances to a town of any size, solitude and remoteness. You won't be able to pop along to the local bread shop, drop into the local bar for a glass of your favourite tipple with the locals or have a choice of restaurants on your doorstep. In a town or large village, the market will be just around the corner, the doctor and chemist close at hand and, if you need help or run into any problems, your neighbours will be close by.

In the country, you will be closer to nature (and there's a great deal of that in South Africa), will have more freedom (e.g. to make as much noise as you wish) and possibly complete privacy, e.g. to sunbathe or swim *au naturel*. Living in a remote area in the country will suit nature lovers looking for solitude who don't want to involve themselves in the 'hustle and bustle' of town life (not that there's much of this in some rural towns). If you're after peace and quiet, however, make sure that there isn't a busy road or railway line nearby or a local church within 'donging' distance. Note also that many people who buy a remote country home find that the peace of the countryside palls after a time and they yearn for the more exciting city or coastal nightlife. If you've never lived in the country, it's wise to rent before buying.

Although it's cheaper to buy in a remote or unpopular location, it's often much more difficult to find a buyer when you want to sell.

GETTING THERE

Although it isn't so important if you're planning to live permanently in South Africa and stay put, one of the major considerations when buying a holiday home is the cost of getting to and from South Africa. In particular, you should ask yourself the following questions:

- How long will it take you to get to a home in South Africa, taking into account journeys to and from airports at either end?
- How frequent are flights, and internal buses and trains if needed, at the time(s) of year when you plan to travel?
- Are direct flights available?
- What is the cost of travel from your home country to South Africa?
- Are off-season discounts or inexpensive charter flights available? Are they likely to be introduced in the future?

If a long journey is involved, you should bear in mind that it may take you a day or two to recover (although jet-lag isn't a problem for visitors coming from Europe, with South Africa in the same time zone as Eastern Europe - GMT + two hours). Obviously, the travelling time and cost of travel to a home in South Africa will be more important if you're planning to spend several periods of time there each year rather than one long stay. You should include the price of getting to and from South Africa in your budget when considering a property purchase, particularly if you're planning to make more than a couple of visits per year.

SURVIVAL TIP
Always allow plenty of time to get to and from airports, ports and railway stations in South Africa, particularly when travelling during peak hours, when traffic congestion can be heavy.

Airline Services

Around 20 scheduled domestic airlines are currently licensed to provide air services within South Africa and around 60 provide scheduled international air services, including Air Afrique, Air Austral, Air Botswana, Air France, Air Gabon, Air Madagascar, Air Malawi, Air Mauritius, Air Namibia, Air Portugal, Air Seychelles, Air Tanzania, Air Zimbabwe, Alitalia, Alliance Express, Angola Airlines, Austrian Airlines, British Airways, Cameroon Airlines, Cathay Pacific, Comair, East African Airlines, Egyptair, El Al, Emirates, Ethiopian Airlines, Ghana Airways, Iberia, KLM, Kenya Airways, Lufthansa, Malaysian Airlines, Olympic Airways, Qantas, Sabena, Saudi Arabian Airlines, Singapore Airlines, Swiss International Airlines and Virgin Atlantic. (For a full and up-to-date list see 💻 www.info.gov.za/yearbook/2004/transport.htm.)

South Africa's national airline is South African Airways (💻 www.flysaa.com) and it enjoys a sound international reputation, currently boasting the world's most modern 747 fleet. According to the rating scheme of Skytrax ('leading research advisors to the world airline industry', 💻 www.airlinequality.com), South African Airways scores four stars out of a maximum of five. South African Airways flies to and from many of the world's major airports, including (from Johannesburg) Aberdeen, Belfast, Dublin, Edinburgh, Glasgow, Inverness, Leeds, London, Manchester and Teesside in the UK and Ireland; Adelaide, Brisbane, Melbourne, Perth and Sydney in Australia; and Atlanta, Baltimore, Boston, Chicago, Cincinnati, Cleveland, Denver, Detroit, Fort Lauderdale, Houston, Las Vegas, Los Angeles, Miami, Minneapolis, New Orleans, New York, Orlando, Pittsburgh, Portland, St Louis, Salt Lake City, San Diego, San Francisco, Seattle, Tampa, Washington and West Palm Beach in the US.

Prices for flying to and from South Africa vary greatly and you're strongly recommended to shop around. The good news is that competition is increasing and prices - especially to and from Europe, North America and Australia - are falling, particularly outside the school holiday months (February, March, May, July, August, October and November). And, since the announcement that South Africa is to host the 2010 World Cup (in football/soccer), some international airlines are already planning to lay on more flights to and from the country, as interest in South Africa grows. British Airways, for example, is adding a further five services per week to Cape Town from October 2004, and others are expected to follow.

In June 2004, Civair (www.civair.com), for example, was offering one-way flights from Stansted, UK to Cape Town for R2,000 (£175). In late October 2004, return flights from the UK to Cape Town were priced as follows: British Airways £650; Civair £430; South African Airways £665; and Virgin Atlantic £650.

The instability of the airline business means that airlines frequently merge or go bankrupt, which often results in a reduction of services or the disappearance of routes. Budget airlines also frequently change their routes and prices. You therefore shouldn't invest in a property if you need to rely on cheap flights to a local airport.

Airports

South Africa has around 730 airports, 145 of which have paved runways. There are over 30 international airports, varying from small airports used just for short, cross-border flights to neighbouring countries to larger airports for flights to more far-flung destinations within Africa and other continents. However, there are just three major international airports: Cape Town, Durban and Johannesburg.

The Airports Company of South Africa (ACSA, www.airports.co.za), which was established in 1993, owns and operates South Africa's nine principal airports – Bloemfontein, Cape Town, Durban, East London, George, Johannesburg, Kimberley, Pilanesberg, Port Elizabeth and Upington – and it also operates Pilanesberg airport on a concession basis. By 2007, the ACSA is expected to have spent R185 million (£16 million) on infrastructure developments at the seven smaller airports; Port Elizabeth, the largest and busiest of the seven, will receive the bulk of the capital. Details of current facilities and services are given below.

Bloemfontein: Bloemfontein Airport (☎ 051-433 2901) in the Free State lies 10km (6mi) east of the city centre and handles around 225,000 passengers per year, mainly business travellers. There are some international flights, but most are domestic.

Cape Town: Cape Town International Airport (☎ 021-937 1200) lies around 22km (14mi) east of Cape Town and in 2003 handled 5 million passengers. That is expected to rise to 6.5 million by the end of 2004 and as many as 14 million by 2015. A new R120 million (£10.4 million) international departures terminal was opened in February 2003.

Durban: Durban International Airport (☎ 031-451 6666) is 16km (10mi) south of central Durban and handles around 2.4 million passengers per year. Construction of a new airport (to be called King Shaka International Airport) at La Mercy, 50km (31mi) outside the city, was due to begin some time in 2004; it will eventually replace the existing airport. Most intercontinental flights come and go from Johannesburg and Cape Town rather than Durban.

East London: East London airport (☎ 043-706 0304) in the Eastern Cape lies 9km (5.5mi) west of the city centre and handles around 350,000 passengers per year, around 200,000 of those business travellers. There are some international flights, but most are domestic.

George: George Airport (☎ 044-876 9310) is between Cape Town and Port Elizabeth on the Garden Route (one of South Africa's premier tourist attractions) and handles over 250,000 passengers per year.

Johannesburg: Johannesburg International Airport (☎ 011-921 6911) is located 24km (15mi) north-east of the city centre and each year handles some 12 million travellers, using 53 airlines, meaning that it's one of the busiest airports in Africa. The ACSA's flagship development is the R750 million (£65 million) domestic terminal at Johannesburg International Airport, which was opened in March 2003 and which will eventually allow overall capacity to reach 18 million passengers per year. The six terminals are used as follows:

- Terminal 1 – International arrivals;
- Terminal 2 – International arrivals;
- Terminal 3 – South African Airways and SA Express arrivals;
- Terminal 4 – Non-South African Airways domestic arrivals;
- Terminal 5 – Domestic departures;
- Terminal 6 – International departures.

Kimberley: Kimberley Airport (☎ 053-830 7100) in the Northern Cape is 6km (3.7mi) south of the city and handles around 85,000 passengers per year, around three-quarters of them business travellers. It caters for some international cargo flights.

Pilanesberg: Pilanesberg Airport (☎ 014-552 1261) serves Sun City in the North West province and handles around 50,000 passengers per year. The majority of flights are to and from Cape Town and Johannesburg, but there are some international flights.

Port Elizabeth: Port Elizabeth Airport (☎ 041-507 7348) in the Eastern Cape lies close to the city's CBD (central business district) and handles around 900,000 passengers per year, 60 per cent of them business travellers.

Upington: Upington Airport (☎ 054-337 7900) in the Northern Cape has the continent's longest runway (4,900m/16.077ft, long enough for a space shuttle to land on – should it ever need to!) and handles around 30,000 passengers per year. It's primarily a cargo airport, some of it international.

GETTING AROUND

Public transport services in South Africa vary considerably according to where you live, and the country is generally geared towards car travel. Public transport is often thin on the ground even in South African cities, although some have reasonably efficient (but not always safe) local bus and rail services.

Domestic Flights

South Africa is a large country and flying between destinations is often the only feasible option if time is limited. Internal flights aren't particularly cheap, but prices compare favourably with the costs of travelling long distances in a rented car, with stopovers en route. Booking through a travel agent is often the way to secure the cheapest flights, and booking three weeks in advance can qualify you for discounts of up to 50 per cent, except at the busiest times of the year.

A number of smaller airlines offer South African domestic flights (e.g. Comair, in conjunction with British Airways, 💻 www.britishairways.com; Nationwide, 💻 www.nationwideair.co.za; and Civair, 💻 www.civair.co.za), but the largest domestic carrier by far is South African Airways (SAA, 💻 www.flysaa.com), with its two associates, SA Airlink and SA Express; reservations for all three are made through SAA. SAA and its associates serve the major airports of Cape Town, Durban and Johannesburg, as well as Bloemfontein, East London, George, Kimberley, Margate, Mmabatho, Nelspruit, Phalaborwa, Pietermaritzburg, Pietersburg, Plettenberg Bay, Skukuza, Sun City, Ulundi, Umtata and Upington.

Expect to pay around R2,700 (£235) for an off-peak, return, economy class flight from Johannesburg to Cape Town (2 hrs 10 mins) or from Cape Town to Durban (2 hrs). Competition on the Johannesburg to Cape Town route from a range of airlines is forcing prices down, however, and you can sometimes buy one-way fares for as little as R600 (£52).

As yet, the airlines don't offer discounts to pensioners, but travellers (of any age) intending to take more than four flights within South Africa can save a lot of money with an African Explorer Pass, available on SAA and SA Express internal and regional flights. In order to qualify for the pass, you must have an international flight ticket to South Africa (on any airline) and must quote the ticket number to a travel agent or SAA office when applying. Passes are valid for 45 days from the date of issue and give up to 60 per cent discount when booking between four and eight flights (and you save on VAT).

Domestic Rail Services

Most intercity rail services in South Africa are run by Spoornet (💻 www.spoornet.co.za) and tickets must be booked in advance, at railway stations or at Spoornet offices in the larger cities. Train travel is one of the slower ways to get around South Africa. For example, the journey from Cape Town to Johannesburg takes around 27 hours, compared with only 19 hours by bus and just over two hours by plane. But it can be a leisurely way to see the country, with a night's sleep thrown in – all for a mere R335 to R495 (£29 to 43), depending on the train.

First and second class compartments have washbasins and seats that convert into bunks at night (third-class travel isn't recommended, being uncomfortable and often unsafe). Some people take sleeping bags, others rent cotton sheets and blankets from the bedding attendant who comes round every evening and who will make up the bed for you (costing around R20/£1.75). Normal second-class cabins accommodate up to six people, first-class four, and first class carriages have a shower. Smaller cabins, called coupés, are available, although more expensive; these take two people in first class, three in second class. First-class rail seats are around the same price as bus tickets for the same journey, while second-class tickets are considerably cheaper.

There are a couple of luxury trains operating in South Africa. The famous Blue Train runs from Pretoria to Cape Town, from Pretoria to Victoria Falls, from Pretoria to Hoedspruit and from Cape Town to Port Elizabeth. The one-way, luxury double cabin fare from Pretoria to Cape Town (a 29-hour journey) is around R20,430 (£1,775) in high season, R17,365 (£1,510) in low season. Passengers need 'smart casual' clothes for the daytime and must don formal attire for dinner. The Blue Train has its own website (💻 www.bluetrain.co.za) with full details of high and low-season fares and timetables.

Another luxury option is Rovos Rail (💻 www.rovos.co.za), which boldly dubs itself 'the most luxurious train in the world'! In fact, there are several trains, which run to and from Cape Town, George, Pretoria and Victoria Falls. The website has details of the timetables and fares, which are in the range of R6,500 (£565) to R14,600 (£1,270) per person.

You must be security-conscious when travelling by train in South Africa. Never leave valuables unattended in your compartment and keep the windows closed because thieves often gain entry through open windows when trains stop at stations (particularly in Gauteng). Some passengers take their own food and drink rather than leaving their possessions to go to the dining car.

Domestic Bus Services

South Africa's leading inter-city bus operators are Greyhound (💻 www.greyhound.co.za), Intercape (💻 www.intercape.co.za) and Translux (💻 www.translux.co.za). Their buses are usually referred to as coaches and the comfortable, reasonably inexpensive service offered by the three companies covers most towns in South Africa. Fares vary according to the distance of the journey and the time of year: peak season is the school holiday periods. A typical peak season fare from Cape Town to Johannesburg is around R415 (£36), with prices around a third less outside the peak season. Greyhound and Translux have similar fares, Intercape's are slightly lower.

The standard of the coaches is high. All Greyhound coaches, for example, have air-conditioning, individual reading lights, toilets, reclining seats, audio and visual entertainment and, on some routes, hostesses. Frequent travellers are recommended to obtain a pass. To join Greyhound's scheme (childishly called the Greyhound Get-A-Round Club), for example, fill in a form at a Greyhound office or online; each journey you make earns points that can be exchanged for a free journey. Greyhound also has a pass that gives seven days' unlimited travel over a 30-day period for around R1,400 (£122), 15 days over 30 days for around R2,700 (£235) and 30 days over 60 days for around R4,500 (£390).

The Baz Bus (💻 www.bazbus.com) runs up and down the coast between Cape Town and Durban, and also from Durban to Johannesburg and Pretoria. It's favoured by backpackers and other budget travellers, despite the fact that the prices aren't 'budget', as it has a useful hop-on/hop-off system.

Domestic Ferry Services

Although South Africa has a long coastline, there are few regular ferry and boat trips around the coast. There are sailings between Cape Town and Durban and Port Elizabeth and Durban (contact Safmarine for details, 💻 www.safmarine.com) but other means of transport are much quicker.

South African Roads

South Africa's road network comprises over 534,000km (331,828mi) of roads and streets. The major roads are generally excellent (unlike much of the driving that takes place on them – see **Driving** below) and make it a country that appeals to people who enjoy long road trips.

There are 9,400km (5,841mi) of national roads (with the prefix 'N'), which are of motorway standard, and there are plans to increase this to 20,000km (12,428mi). Toll sections cover around 2,200km (1,367mi). Toll roads are shown by a black 'T' in a yellow circle and the tolls are based on distance and vehicle type – an extensive list of toll charges can be found on the website of the South African National Roads Agency Limited (🖳 www.nra.co.za). There's always an alternative route to a toll road, and the turn-off is indicated by a black 'A' in a yellow circle. Provincial roads carry the prefix 'R', followed by a number (usually three-digit) and metropolitan routes in urban areas have the prefix 'M'.

Many petrol stations in cities, large towns and along N roads are open 24 hours per day, but those in rural areas are usually open from around 8am to 6pm, sometimes later.

Driving

South Africa has one of the world's worst road accident rates, mainly because of reckless (sometimes suicidal) driving, drunk or drugged driving and unsafe and/or overloaded vehicles. Other hazards include animals and pedestrians on the roads, particularly in rural areas; fog, especially during the rainy season in Kwazulu-Natal; drivers falling asleep at the wheel because of the long distances between major towns; and carjacking, particularly in Johannesburg.

Official government figures put the annual death toll on South Africa's roads at around 10,000, but according to research by the country's Medical Research Council, approximately 18,000 people died in road accidents in 2000. To put this in context, the UK has around 3,400 road accident deaths per year, with a population 30 per cent greater than South Africa's. South Africa's rate of accidents per vehicle is also among the highest on the continent, with over 500,000 accidents every year – a very high number in a country where the great majority of the population doesn't own a vehicle.

Even passengers on organised tours aren't immune from the carnage on South Africa's roads. For example, in September 1999, 26 British tourists and their local guide were killed when their tour bus skidded off a wet road and down the side of a mountain on the notorious Long Tom Pass in Mpumalanga. And in 2003, ten travellers were killed when their bus left the road at Piet Retief. Unfortunately, such incidents are common in South Africa. The government has recognised the problem and tried to reduce the death toll on its roads. In 1997, for example, it launched the emotively-named 'Arrive Alive' campaign, but it has had little effect and, in late 2003, South Africa's transport minister asked the UK government for assistance in improving the country's road safety!

December is the most dangerous month on South Africa's roads because of excessive alcohol consumption during the holiday period and the increase in the number of long-distance journeys due of migrant workers returning home. Bus and taxi driver fatigue is a cause of many of these festive period accidents, when it's common practice for taxi drivers to make the 600km (373mi) trip between Johannesburg and Durban three times in 24 hours. Alcohol plays a part in over half the accidents recorded in December, when people walking (or staggering) in the road and drunks lying on it are involved in over 30 per cent of fatal accidents. See also page 255.

South Africa's Automobile Association (www.aasa.co.za) offers a range of membership options, including a reliable breakdown recovery service, with annual fees ranging from R215 (£18.70) to R825 (£71.73).

Those who decide to brave South Africa's roads should bear in mind the following rules and conventions:

- South Africans drive on the left-hand side of the road and overtake on the right, meaning that driving is familiar to natives of Australia, Japan and the UK, among others.
- Speed limits are 60kph (37mph) in built-up areas, 100kph (62mph) on rural roads and 120kph (75mph) on major roads, but the majority of traffic travels much slower or much faster than these figures. The traffic police use cameras and radar in some areas to try to enforce speed limits.
- The legal blood/alcohol level for drivers is 0.5mg of alcohol per ml of blood (the same as France, for example) and there are fines and/or prison sentences for exceeding this level.
- Drivers and passengers are required to wear seat (safety) belts at all times.
- One of the most important road rules to be aware of in South Africa is the 'four-way stop' (at crossroads). In many countries, drivers on the major road have priority at such junctions, but not in

South Africa. When you reach a four-way stop, you must stop. If there are other vehicles at the junction, the ones arriving first may cross first.

- If your home country driving licence is printed in English and carries your photograph, you can use it in South Africa for up to six months; if not, you require an International Driving Permit (apply to a national motoring organisation in your home country).
- When driving, always carry your driving licence and passport.

ESTATE AGENT
BEWARE SHARKS!

3.

Your Dream Home

Once you've chosen a location for your dream home in South Africa, you must decide on the type of property that will best suit your requirements and consider the purchase options and the fees associated with buying. When buying a home anywhere, it isn't wise to be in too much of a hurry - and South Africa is no exception. Although it's a common practice, mixing a holiday with property purchase isn't wise, as most people are inclined to make poor decisions when their mind is fixed on play rather than business.

Some people make expensive (even catastrophic) errors when buying a home in South Africa, usually because they don't do sufficient research and are simply in too much of a hurry - often setting themselves ridiculous deadlines such as buying a home during a week's holiday.

Many people have had their fingers burnt by rushing into property deals without proper care and consideration. It's all too easy to fall in love with the beauty and allure of South Africa and sign a contract without giving it sufficient thought. Don't allow yourself to be rushed into making a hasty decision, e.g. by fears of an imminent price rise or because someone else is supposedly interested in a property. It's vital to do your homework thoroughly and avoid the 'dream sellers' (often fellow countrymen) who will happily prey on your ignorance and tell you anything in order to sell you a home.

It's a lucky person who gets his choice absolutely right first time, which is why most experts recommend that you rent before buying unless you're absolutely sure of what you want, how much you can afford to pay and where you want to live (see **Renting Before Buying** on page 120). Have a good look around in your chosen region(s) and obtain an accurate picture of the types of property available, their relative prices and what you can expect to get for your money. However, before doing this, you should make a comprehensive list of what you want (and don't want) from a home, so that you can narrow the field and save time on wild goose chases.

There's no shortage of properties for sale in South Africa (although desirable properties in parts of Cape Town are sometimes in short supply) and, whatever kind of property you're looking for, you're likely have an abundance to choose from. In most areas, properties for sale include derelict farmhouses, un-modernised village homes, modern apartments with all mod cons, and a wide choice of detached villas. Another option is to buy a plot and have a house built to your specifications (see page 166).

Wait until you find something you fall head over heels in love with and then think about it for a week or two before rushing headlong into the purchase. One of the advantages of buying property in South Africa is that there's often another 'dream' home around the next corner – and the second or third dream home is often even better than the first. What seems at first to be the opportunity of a lifetime can turn out to be an expensive pile of stones. **Don't dally too long, however, as good properties at the right price don't remain on the market for long.**

If you're looking for a holiday home, you may wish to investigate a scheme that restricts your occupancy of a property to a number of weeks each year. These include shared ownership, leaseback and timesharing (see page 152).

Don't rush into any of these schemes without fully researching the market and before you're absolutely clear about what you want and what you can realistically expect to get for your money.

RESEARCH

The secret of successfully buying a home in South Africa (or anywhere) is research, research and more research. A successful purchase is much more likely if you thoroughly investigate the various regions, the types of property available, prices and relative values, and the procedure for buying property. The more research you do before committing yourself the better; this should (if possible) include advice from those who already own a home in South Africa, from whom you can usually obtain invaluable information (often based on their own mistakes), as well as by reading publications and visiting property exhibitions.

Property exhibitions are now commonplace in the UK and Ireland, and are increasingly popular with prospective buyers who can get a good idea of what's available and make contact with estate agents and developers. **Appendix A** includes a list of the main exhibition organisers in the UK and Ireland. Property is also advertised in many newspapers and magazines in South Africa and abroad (see **Appendix B**) and on the internet (see **Appendix C**).

SURVIVAL TIP

The cost of investing in a few books or magazines (and other research) is tiny compared with the expense of making a big mistake.

AVOIDING PROBLEMS

The problems associated with buying property abroad have been highlighted in the last few decades, during which the property market in some countries has gone from boom to bust and back again. From a legal point of view, South Africa is one of the safer countries in which to buy a home, and buyers have a high degree of protection under law. However, you should take the usual precautions regarding contracts, deposits and obtaining proper title.

Among the most common problems experienced by buyers in South Africa are:

- Buying in the wrong area (rent first!);
- Buying a home that's difficult to resell: a property with broad appeal in a popular area is usually easiest to sell. A modest, reasonably priced property is usually likely to be much easier to sell than a large expensive home, particularly one requiring restoration or modernisation.
- Buying a house and garden much larger than you need because they seem to offer such good value. Although buying a house with umpteen rooms and several acres of land may seem like a good investment, bear in mind that, should you wish to sell, buyers may be thin on the ground, particularly if the price has doubled or trebled after the cost of renovation (see below). You should think carefully about what you're going to do with a large house and garden. Both will require a lot of maintenance, and your heating and/or air-conditioning costs will be high. After you've installed a swimming pool, tennis court and croquet lawn, you will still have a lot of change left out of even a couple of acres. Do you like gardening or are you prepared to live in a jungle? Can you afford a gardener? Do you plan to make money from the land, e.g. by planting an orchard or a vineyard, or creating a fishing lake, and will you be able to?

  Don't, on the other hand, buy a property that's too small; when you have a home in South Africa, you will inevitably discover that you have many more relatives and 'friends' than you realised!
- Paying too much (due to overcharging by vendors and agents, particularly when selling to foreigners);
- Taking on too large a mortgage;
- Buying a property for renovation and grossly underestimating the restoration costs (see page 164);
- Buying a property for business, e.g. to convert to self-catering accommodation, and being too optimistic about the income;

- Buying a property that doesn't have a reliable water supply (see page 286);
- Not having a survey done on an old property (see page 154);
- Not taking legal advice (see below);
- Not including the necessary conditional clauses in the contract;
- Buying a property without legal title (see page 115);
- Buying a property that's subject to embargoes or an undischarged mortgage, is part of the assets of a company, has been sold illegally by a bankrupt builder or company, is subject to claims by relatives or has been sold to more than one buyer;
- Buying a property that has been built or extended without planning permission;
- Buying from a builder who absconds with your money before completing a property.

Always beware when a property is offered at a seemingly bargain price by a builder, developer or other businessman, in which case you should run a thorough credit check on the vendor and his business.

Land & Title

The right to property is enshrined under section 25 of the Constitution of the Republic of South Africa Act, 1996. It states (somewhat evasively) that nobody may be deprived of property except in terms of law of general application, and no law may permit arbitrary deprivation of property. The registration of rights in land and other immovable property is regulated by the Deeds Registries Act, 1937, and South Africa boasts one of the world's most efficient and sophisticated systems of land registration. Every piece of land is shown on a diagram and ownership recorded in one of the regional Deeds Registries, where documents are available for public viewing, and the system does provide owners with security of title (unlike those of some other countries!).

Although South Africa still recognises an old system of 99-year leasehold, the main real right in land is that of ownership, similar to the UK system of freehold title, and most land in South Africa is privately held by outright ownership. The separate ownership of buildings or parts of buildings in a development is recognised by the Sectional Titles Act, 1986 (see page 143).

South Africa is rich in mineral wealth and the Minerals Act, 1991 (soon to be superseded by the Mineral and Petroleum Resources Act) separates the rights to minerals in and under land from the ownership of the surface rights to the land, so buying a property in South Africa doesn't entitle you to set up a gold mine in the garden!

Redistribution

Since 1994, the ownership of land in South Africa has been the subject of a number of legal and administrative changes, and the international media sometimes carry scare stories claiming that South Africa's policy of 'land redistribution' might lead to a Zimbabwe-style land grab, white owners being thrown off their land with no compensation or, worse, being attacked and perhaps even killed. Ironically, the disastrous situation in Zimbabwe and the resulting international outcry have probably done as much as anything to ensure that South Africa will not be tempted to go down the same path.

Under the old colonial system, 87 per cent of South African land was owned by around 60,000 white farmers or by the state. In 1993 the World Bank warned that, if South Africa didn't undertake 'a major restructuring of the rural economy centred on significant land transfers and smaller scale agricultural production units', the country would be in danger of rural violence, perhaps even civil war. The following year, with the Restitution of Land Rights Act, the first post-apartheid government undertook to consider claims from people who believed they'd been unfairly forced from their land during the apartheid years, and to transfer state-owned land to disadvantaged communities.

The original idea was for a redistribution of land through voluntary sales, called the 'willing buyer/willing seller' approach. The goal was to transfer a third of white-owned farmland over five years. But a decade later, only 2 to 3 per cent has been transferred by this method, and it's estimated that around 90 per cent of South Africa's commercial farmland is still in the hands of 50,000 white farmers. The South African government's stated aim is to settle outstanding individual land claims by the end of 2005, but this seems unrealistic.

This has forced the government to consider different approaches to speed up the process. Financial grants have been increased to make it easier for individuals to buy land and, more controversially, amendments to the 1994 Act were signed, empowering the Minister of Agriculture to expropriate farms without recourse to the courts. This extreme measure is only to be used as a last resort, as an 'encouragement' to white farmers, many of whom are thought to be unwilling to sell their land. Expropriation is allowed only if black South

Africans can demonstrate that the land was once theirs and was unfairly seized; and the existing owner must be fully compensated. An alternative plan is for the government to buy land itself and redistribute it to promote black farming; the goal is to redistribute a third of agricultural land by 2015, but the current funds available are far short of the amount needed to achieve this.

In opposition to these measures, the Transvaal Agricultural Union was recently set up by white farmers to resist land claims, while on the other hand the Landless People's Movement, which claims 100,000 members, has threatened farm invasions in 2005 . . .

Much of the publicity about land redistribution has focused on rural claims, but not all of the land claims are for agricultural land. One of South Africa's biggest land claims concerns Richards Bay in Kwazulu-Natal, the country's largest deepwater harbour. Another claim is for a section of prime land on the Kwazulu-Natal South Coast (south of Durban), affecting around 5,000 mostly white-owned properties, and another is for land at Prince's Grant, one of South Africa's leading golf and housing developments on the Dolphin Coast, around an hour north of Durban.

Property buyers need to be aware of this situation but using a lawyer (see below) will alert you to any claims on property or land that you intend to buy.

Foreign Ownership Limitations

Foreigners intending to buy property in South Africa also need to take heed of rumours that the government has been planning to limit foreign ownership of land in South Africa in order to control escalating property prices. The rumours began circulating in June 2004 but little has been heard since, following an understandable outcry. It seems likely, however, that any mention of such plans was in order to acknowledge the fears of some South Africans about rapidly rising house prices rather than being a serious proposal. Indeed, the suggestion flies in the face of recent government policy to attract more investment into the country, including encouraging foreigners to invest in the commercial as well as the residential property market. Moreover, the most rapid property price inflation has been in the middle and top end of the market and not in lower-price housing, so most South Africans haven't been affected. It's even possible that the whole matter was a scare story, whipped up by the press or the result of crossed lines and poor communication.

Legal Advice

It cannot be emphasised too strongly that anyone planning to buy property in South Africa must take expert, independent legal advice. If you aren't prepared to do this, you shouldn't even think about buying a property! Some people who buy a home in South Africa don't obtain independent legal advice and most of those who experience problems take no precautions whatsoever. Of those who do take legal advice, some do so only after having paid a deposit and signed a contract or, more commonly, after they've run into problems.

SURVIVAL TIP

Never sign anything, or pay any money, until you've sought advice from a lawyer who's experienced in South African property law.

You will find that the relatively small cost (in comparison with the cost of a home) of obtaining legal advice is excellent value, if only for the peace of mind it affords. Trying to cut corners to save a few rand on legal costs is foolhardy in the extreme when a large sum of money is at stake.

Your lawyer will carry out the necessary searches regarding such matters as ownership, debts and rights of way. It isn't wise to use the vendor's lawyer, even if this would save you money, as he's primarily concerned with protecting the interests of the vendor.

Enquiries must be made to ensure that the vendor has registered title and that there are no debts against a property. It's also important to check that a property has the relevant building licences, conforms to local planning restrictions and that any changes (alterations, additions or renovation) have been approved by the local authorities and have planning permission. If a property is owned by several members of a family, all owners must give their consent before it can be sold. See **Conveyancing** on page 193.

Before hiring a lawyer, compare the fees charged by a number of practices and obtain quotations in writing. Always check what's included in the fee and whether it's 'full and binding' or just an estimate (a low basic rate may be supplemented by much more expensive 'extras'). A lawyer's fees may be calculated as an hourly rate (e.g. R1,000/£87 per hour) or as a percentage of the purchase price of a property, e.g. 1 to 2 per cent, with a minimum fee of R2,000 (£175) to R4,000 (£350). You could employ a lawyer just to check the preliminary contract (see below) before signing it to ensure that it's correct and includes everything necessary, particularly regarding conditional clauses.

You may be able to obtain a list of lawyers who speak your language and are experienced in handling South African property sales, either in South Africa or in your home country, e.g. British buyers can obtain a list from the Law Society in the UK. Note, however, that if you use a lawyer in your home country, you may have to pay extra fees, as your lawyer will almost certainly have to use the services of a lawyer in South Africa too.

Be careful who you engage, as some lawyers are part of the problem rather than the solution (overcharging is rife)! Don't pick a lawyer at random, but engage one who has been recommended by someone you can trust.

Professionals

There are professionals speaking English and other languages (particularly Dutch and German) in most areas of South Africa, and some expatriate professionals (e.g. architects, builders and surveyors) also practise there. However, don't assume that a fellow countryman will offer you a better deal or do a better job than a South African (the contrary may be true). It's wise to check the credentials of professionals you employ, whether South African or foreign. It's important to deal only with a qualified and licensed estate agent (see page 128). A surveyor may also be necessary, particularly if you're buying an old property or a property with a large plot (see **Inspections & Surveys** on page 154).

It's never wise to rely solely on advice proffered by those with a financial interest in selling you a property, such as a builder or estate agent, although their advice may be excellent and totally unbiased.

Finance

It's recommended to have your finance in place before you start looking for a property and, if you need a mortgage, to obtain a mortgage guarantee certificate from a bank (see **Mortgages** on page 184).

Buying Off Plan

Many problems can arise when buying off plan (i.e. an unbuilt property) or a property on an unfinished development. Because of the problems associated with buying off plan, such as the difficulty in ensuring that you actually get what's stated in the contract and that the developer doesn't go broke, some experts have advised buyers against buying an unfinished property. If you wish to buy a home in a popular development, however, it's essential to buy off plan.

Although there are many satisfied buyers of off-plan property, the process is usually more time-consuming and stressful than buying a resale property.

An off-plan property isn't finished until the building is complete in every detail (as confirmed by your own lawyer or architect), communal services have been installed, and all the infrastructure is in place, such as roads, parking areas, external lighting and landscaping. A builder is supposed to provide buyers with an insurance policy or banker's 'termination' guarantee, which protects them against the builder going broke before construction is completed. However, some builders fail to obtain insurance, and insurance certificates have even been found to be forged! See **Buying A New Home** on page 139

Buying Land

Before buying building land, ensure that it has planning permission or that planning permission will be a formality. Don't take the vendor's word for this, but make it a condition of the purchase of a building plot. (see **Building Your Own Home** on page 166).

RENTING BEFORE BUYING

To reduce the chance of making an expensive error when buying in an unfamiliar region, it's usually prudent to rent a house for a period, taking in the worst part of the year (weather-wise), especially if you're uncertain about exactly what sort of home you want and where you wish to live. This allows you to become familiar with the region and the weather and gives you plenty of time to look around for a home at your leisure.

SURVIVAL TIP

Renting before buying is even more important for those planning to live permanently or set up a business in South Africa, when it isn't wise to buy a home until you're sure that the business will be a success.

If possible, you should rent a similar property to that which you're planning to buy, during the time of year when you intend to occupy it. Renting allows you to become familiar with not only the weather but also the amenities and the local people, to meet other foreigners who have made their homes in South Africa and share their experiences, and, not least, to discover the lifestyle and the cost of living for yourself. Renting 'buys' you time to find your dream home at your leisure. You may even wish to consider renting a home in South Africa long-term (or 'permanently'), as it saves tying up your capital and can be surprisingly inexpensive in many regions. Some people let their family homes and rent one in South Africa for a period (you may even make a profit!).

If you're looking for a rental property for three to six months, it's best not to rent unseen but to rent a holiday apartment for a week or two to allow yourself time to look around for a long-term rental. Properties for rent are advertised in South African newspapers and magazines, including expatriate publications, and can also be found through property publications in many countries. Many estate agents offer short-term rentals, and builders and developers may rent properties to potential buyers. Short-term rentals (i.e. up to three months) can be found through local tourist offices in South Africa and the South African State Tourist Offices abroad, travel agents, the internet and many overseas newspapers. The best newspapers in the UK are the *Sunday Times*, *Sunday Telegraph* and *Observer*, all of which contain holiday rental classifieds from British homeowners in South Africa.

Long-Term Rentals

If you're looking for a long-term rental (i.e. over three months), you're generally spoilt for choice: it's possible to rent every kind of property, from a tiny studio apartment to a huge, rambling country pile. Rental costs vary considerably according to the size (number of bedrooms) and quality of a property, its age and the facilities provided. However, the most significant factor affecting rents is the region of South Africa, the city and the neighbourhood. Most rents are negotiable and you should try to obtain a reduction. Sometimes an agent will suggest offering a reduced rent (he may even tell you what to offer!). South African landlords often prefer renting to non-resident foreigners, who pay higher rents and are easier to evict! Long-term rents are roughly as follows:

Size Of Property	Monthly Rental (R)	Monthly Rental £
1-bedroom	3,000 – 6,000	260 – 520
2-bedroom	5,000 – 10,000	430 – 870
3-bedroom	8,000 – 17,000	700 – 1,480

Rental Housing Act

When you've chosen a property to rent, you must make an offer in writing. If an estate agent is handling the transaction, he will usually draw up a lease for you to sign (and might ask you for credit references and/or proof of income). If you aren't buying through an agent, you can ask a lawyer to draft a lease or you can do so yourself, using the Rental Housing Act for guidance. All residential leases are governed by the Rental Housing Act, which stipulates that a rental lease must contain the following:

- The landlord's name and address;
- The tenant's name and address;
- The address of the property;
- The rent and any escalation (increases in rent over a period of time);
- Any other costs that the tenant must pay;
- When the rent must be paid, usually the first day of every calendar month;
- The amount of any deposit required;
- The period of the lease;
- The landlord's and tenant's obligations to each other (see below);
- A list of the property's existing defects, if any;
- Any house rules that the tenant has to obey;
- A list of fixtures and furniture (if applicable).

The law imposes the following obligations on landlords and tenants:

- The landlord must issue a detailed written receipt for every payment received from the tenant.
- If a deposit is paid, the landlord must invest it in an interest-bearing bank account and must give the tenant a written statement of the interest earned whenever the tenant asks for one.
- Before the tenant moves in, he and the landlord must inspect the property and compile a list of any defects, which must be attached to the lease.
- When the tenant moves out, he and the landlord must inspect the property again to assess whether any damage has been done. If no damage has been done, the landlord must refund the tenant's deposit and the interest within seven days; if there's damage, the landlord can pay for any repairs out of the deposit and refund the balance and the interest within 14 days.

Short-Term Rentals

South Africa has an abundance of self-catering accommodation for short-term rental (i.e. less than three months) – an overabundance in some coastal holiday areas. You can choose from literally thousands of cottages, apartments, villas, bungalows, mobile homes, chalets, and even the odd stately home or castle. Most property is available for holiday lets only, however, particularly during the peak summer season, and little property is let for more than a few weeks: some foreign owners will let their homes for a few months at a time outside peak periods.

A typical holiday rental is a small cottage or self-contained apartment with one or two bedrooms (sleeping two to four and usually including a sofa bed in the living-room), a large living-room/kitchen with an open fire or stove, and a toilet and bathroom. Always check whether a property is fully equipped (which should mean whatever you want it to mean!) and whether it has some sort of heating, preferably central heating, if you're planning to rent in winter.

Standards vary considerably, from dilapidated, ill-equipped cottages to luxury villas with every modern convenience. Charges are usually levied on a weekly basis (Saturday to Saturday) and vary widely according to the standard, location, number of beds and the facilities provided. For example, a two-bedroom house or apartment in an average area could be rented for R1,150 (£100) per week or less out of season, whereas a similar property in a popular area (e.g. Camp's Bay) might cost up to seven times as much in high season.

Hotels & Hostels

Hotels aren't a cost-effective solution for home hunters, although there's often little choice if you need accommodation for a few days only. Hotel rates in South Africa vary according to the time of year, the location and the individual establishment, although you may be able to negotiate rates outside the high season and for long stays. In most rural towns, a single room in a three-star hotel costs from around R250 (£22) and double rooms from R325 (£28) per night. You should expect to pay at least twice as much in a major city, where cheap hotels are sometimes used as permanent accommodation. South Africa's luxury hotels charge the same high rates as those in London, New York and other expensive cities.

Bed and breakfast accommodation is also available, although it isn't usually budget accommodation. For budget accommodation (around R150/£13 per night) you need to choose a hostel or residence, which is similar to a hotel but contains self-catering apartments or studios. There are also apartment hotels, listed in the yellow pages and on the internet.

HOME EXCHANGE

An alternative to renting is to exchange your home abroad with one in South Africa for a period. This way you can experience home living in South Africa free or for a small cost (if you use an agent) and may save yourself the expense of a long-term rental. Although there's an element of risk involved in exchanging your home with another family (depending on whether your swap is made in heaven or hell!), most agencies thoroughly vet clients and have a track record of successful swaps.

There are home exchange agencies in most countries, many of which are members of the International Home Exchange Association (IHEA). Home exchange companies in the US include HomeLink International, with over 12,500 members in around 50 countries (☎ 813-975 9825, 💻 www.swapnow.com). Two long-established home exchange companies in the UK are HomeLink International, Linfield House, Gorse Hill Road, Virginia Water, Surrey GU25 4AS, UK (☎ 01344-842642, 💻 www.homelink.org.uk), which publishes a directory of homes and holiday homes for exchange, and Home Base Holidays, 7 Park Avenue, London N13 5PG, UK (☎ 020-8886 8752, 💻 www.homebase-hols.com), which has a representative in South Africa.

TYPES OF PROPERTY

There's a wide variety of residential property available in South Africa, including apartments, townhouses, detached houses, 'cluster housing' (freehold houses in a complex, sometimes with shared facilities, e.g. gardens and swimming pool), sectional title units (see **Community Properties** on page 143), retirement properties, farmhouses, villas, mansions and castles.

Apartments

Apartments are ubiquitous in South Africa's towns, cities and coastal resorts. As well as continuing to build new apartments, developers are increasingly converting non-residential buildings, e.g. factories or warehouses, into luxury apartments - especially in inner cities. Apartments in older buildings tend to have higher ceilings than those in modern apartment blocks and either have smaller rooms or, in the case of converted factory or warehouse apartments, are open-plan.

Apartments are generally good value and, if they're in a popular tourist location, offer year-round rental potential. Advantages of apartment living include low maintenance (once you've carried out any necessary work), security (especially if the block has 24-hour security or a *concierge*) and the use of communal gardens and pool (and possibly other facilities such as tennis courts). Apartments in towns have the added advantage of local facilities and amenities within walking distance.

Disadvantages can include noisy neighbours, poorly-maintained buildings and grounds, crowded complexes during holidays and little storage space (although many new apartments have fitted wardrobes). Owners of properties in most apartment blocks in South Africa are members of a community of owners and must abide by the community's rules, and pay community (see **Community Properties** on page 143).

Houses

South Africa has a range of semi-detached houses and detached houses with small gardens or patios, which usually form part of a purpose-built residential area. Construction is generally of excellent quality – marble floors and top-of-the-range kitchens are the norm. Resort developments, some of which are extremely upmarket, often have communal gardens with a swimming pool and sports facilities such as tennis courts. There may also be 24-hour security on the complex.

The advantages of a modern home on a residential complex include little upkeep (and no restoration work!), spacious living, use of communal gardens and pool without maintenance costs or work, and community living with fewer neighbours than in an apartment.

Among the disadvantages are high community fees and a lack of historic architecture. As in the case of apartments, owners of properties in some residential complex in South Africa are members of a community of owners and must abide by the community's rules, and pay community fees (see **Community Properties** on page 143).

Country Properties

Some foreign buyers in South Africa avoid the coastal resorts of the Western Cape, the Garden Route and Kwazulu-Natal and opt for a country property, of which there are many in South Africa's vast hinterland. They range from humble cottages huts to vast estates, particularly in those areas where there's high rural unemployment and the population is migrating from the country to the cities. Almost all country properties come with large plots and many include fruit trees, vineyards, other crops or pasture. Renovation is sometimes necessary, unless you pay a premium for a property that has already been modernised.

Advantages of country properties include lower prices (in most areas), peace and quiet, lower local taxes (usually) and the opportunity to live in the 'real' South Africa. On the other hand, rural properties sometimes involve extensive maintenance as well as restoration work, utilities may be poor or non-existent, amenities and facilities are often some distance away and you don't have the advantage of a ready-made community.

The good news is that South African small town and village communities are generally friendly, although sometimes after an initial period of 'sussing you out'. In some rural areas, e.g. the Winelands (see page 86), there are established expatriate communities, particularly English or German-speaking, for those who are reluctant to sever all ties with 'home'.

Architectural Styles

South Africa has a wide range of architectural styles, which is a reflection of the many and various cultural influences that have shaped the country: indigenous, British, Dutch, French, German, Malay and others. There are mud buildings with roofs made from a variety of materials (e.g. sticks, thatch and corrugated iron), wattle-and-daub huts, thatched houses with whitewashed walls and gables, Victorian and Edwardian mansions, Mediterranean villas and modern high-rises, the functional but attractive' Cape Malay' styles found in parts of Cape Town, Art Deco elegance in Durban, and ornate 'Cape Dutch' houses (see below).

Cape Dutch

South Africa's emblematic architectural style, much loved by tourist brochure photographers, is Cape Dutch. The style is an amalgamation of influences: Dutch, German, Huguenot and Indonesian. The earliest Cape Dutch houses are single-storied and utilitarian, usually three rooms in a row, with steeply pitched roofs supported by rafters and walls made of clay or thick rubble; later buildings are made of burnt brick, with sea shells used as the basis of the lime mortar and reeds for the thatched roofs.

With increasing prosperity (from the beginning of the 18th century), houses began to grow in size and reflect the individual needs and taste of each owner. Front gables began to be added, largely made by craftsmen brought over from the Far East, and a variety of styles began to develop. By the mid-18th century, owners began to add wings onto either end of the basic structures, leading to the so-called U-plan. Floors were made of compacted earth or Robben Island slate, and shutters were added to windows. Other styles of building plan also evolved, including the T-plan and H-plan.

Later still, outbuildings began to be added, including a house (*jonkershuis*) for the eldest son, stables, coach houses, slaves' quarters and wine cellars. The very best Cape Dutch buildings are found in parts of the Cape Peninsula and the nearby Winelands.

HOUSE HUNTING

There are many ways of finding homes for sale in South Africa, including the following:

- **Newspapers & Magazines** – Useful publications include *Cape Argus* and *Cape Times* (Cape Town), *Daily Dispatch* (East London), *Mail & Guardian, Sunday Times* and *The Star* (Johannesburg), and *Daily News* and *Natal Mercury* (Durban).
- **Property Exhibitions** – See **Appendix A** for details;
- **The Internet** – There are literally thousands of sites dedicated to property in South Africa. These can be found by typing in 'South African property' or, for example, 'Cape Town property' in a search engine such as Google (💻 www.google.com), Yahoo (💻 www.yahoo.com) or Altavista (💻 www.altavista.com). Most sites belong to or are linked to an estate agent or agents.
- **Property Tours** – Tours are organised by some agents, usually concentrating on a particular area in South Africa over several days, during which you get a good idea of what's available and an insight into local life. Some tours include visits to tourist attractions as well as the chance to sample local food and drink.
- **Visiting An Area** – Some property owners in South Africa sell privately to avoid paying an agent's commission and put 'For Sale' signs outside the property. This is particularly common in rural areas, where properties may also be advertised in bars. Ask local people if they know of any properties for sale.
- **Estate Agents** – See below.

Public Holidays

If you're making a house-hunting trip, make sure you avoid public holidays (if any fall on a Sunday, the following Monday is deemed a public holiday). South African public holidays are as follows:

Date	Holiday
1st January	New Year's Day
21st March	Human Rights Day
March or April	Good Friday
12th April	Family Day
27th April	Freedom Day
1st May	Workers' Day
16th June	Youth Day
9th August	National Women's Day
24th September	Heritage Day
16th December	Day of Reconciliation
25th December	Christmas Day
26th December	Day of Goodwill

ESTATE AGENTS

There are around 36,000 registered estate agents in South Africa - no doubt attracted by the average commission of around 7.5 per cent - ranging from huge national and international chains to small, local operations. South Africa's largest estate agents (in alphabetical order) include Aida (💻 www.aida.co.za), ERA (💻 www.era.co.za), Homenet (different website addresses in different regions), Nationlink (💻 www. nationlinkproperty.com), Pam Golding (💻 www.pamgolding.co.za), Rawson (💻 www.rawson.co.za), REMAX (different website addresses in different regions) and Seeff Property Services (💻 www.seeff.com). If you wish to find an agent in a particular town or area, look in the local telephone book or yellow pages or use the internet.

Dealing with an estate agent in South Africa is similar to dealing with one in Australia, Europe or the United States: most are well organised and professional (some are positively sleek). The industry is controlled by the government-established Estate Agency Affairs Board (☎ 011-880 9994, 💻 www.eaab.org.za), with which all estate agents must be registered. All agents are issued (annually) with a fidelity fund certificate and must comply with the Board's Code of Conduct. A current certificates should be displayed; if it isn't, check with the Board that an agent is registered. Agents must also have either undertaken an examination course in the principles of estate agency or completed a year's practical training under the guidance of a qualified 'full status' estate agent. If you have a complaint against an estate agent or believe that he has mismanaged your money, you should contact the Board.

Some people, particularly the UK, use an agent in their own country with an office in South Africa or who works with one or more South African agents. You may pay higher fees when dealing with a foreign agent, as there may be more people involved and local property owners may inflate the price when they think a 'rich' foreigner is interested in buying their home.

> **SURVIVAL TIP**
> **If you're using a foreign agent, confirm (and reconfirm) that a particular property is still for sale and the price before travelling to South Africa to view it.**

Obtain details of as many properties as possible in your chosen area and make a shortlist of those you wish to view (it's also wise to mark them on a map). Details provided by South African estate agents are usually extensive, although in the case of old properties in need of renovation, there obviously isn't much information that can be given except the land area and the number and size of buildings. Most serious agents have extensive websites providing details of properties they offer (as well as information about the legal and financial aspects of buying and selling property, and quite often general information about life in South Africa), although not all properties are included on them and you may need to register to view those that are. South African agents who advertise in foreign journals or who work closely with overseas agents may provide colour photographs and a full description, particularly for expensive properties.

> **SURVIVAL TIP**
> **Whoever you buy through, make sure that you know the local market value of property, as it's easy to pay over the odds in popular areas.**

Never allow yourself to be pressurised into a purchase and always take independent expert legal advice (see page 117). Some agents pressurise clients into signing contracts and paying deposits quickly, alleging that there are queues of other clients waiting to buy the property (which may be true!). Some even claim that legal advice is unnecessary or that they provide it themselves, which is both illegal and unethical. Your chance of solving any problems is greater if you take legal advice, and registered lawyers have professional indemnity insurance. There are, however, many reputable estate agents in South Africa, who provide an excellent and reliable service.

Commission

The commission charged by estate agents varies, the average being around 7.5 per cent plus Value Added Tax (VAT), which is invariably paid by the seller. Some sellers charge a fixed commission, e.g. R15,000 on properties costing up to R300,000 and up to R65,000 on properties costing up to R2 million. The cheaper the property, the higher the fee tends to be as a percentage of the sale; on the most expensive properties fees tend to be more negotiable. In any case, you're free to negotiate the agent's commission (whether a fixed fee or a percentage).

Before using an agent, check whether he makes extra charges (apart from the normal fees and taxes associated with buying a property in South Africa - see **Fees** on page 138) for services such as additional viewings, checking the property on your behalf, and arranging for the connection of utilities.

Viewing

Some South African agents expect customers to know where they want to buy within a 30 to 40km (20 to 25mi) radius and may even expect you to narrow your choice down to certain towns or villages. If you cannot define where and what you're looking for, at least tell the agent so that he will know that you're undecided. If you're 'just looking' (window shopping), say so. Most agents will still be pleased to show you properties, as they're well aware that many people fall in love with (and buy) a property on the spot.

A South African agent may ask you to sign a document before showing you any properties; this is simply to protect his commission should you obtain details from another source or try to do a deal directly with the owner. You're usually shown properties personally by agents and won't be given the keys (particularly to furnished properties) or be expected to deal with tenants or vendors directly.

You should make an appointment to see properties, as agents don't like people simply turning up and asking to view a property. **If you make an appointment, you should keep it or call and cancel it.** If you're on holiday, you can drop in unannounced to have a look at what's on offer, but don't expect an agent to show you properties. If you view properties during a holiday, it's wise to do so at the beginning so that you can return later to inspect any you particularly like a second or third time. South African estate agents usually work on Saturdays and even on Sundays in some areas during the peak season.

You should try to view as many properties as possible during the time available, but allow sufficient time to view each property thoroughly, to travel (and get lost) between houses, and for breaks for sustenance. Although it's important to see sufficient properties to form an accurate opinion of price and quality, don't see too many in one day (between four and six is usually a manageable number) as it's easy to become confused as to the merits of each property. If you're shown properties that don't meet your requirements, tell the agent immediately. You can help the agent to narrow the field by telling him exactly what's wrong with the properties you reject.

It's wise to make notes of both the good **and** bad features, and take lots of photographs of the properties you like, so that you're able to compare them later at your leisure, but keep a record of which photos are of which house! It's also wise to mark each property on a map so that, should you wish to return, you can find them without getting lost (too often). The more a property appeals to you, the more you should look for faults and negative points; if you still like it after stressing the negative points, it must have special appeal!

PROPERTY PRICES

The figures in the table below are average property prices (published by ABSA bank) in each province during the period 2000–2003.

Province	Average Property Price (R)	(£)
Western Province	392,500	34,130
Gauteng	373,720	32,500
Kwazulu-Natal	295,060	25,650
North West	282,421	24,558
Eastern Cape	278,820	24,245
Mpumalanga	250,790	21,800
Limpopo (Northern Province)	246,490	21,435
Free State	243,865	21,200
Northern Cape	225,792	19,635

The sections below indicate the types of property that can be bought in secure, desirable areas in a variety of price ranges; all prices are in rand (to convert to sterling, divide by 11.5; for US dollars, divide by 6). For details of prices in particular areas, see **Provinces** on page 60.

250,000 – 500,000

- 1-bed apartment in Bellville (Cape Town);
- 1-bed apartment in Muizenberg (Western Cape);
- Isolated 4-bed house near Mossel Bay (Western Cape);
- 1-bed apartment in George (Western Cape);
- 2-bed house in Jeffreys Bay (Eastern Cape);
- 2-bed townhouse in Port Elizabeth (Eastern Cape);
- 2-bed apartment in East London (Eastern Cape);
- Basic 3-bed house in Amanzimtoti (Kwazulu-Natal);
- 2-bed house in Hibberdene (Kwazulu-Natal);
- 1-bed apartment in Uvongo (Kwazulu-Natal);
- 1-bed apartment in Margate (Kwazulu-Natal).

500,000 – 750,000

- 2-bed apartment in Simon's Town (Western Cape);
- 3-bed apartment in Mossel Bay (Western Cape);
- 2-bed apartment in Plettenburg Bay (Western Cape);
- 3-bed house in St Francis Bay (Eastern Cape);
- Small 3-bed house in Port Elizabeth (Eastern Cape);
- 2-bed apartment in Amanzimtoti (Kwazulu-Natal);
- 5-bed house in Hibberdene (Kwazulu-Natal);
- 4-bed house in Port Shepstone (Kwazulu-Natal);
- 3-bed townhouse in Uvongo (Kwazulu-Natal);
- 3-bed house in Margate (Kwazulu-Natal).

750,000 – 1 Million

- Small house or apartment in City Bowl or Gardens Suburbs (Cape Town);
- 2-bed house in Jongensfontein or Stilbaai (Western Cape); 3-bed beachfront apartment in Mossel Bay (Western Cape);
- 3-bed house in George (Western Cape);

- 3-bed apartment in Plettenburg Bay (Western Cape);
- 2-bed house near port in St Francis Bay (Eastern Cape);
- 3-bed house in Kenton-on-Sea (Eastern Cape);
- 3-bed house in East London (Eastern Cape);
- 3-bed house with pool in Amanzimtoti (Kwazulu-Natal);
- 4-bed townhouse in Margate (Kwazulu-Natal).

1 – 2 Million

- House or apartment in Gardens Suburb (Cape Town);
- 3-bed house in northern suburbs (Cape Town);
- 3-bed bungalow in southern suburbs (Cape Town);
- 3-bed house in Green Point or Sea Point (Cape Town);
- 3-bed house in Pinelands (Western Cape);
- 2-bed apartment in Muizenberg or Fish Hoek (Western Cape);
- 5-bed mansion in Fish Hoek (Western Cape);
- 3-bed townhouse in Simon's Town (Western Cape);
- 2-bed apartment in Stellenbosch (Western Cape);
- 3–4-bed house in the Winelands (Western Cape);
- 5-bed house in Gaansbaai (Western Cape);
- 3-bed house in Mossel Bay (Western Cape);
- 4-bed house in Jongensfontein or Stilbaai (Western Cape);
- Stylish 3-bed house in George (Western Cape);
- 3-bed house in Knysna (Western Cape);
- 4-bed house near beach in Port Elizabeth (Eastern Cape);
- 4–5-bed house in Kenton-on-Sea (Eastern Cape);
- 4-bed house in East London (Eastern Cape);
- 3–4-bed house in Uvongo (Kwazulu-Natal);
- 3-bed house in Durban North or Umhlanga Rocks (Kwazulu-Natal);
- 3-bed apartment or 3-bed house with pool in Ballito (Kwazulu-Natal).

2 – 3 Million

- 4-bed house in Southern Suburbs (Cape Town);
- 3–4-bed house in Muizenberg (Western Cape);

- 4-bed house in Simon's Town (Western Cape);
- Mansion in Jongensfontein or Stilbaai (Western Cape);
- 4-bed house in Plettenburg Bay (Western Cape);
- 5-bed house in prime location in Hibberdene (Kwazulu-Natal);
- 4-bed house in Westville (Kwazulu-Natal).

3 - 5 Million

- 3-bed house in Waterfront (Cape Town);
- 4-bed house in Southern Suburbs (Cape Town);
- 5-bed house in Noordhoek (Western Cape);
- 3-bed apartment on East Peninsula Coast (Western Cape);
- 5-bed seafront mansion in Fish Hoek (Western Cape);
- 5-bed house in Simon's Town (Western Cape);
- 4–5-bed waterfront apartments in St Francis Bay (Eastern Cape);
- 5-bed seafront apartment in Jeffreys Bay (Eastern Cape);
- 4-bed beachfront house in Amanzimtoti (Kwazulu-Natal);
- 5-bed house in Uvongo (Kwazulu-Natal);
- 5-bed house in Durban North or Umhlanga Rocks (Kwazulu-Natal).

5 - 10 Million

- Mansion in Clifton or Camp's Bay (Western Cape);
- 3-bed house in Llandudno (Western Cape);
- 3-bed house in Hout Bay (Western Cape);
- 3-bed beachfront apartment on East Peninsula Coast (Western Cape).

Over 10 Million

- Mansion in Southern Suburbs (Cape Town);
- Mansion in the Winelands (Western Cape).

With prices in the Western Cape now beyond the reach of some people and Garden Route prices increasing too, more buyers are looking to the coasts either side of Durban and prices are expected to rise imminently, although predicting what will happen to the property market is a reliable way to make yourself look foolish. The same data can be open to very different interpretation: for example, some people think that the strengthening rand will lead to an imminent reduction in the number of foreign property buyers in South Africa, while others believe that the stronger rand will boost confidence in the South African economy and attract more foreigners to buy.

Garages & Parking Bays

The cost of parking is an important consideration when buying in a town or resort in South Africa, particularly if you have a number of cars. A garage or private parking space isn't always included in the price when you buy a new apartment or townhouse in South Africa, although secure parking may be available at an additional cost, possibly in an underground garage. Modern detached homes usually have a garage or a basement that can be used as a garage. Smaller homes normally have a single garage, while larger properties may have garaging for up to four cars. A lock-up garage is important in areas with a high incidence of car theft and theft from cars (e.g. most cities) and is also useful to protect your car from climatic extremes – particularly too much sun and heat.

Without a private garage or parking space, parking can be a nightmare (and dangerous), particularly in cities and during the summer in busy resorts or developments. Free on-street parking can be difficult or impossible to find in cities and large towns, and in any case may be inadvisable for anything but a wreck. If you're buying in a large development, note that the nearest parking area may be some distance from your home. This may be an important factor, particularly if you aren't up to carrying heavy shopping hundreds of metres and possibly up several flights of stairs.

It's usually cheaper to rent a parking bay than a garage, but even these can be expensive: in outlying areas of Cape Town, for example, the price of a parking bay is between R38,000 (£3,300) and R45,000 (£3,900) and in the City Bowl or the fashionable central area of Long Street, a bay can cost between R70,000 (£6,00) and R100,000 (£8,700).

The cost of a garage or parking space isn't always recouped when selling, although it makes a property more attractive and may clinch a sale. Parking isn't usually a problem when buying an old home in a rural area, although there may not be a purpose-built garage.

Negotiating The Price

When buying a property in South Africa it pays to haggle over the price, even if you think it's a bargain. Don't be put off by a high asking price, as most sellers are willing to negotiate. Many properties sell for a lot less than their original asking prices, particularly luxury properties. Sellers generally presume that buyers will bargain and rarely expect to receive the asking price (although some vendors ask an unrealistic price and won't budge a rand!). In popular areas (e.g. the Waterfront in Cape Town), asking prices may be unrealistically high particularly to snare the unsuspecting and ignorant foreign buyer. There has been evidence of dual pricing (the practice of quoting higher prices to foreigners) in the past and, although now rare, it still occurs. To get an idea of property prices in different regions of South Africa, check the prices of properties advertised in property magazines and South African newspapers, magazines and property journals. It may be worthwhile obtaining an independent valuation (appraisal) to determine a property's 'true' value. **Always be prepared to walk away from a deal rather than pay too high a price.**

An offer should be made in writing, as it's likely to be taken more seriously than a verbal offer. If you're using an agent, you should ask him what to offer, although he may not tell you (and indeed shouldn't if he's also acting for the seller). If you make an offer that's too low, you can always raise it, but it's usually impossible to lower an offer once it has been accepted (if your first offer is accepted without discussion, you will never know how low you could have gone!). On the other hand, if you make a very low offer, an owner may feel insulted and refuse to do business with you! If you make a low offer, it's wise to indicate to the owner a few points of weakness (without being too critical) that merit a reduction in price. If an offer is rejected, it may be worth waiting a week or two before making a higher offer, depending on the market and how keen you are to buy a particular property. If a property has been realistically priced, you shouldn't expect to obtain more than a 5 or 10 per cent reduction, although cash buyers in some areas may be able to negotiate a considerable reduction for a quick sale, depending on the state of the local property market and the urgency of the sale.

If you're seeking an investment property, it's best to buy in an area that's in high demand, preferably with both buyers and renters. For the best resale opportunities, it's usually best to buy in an area or community (and style) that's attractive to South African buyers. Buying a 'distress sale' from an owner who simply must sell is likely to result in the best deal. Obviously you will be in a better position if you're a cash buyer and are able to close quickly.

Whatever your reason for buying and whatever type of property you're seeking, you should find out as much as possible about a property before making an offer, including the following:

- When it was built;
- How long the owners have lived there;

- Whether it's a permanent or holiday home;
- Why they're selling (they may not tell you outright but may offer clues);
- How keen they are to sell (again, you might need to infer this);
- How long the property has been on the market;
- The condition of the property;
- What the neighbours and the neighbourhood are like;
- Local property taxes and insurance rates;
- Not least, whether the asking price is realistic.

Timing is of the essence in the bargaining process and it's essential to find out how long a property has been on the market (generally the longer it has been for sale, the more likely a lower offer will be accepted) and how desperate the vendor is to sell. Some people will tell you outright that they must sell by a certain date and that they will accept any reasonable offer. You may be able to find out from neighbours why someone is selling, which may help you to decide whether an offer would be accepted. If a property has been on the market for a long time, e.g. longer than six months in a popular area, it may be overpriced (unless it has obvious problems). If there are many desirable properties for sale in a particular area or development that have been on the market a long time, you should find out why.

For your part you must ensure that you keep any 'sensitive' information from a seller and give the impression that you have all the time in the world (even if you're desperate to buy immediately!). All this 'cloak and dagger' stuff may seem unethical, but you can be assured that if you were selling and a prospective buyer knew you were desperate and would accept a low offer, he certainly wouldn't be in a hurry to pay you any more!

If applicable, have fixtures and fittings listed in the contract. It's also wise to take photographs if a property contains original architectural details such as stone fireplaces, door and window lintels, and garden statuary, which may be removed or replaced by copies. See also **Final Checks** on page 194.

Before deciding on the price, make sure you know exactly what's included, as it isn't unheard of for people to strip a house or apartment bare when selling, including the kitchen sink, toilets, light fittings and even the light switches!

FEES

A variety of fees (also called closing or completion costs) are payable when you buy a property in South Africa, including those detailed below. **Before signing a preliminary contract, check exactly what fees are payable and have them confirmed in writing.**

In addition to the fees associated with buying a home, you must also take into account the running costs. These include local property taxes (see page 217), building insurance (see page 232), contents insurance (see page 233), standing charges for utilities (see page 139), community fees for a community property (see page 144), garden and pool maintenance costs, and a caretaker's or management fees if you leave a home empty or let it (see page 237). Annual running costs usually average around 2 to 4 per cent of the cost of a property.

Transfer Duty

Transfer duty is a tax levied on the transfer of ownership of fixed property. If you're buying as a company, a close corporation or a trust (sometimes called a 'legal entity'), transfer duty is levied at a flat rate of 10 per cent of the purchase price. If you're buying as an individual (officially termed a 'natural person'!), duty is calculated on the following scale: If you buy a home in South Africa, you must pay transfer duty on the value of the property above R140,000 (£12,173). Duty is levied at 5 per cent on the value between R140,000 and R320,000 (£27,826), and at 8 per cent on any value over R320,000. For example, on a property costing R500,000 (£43,500), you will pay R31,700 (£2,756) in stamp duty.

Value (R)	Duty Rate (%)	Cumulative Duty (R)
Up to 150,000	0	0
150,001 - 320,000	5	8,500
Over 320,000	8	

Legal Or Conveyancing Fees

These are calculated on a sliding scale and amount to between 1 and 2 per cent of the purchase price, depending on the value of the property.

Bank & Mortgage Costs

Bank inspection fees are around 0.2 per cent of the valuation, and the mortgage arrangement fee is around 1 to 1.5 per cent of the loan amount.

Utility Fees

If you buy a new property, you must usually pay for electricity and water connections (and occasionally gas, but it's little used in South Africa) and the installation of meters. You should ask the builder or developer to provide the cost of connection to services in writing. If you buy a resale property, you must usually pay for the cost of new contracts, particularly water (see **Utilities** on page 281).

Other Fees

Other fees may include surveyor's or inspection fees (see **Inspections & Surveys** on page 154), architect's fees and the cost of moving house (see **Chapter 6**).

Note that stamp duty was abolished in the 2004 budget but is still (erroneously) mentioned on many websites dealing with buying property in South Africa.

BUYING A NEW HOME

Although new properties may lack the charm and character of older buildings, they offer attractive financial and other advantages. There are no costs or problems associated with renovation or modernisation, and they're cheaper to heat and maintain due to the modern building methods and materials employed. The standard of new buildings in South Africa is strictly regulated and is generally higher than that of old houses. New homes usually have good insulation and ventilation, providing lower heating bills in winter and keeping homes cooler in summer. It's often cheaper to buy a new home than to restore a derelict property, as the price is fixed, unlike the cost of renovation, which can soar way beyond original estimates – as many people have discovered to their cost! If required, a new property can usually be let immediately and modern homes have good resale potential and are considered a good investment by South African buyers. On the other hand, new homes are usually smaller than old properties and rarely come with a large plot.

A huge variety of new properties is available in South Africa, including coastal and city apartments, sports developments (e.g. golf), and a wide range of individually designed detached houses. Many new properties are part of purpose-built, gated developments, often located near the coast or in the mountains, and offer a range of sports facilities, which may include a golf course, swimming pool, tennis and squash courts, a gymnasium or fitness club and a restaurant (see **Community Properties** on page 143).

Some purpose-built developments are planned as holiday homes and may not be attractive as permanent homes (they're also generally expensive).

If you're buying an apartment or a house that's part of a development, check whether your neighbours will be mainly South African or other foreigners. Some people don't wish to live in a 'ghetto' of their fellow countrymen and this might also deter South African buyers when you want to sell.

Some new properties are sold by property developers or builders, although they're also marketed by estate agents. It's possible to check a developer's or builder's financial status, although your best insurance is their reputation. Ask for details of their previous developments and, if possible, visit them and ask owners whether they're satisfied with their homes. New developments have a sales office and may have a show house or apartment.

Buying Off Plan

When buying a new property in a development, you're usually obliged to buy it 'off plan', i.e. before it's built. In fact, if a development is built and largely unsold, particularly a quality development in a popular area, it usually means that there's something wrong with it! The contract contains the timetable for the property's completion, payment dates, the completion date and penalties for non-completion, guarantees for building work, and a copy of the plans and drawings. The floor plan and technical specifications are signed by both parties to ensure that the standard and size of construction is adhered to.

Payments are spread over 12 to 18 months, although the payment schedule can vary considerably. A typical payment schedule may consist of a 5 per cent reservation fee, 15 per cent on signing the preliminary contract, 30 per cent during construction and 50 per cent on completion. If a property is already partly built, the builder will ask for a higher initial payment, depending on its stage of completion. You may be able to persuade a builder to agree to your withholding 5 or 10 per cent of the final payment for a period (e.g. six months) as an insurance against defects.

If you're buying a property off plan, you can usually choose your bathroom suite, kitchen, fireplace, wallpaper and paint, wall and floor tiles, and carpet in bedrooms, some of which may be included in the price. You may also be able to alter the interior room layout, although this will increase the price. Some developers will negotiate over the price or include extras free of charge (such as a fitted kitchen when it isn't included in the price), particularly if a development isn't selling well.

SURVIVAL TIP
You should make any changes or additions to a property, such as including a chimney or additional shower room, during the design stage, as they will cost much more to make later.

BUYING A MODERN RESALE HOME

The vast majority of homes for sale in South Africa are 'resale' homes, i.e. they've been previously owned and occupied. There are many advantages to buying a modern resale home compared with a brand new home; these may include the following:

- An established development with a range of local services and facilities in operation;
- More individual design and style;
- No 'teething troubles';
- Savings on the cost of installing water and electricity meters and telephone lines, or the cost of extending these services to the property;
- Furniture and other extras included in the price;
- A mature garden and trees;
- A larger plot.

With a resale property you can see exactly what you will get for your money, and the previous owners may have made improvements or added extras such as a swimming pool, which may not be fully reflected in the asking price.

Resale properties often represent good value, particularly in resort areas, where many apartments and townhouses are sold fully furnished, although the quality of furnishings varies considerably – from luxurious to junk – and may not be to your taste. (Luxury properties and villas are rarely sold furnished).

When buying a resale property in a development, it's wise to ask the neighbours about any problems, community fees, planned developments and anything else that may affect your enjoyment of the property (see **Community Properties** on page 143). Most residents are usually happy to tell you – unless of course they're trying to sell you their own property!

You should consider having a survey done on a resale property, as major problems can be found even in properties less than five years old (see **Inspections & Surveys** on page 154).

BUYING AN OLD HOME

In South Africa, the term 'old home' usually refers to a building that's pre-war and possibly hundreds of years old, which either is in need of restoration and modernisation or has already been restored. If you want a property with abundant charm and character, a building for renovation or conversion, outbuildings or a large plot, you must usually buy an old property. Note, however, that if an old building is listed (preserved or protected by local or national statute) there may be limitations on its use and any changes you may wish to make to it (see **Conveyancing** on page 193).

South Africa has a fair amount of beautiful historic buildings, particularly from the 17th to 19th centuries, covering the whole spectrum from tiny village houses to rambling mansions. In some rural areas, it's still possible to buy old properties for as little as R150,000 (£13,000), although you will need to carry out major renovation work, which will double or treble the price. Because the purchase price is often low, some foreign buyers believe they're getting a wonderful bargain, without fully investigating the renovation costs.

Renovation or modernisation costs will invariably be higher than you imagined or planned. Taking on too large a task in terms of restoration is a common mistake among foreign buyers in all price brackets. If you're planning to buy a property that needs restoration or renovation and you won't be doing the work yourself, obtain an accurate estimate of the costs before signing a contract.

If the property is off the beaten track, you may need to include the cost of building or at least resurfacing a road so that heavy vehicles can reach the site. The cost of building the most basic road is at least R200 (£17) per metre.

In any case, it isn't usually cheaper to buy and restore an old building than to buy a new one, and it can be much more expensive. If you buy and restore a property with the intention of selling it for a profit, you must take into account not only the initial price and the restoration costs, but also the fees and taxes included in the purchase, plus possibly capital gains tax (see page 215). It's often difficult to sell an old renovated property at a higher than average market price, irrespective of its added value.

Don't buy a derelict property unless you have the courage, determination and money to overcome the many problems you will certainly face. Unless you're prepared to wait until you can occupy it or are willing to live in a caravan for a long time while you work on it, it's better to spend a bit more and buy something habitable but untidy than to buy a property that needs gutting before you can live in it.

On the other hand, old properties may provide better value than new homes, although you must check their quality and condition carefully. As with most things in life, you generally get what you pay for, so you shouldn't expect a fully restored property for peanuts.

COMMUNITY PROPERTIES

In South Africa, apartments and townhouses are sometimes part of what are known as sectional title schemes or sectional title development schemes, in accordance with the Sectional Titles Act No 95 of 1986. This means that properties are part of a community, where individuals own their own apartment or house but share common areas, e.g. driveways, gardens, swimming pools, corridors, gardens, lifts (elevators), entrance foyers, parking areas, outer walls, foundations and the roof. In South Africa, a sectional title development is called a 'unit' and an individual property is called a 'section'; to avoid confusion, however, developments will be referred to as 'schemes' and individual properties as 'properties'.

Parts of a scheme are sometimes designated as 'exclusive use areas'. These include gardens, patios, parking bays, garages and storerooms. If this is the case, you don't own the area concerned but have exclusive use of it. Under the terms of the 1986 Act, an owner can sell the use of an exclusive use area to another owner in the scheme but not to an outsider. This doesn't apply to owners in schemes registered under the previous (1971) Act.

The common property of a sectional title scheme is controlled and run by the scheme's 'body corporate' – the collective name given to all of the owners of properties in a scheme. But the everyday running of the scheme is entrusted to 'trustees', who are appointed by the body corporate. People familiar with Spanish urbanisations will recognise this way of doing things: residents of a group of apartments and/or townhouses appoint a committee with a president (from their own number) to run common affairs.

Trustees are almost always owners of properties in a scheme. The minimum number of trustees in each scheme is two, but the Act doesn't specify a maximum number. To be a successful trustee, you should have knowledge of at least some of the following (in which case you may save the scheme money on professional fees): the law, accountancy, electrical and mechanical devices and problems, bookkeeping and general administration. Trustees often receive no payment for their work (except expenses), although the body corporate will sometimes agree to pay a trustee or trustees.

Major decisions concerning sectional title schemes are made by the body corporate at an annual meeting, usually called the Annual General Meeting (AGM), or at a Special General Meeting, presided over by the chairman of the trustees. These gatherings are held to approve budgets, appoint trustees and consider changes to the rules (provided that these aren't contrary to the intentions and spirit of the Sectional Titles Act). Discussions on these occasions are sometimes lively, occasionally confrontational, and all members of the body corporate are entitled to vote (unless they're in arrears with fee payments or in serious breach of the rules). Unless otherwise decided, an individual owner's voting power is determined by his percentage ownership of the entire scheme (for example, he might own more than one apartment or townhouse) – known as his Participation Quota (PQ).

Managing Agents

Running a large sectional title scheme can be complicated and time-consuming and, unless the body corporate is particularly well supplied with people with a wide range of specialist knowledge and experience, it can prove impossible to do successfully. As a result, some bodies corporate appoint a managing agent to carry out some or all of the work – usually a company that specialises in sectional title administration. A managing agent must be registered with The Estate Agents Board (see page 128) and hold a fidelity fund certificate issued by the Board.

The managing agent sends out monthly statements of work and accounts, carries out bookkeeping, recovers unpaid debts, arranges quotes for maintenance and repairs, and helps the trustees with the many tasks involved in administering the scheme. A good managing agent can save a body corporate a lot of time, trouble, stress and expense. On the other hand, a frequent criticism of sectional title schemes is the low standard of managing agents.

Fees

Payment for the administration and running of a sectional title scheme is shared among the owners. Costs incurred include insurance premiums, repairs and maintenance charges, the wages of cleaning, maintenance and gardening staff, and water and electricity used on the common property. These are paid for by a monthly levy, which every owner must pay. Any costs incurred in the upkeep and maintenance of exclusive use areas are recovered from the user of the area.

As well as dealing with these expenses, the body corporate must establish a fund to pay for future maintenance and to cover unexpected expenses. The Sectional Titles Act doesn't specify a size for this fund and doesn't allow any part of it to be refunded; any surplus must be used to subsidise future levies or to improve the common property. In an emergency, the trustees can impose a special levy to cover unforeseen expenses.

Before every AGM, the trustees prepare a budget for the following year and this determines the size of the levy. The budget is sent to all members of the body corporate before the meeting for their consideration and discussed and approved at the meeting. Once this is done, the total cost is divided into monthly amounts and split among owners according to their PQ (see above).

Insurance

The Sectional Titles Act requires the body corporate to ensure that the buildings are insured for their replacement cost. This insurance must cover all properties and improvements to the common property but it covers only buildings; individual owners must insure their contents. The premiums are included as part of the monthly levy (see above).

Rules

Owners in a sectional title scheme must obey common rules, which usually include those detailed below. If an owner fails to maintain his property or exclusive use area, the body corporate can carry out the necessary maintenance and repairs, and charge the owner. A body corporate is even allowed to apply to the Supreme Court for an order instructing an owner to comply with a scheme's rules. Most disputes, however, are settled without recourse to such measures: it's in the interest of all owners that the scheme runs smoothly.

Air-Conditioning

Property owners must obtain permission from the body corporate to install air-conditioning units, as these must be mounted externally and can therefore be unsightly as well as making a noise, which can affect neighbours.

Alterations

It's usually unnecessary to obtain permission to make alterations inside a property. Alterations involving structural changes or affecting the water or electricity supply, however, might require consent and you may be obliged to use a professional; in any case, if the work will disturb or inconvenience neighbours, it's recommended to advise them as a courtesy. If any of your proposed alterations affect common property, you must seek consent from the body corporate. For example, fitting an awning outside a window needs consent because outer walls are part of common property; you might even be restricted as to the type and colour of awning you can install. Similarly, any alterations to windows need consent, and this is often refused if the changes will make them noticeably different from the other windows in a scheme.

Balconies: Many owners wish to enclose their balconies, wholly or partly, to make them more private. Whether or not you're entitled to do this without the consent of the body corporate is a complicated matter, as a balcony may form part of a property or part of the common property or it may be an exclusive use area. Even if it forms part of a property, there may be rules to say that it cannot be enclosed, because that would be deemed to be converting it from a non-habitable to a habitable area, which would require municipal planning permission. In any case, enclosing a balcony alters the outer appearance of the scheme and would often require the unanimous agreement of the body corporate.

Pets

The question of the keeping of pets is covered under Rule 1 of the Sectional Titles Act – an indication of the importance given to the matter. An occupant of a sectional title property may not keep a pet without the written consent of the trustees, but the trustees must not refuse consent without good reason. In granting consent, however, the trustees may impose special conditions (e.g. that a dog be kept on a lead while in communal areas, where its poop must be scooped), and can withdraw the consent if the pet causes a nuisance to other owners.

Rental & Sale

You may rent your property to a tenant but you must tell the body corporate that the property is being rented. As the owner, you remain a member of the body corporate and are responsible for paying the levy, and you're also responsible for the behaviour of the tenant; you're recommended to give him a copy of the scheme's rules. You should check whether there are any restrictions regarding rentals or leaving a property unoccupied for a long time.

You may of course sell your property, but you must notify the body corporate that you've sold it. The Sectional Titles Act requires that owners of sectional title properties notify the body corporate about any changes in the status of a mortgage (bond) held in respect of the property.

Satellite Dishes

These cannot be installed and you must use the communal dish or dishes (if there are any).

Advantages & Disadvantages

The advantages of owning a community rather than an individual property usually include:

- Increased security;
- Lower property taxes than detached homes;
- A range of community sports and leisure facilities;
- Community living with lots of social contacts and the companionship of close neighbours;
- No garden, lawn or pool maintenance;
- Properties are often situated in locations where owning a detached home would be prohibitively expensive, e.g. a beach-front or town centre.

The disadvantages of community properties may include:

- Excessively high community fees (levy);
- Restrictive rules;
- A confining living and social environment and possible lack of privacy;
- Overuse of communal facilities, especially in a large section or at peak periods: a large swimming pool won't look so big when 100 people are using it, and getting a game of tennis or booking a fitness room may be difficult;
- Noisy neighbours;
- Limited living and storage space;
- Limited covered or secure parking (or insufficient off-road parking);

- Time-consuming and stressful administrative duties if you're a member of the body corporate (critics of sectional title schemes argue that it's impractical for ordinary homeowners to manage often multi-million rand schemes themselves, in their spare time);
- Acrimonious owners' meetings, where management and factions may try to push through unpopular proposals (sometimes using proxy votes).

If you're planning to live permanently in a scheme, you should avoid buying in a section with a high percentage of rental units, i.e. units that aren't owner-occupied, as these they may be filled with rowdy holidaymakers and the owners may be unconcerned with the running of the section.

Checks

Before buying a sectional title property, you should check (or ask your lawyer to check) the following:

- That the seller owns the property he claims to own by asking the trustees to show you a copy of the registered section plan. You should also check the exclusive use areas to which you will be entitled.
- If the section has been extended or altered, that the work had the requisite consent and has been registered;
- Whether a Section 25 Right To Extend The Scheme has been registered, meaning that the developer has reserved the right to add extra buildings or extend existing ones. A Section 25 Right is quite rare, but you should know about it if it exists, as it might change the nature of the scheme you're thinking of buying into.
- The condition of the common property (e.g. brickwork, paintwork, plaster, gardens, driveways, lifts, swimming pool). If these are in poor condition, it's a sign of poor management and high future expenses.
- Whether satellite TV is included. If not, it can be difficult or impossible to obtain agreement to introduce it and you cannot install your own dish.
- How good the security is;
- The rules of the scheme. Is there anything you would find difficult to comply with, or don't want to comply with?
- The monthly levy. You should also ask to see a copy of the latest audited accounts, paying special attention to the financial reserves for

future maintenance and repairs. A healthy reserve fund is often a sign of a well run scheme.

- If you're planning to buy an apartment above the ground floor, whether the building has a lift. Note that upper floor apartments are both colder in winter and warmer in summer and may incur extra charges for the use of lifts. On the other hand, they offer more security than ground floor apartments. An apartment that has other apartments above and below it will generally be more noisy than a ground or top floor apartment. Under-roof apartments may also have temperature control problems (hot in summer, cold in winter), although they enjoy better views. If the building has lifts, check whether they're covered by a full maintenance contract, as lift repairs can be very expensive.
- Whether there's any pending legislation against the body corporate.

You may also wish to check on your prospective neighbours!

SURVIVAL TIP
If you're planning to buy a community property, it's important to ensure that it's well managed and that there aren't any major problems with the common property. If there are, you could be liable to contribute towards the cost of repairs, which could run into many tens of thousands of rand.

RETIREMENT HOMES

There's a steady demand in South Africa for retirement homes, from both South Africans and foreigners. Retirement homes are generally purpose-built communities (sheltered housing) and are becoming more common, particularly in resort areas, although they're still fairly rare. Some retirement developments are managed by foreign companies for foreigners. Many sheltered housing developments attract elderly people, e.g. aged 70 plus, with limited mobility. Developments usually consist of one and two-bedroom apartments or a combination of apartments, townhouses and villas, which can be purchased freehold or leasehold, i.e. a lifetime occupancy (see **Land & Title** on page 115).

Properties usually have central heating, air-conditioning, fully-fitted kitchens and satellite TV. A wide range of communal facilities and services is provided, including medical and dental clinics (possibly with a resident doctor and dentist), nursing services, lounges, laundry, housekeeping, sauna, Jacuzzi, restaurant, bar, meal delivery, handyman, mini-supermarket, post office and banking services, guest apartments, free local transport, 24-hour security with closed-circuit television (CCTV), intercom, personal emergency alarm system and a 24-hour multi-lingual reception. Sports and leisure facilities may include swimming pools, tennis courts, lawn bowling, a gymnasium, video room, library and social club.

Most sheltered housing developments levy monthly service charges, e.g. between R1,000 (£87) and R4,000 (£350), which may include a number of weeks' (e.g. six) nursing care per illness per year. Charges usually include heating and air-conditioning, hot and cold water, satellite TV, and all the other services listed above.

PART-OWNERSHIP

If you're looking for a holiday home, you may wish to investigate a scheme that provides sole occupancy of a property for a number of weeks each year. Schemes include co-ownership, leaseback and timesharing.

Don't rush into any of these schemes without fully researching the market and before you're absolutely clear what you want and what you can realistically expect to get for your money.

Co-Ownership

Co-ownership is where a number of people - not necessarily related - buy a property together, sharing both the costs and the occupancy. A common deal is a four-owner scheme (many consider four to be the optimum number of co-owners), where you buy a quarter of a property and can occupy it for up to three months a year. However, there's no reason why there cannot be as many as 12 co-owners with a month's occupancy each per year (usually shared between high, medium and low seasons).

Co-ownership provides access to a size and quality of property that would otherwise be unimaginable, and it's even possible to have a share in a substantial mansion, where a number of families could live together simultaneously and hardly ever see each other if they didn't want to. Co-ownership can be a good choice for a family seeking a holiday home for a few weeks or months a year and has the added advantage that (because of the lower cost) a mortgage may be unnecessary.

It's usually cheaper to buy a property privately with friends than through a developer, when you may pay well above the market price for a share of a property, although some developers offer a 'turnkey' deal, whereby a home is sold fully furnished and equipped.

> **SURVIVAL TIP**
> **A water-tight contract must be drawn up by an experienced lawyer to protect the co-owners' interests.**

One of the best ways to get into co-ownership (if you can afford it) is to buy a house yourself and offer shares to others. This overcomes the problem of getting together a consortium of would-be owners and trying to agree on a purchase in advance, which is difficult unless it's just a few friends or family members.

Some people form a South African company to buy and manage the property, which can in turn be owned by a company in the co-owners' home country, thereby allowing disputes to be dealt with under local law. Each co-owner receives a number of shares according to how much he has paid, entitling him to so many weeks' occupancy a year. Owners don't need to have equal shares and can all be made direct title holders. If a co-owner wishes to sell his shares, he must usually give first refusal to other co-owners. However, if they don't wish to buy them and a new co-owner cannot be found, the property must be sold.

Co-ownership is usually much better value than timesharing (see below) and needn't cost a lot more.

Leaseback

Leaseback (or sale-and-leaseback) schemes are designed for those seeking a holiday home for a limited number of weeks each year who don't want to involve themselves in a co-ownership scheme or buy a timeshare. A leaseback scheme allows you to buy a new property at less than its market value, e.g. 30 per cent less. In return for the discount, you must lease the property back to the developer, normally for around ten years, so that he can let it as self-catering holiday accommodation. You own the freehold of the property and the full price is shown in the title deed. You also have the right to occupy the property for a period each year, e.g. two to eight weeks, spread over high, medium and low seasons. These weeks can usually be let to provide income or possibly even exchanged with accommodation in another resort (as with a timeshare scheme – see below). The developer furnishes and manages the property, and pays the maintenance and bills (e.g. for utilities) during the term of the lease, even when the owner is in occupation.

Properties sold under a leaseback scheme are usually located in popular resort areas, e.g. golf or coastal resorts, where self-catering accommodation is in high demand.

It's important to have a contract checked by your lawyer to ensure that you receive vacant possession at the end of the leaseback period without having to pay an indemnity charge, or you could end up paying more than a property is worth.

Timesharing

Timesharing, where you purchase the right to occupy a property at designated times, isn't as popular in South Africa as in some other countries, notably Spain and the US, but it has been experiencing an increase in popularity in recent years and there are currently over 200 resorts/developments operating on a timeshare basis in the country.

The best timeshare developments are on a par with luxury hotels and offer a wide range of facilities, including bars, restaurants, entertainment, shops, swimming pools, tennis courts, health clubs, and other leisure and sports facilities. If you don't wish to take a holiday in the same place each year, you can choose a timeshare development that's a member of an international organisation such as Resort Condominium International (RCI, ☎ UK 0870-609 0141, 🖳 www.rci.com), Interval International (☎ UK 0870-744 4222, 🖳 www.intervalworld.com) or Marriott (🖳 www.marriott.co.uk), which allow you (usually for an additional fee) to exchange your timeshare with one in another area or country.

Timesharing (also called 'holiday ownership', 'vacation ownership' and 'holidays for life') has earned a poor reputation in the last few decades, although regulatory bodies have been formed to try to 'clean up' the industry and impose a code of ethics. Buyers often have secure occupancy rights and their money is properly protected before the completion of a new property, and timeshare companies are required to allow prospective buyers a 'cooling-off period' (normally ten days), during which they may cancel a sales agreement without penalty. However, although such directives technically bind timeshare companies, if they flout them you must usually seek redress in a court of law, which may not be something you want (or can afford) to do!

The Timeshare Institute of South Africa (TISA, www.tisa.co.za) is based in Cape Town and has around 140 members (listed on the website). Its mission is to 'foster and promote the growth of the industry in South Africa and to serve both the general public and its members through education; mediation; public relations; communication; legislative information; and enforcement of the Code of Conduct.' A copy of this code can be downloaded from the website.

South Africa isn't plagued by the timeshare touts common is some countries. However, you may be invited to a 'presentation' (i.e. sales pitch) in a popular resort and should know what to expect. If you're tempted to attend a sales pitch (usually lasting at least two hours), you may be subjected to some of the most persuasive, high-pressure sales methods employed anywhere on earth and many people are simply unable to resist. If you do attend, don't take any cash, credit cards or cheque books with you so that you won't be pressured into paying a deposit without thinking it over. Although it's supposed to be illegal for a timeshare company to accept a deposit during the cooling-off period, many companies will try to get you to pay one. If you pay a deposit, your chance of getting it back is slim (particularly if you pay by credit card); if it is repaid, it's likely to take a long time. Note that, of those who 'agree' to buy a timeshare, around half cancel within the cooling-off period.

It isn't difficult to understand why there are so many timeshare companies and why salespersons often employ such intimidating, hard-sell methods. A week's timeshare in an apartment worth around R1 million (£87,000) can be sold for R150,000 (£13,000) or more, making a total income of some R7.5 million (£650,000) for the timeshare company if they sell 50 weeks, plus management and other fees. Top-quality timeshares usually cost at least R100,000 (£8,700) for one week in a one- or two-bedroom apartment in a top-rated resort at a peak period, to which must be added annual management fees, e.g. R1,500 (£130) to R4,000 (£350) or more for each week, plus 'miscellaneous' charges and hefty levies, which can run into thousands of rand per owner.

Most experts believe that there's little or no advantage in a timeshare over a normal holiday rental and that it's simply an expensive way to pay for your holidays in advance.

Most financial advisers believe that you're better off putting your money into a long-term investment, where you retain your capital and may even earn sufficient interest to pay for a few weeks' holiday each year. If you wish to buy a timeshare, it's best to buy a resale privately from an existing owner or a timeshare resale broker, which sell for a fraction of their original cost. When buying privately, you can usually drive a hard bargain and may even get a timeshare 'free' simply by assuming the current owner's maintenance contract.

Often timeshares are difficult or impossible to sell at any price and 'pledges' from timeshare companies to sell them for you or buy them back at the market price are usually just a sales ploy, as timeshare companies aren't interested once they've made a sale. Worse, timeshare companies occasionally go bust, leaving 'owners' with nothing to show for their money.

The resale market for timeshares is practically non-existent (despite promises to the contrary by sales people) and, if you need to sell, you're highly unlikely to get your money back.

Further information about timesharing can be obtained from the Timeshare Council (🖳 www.timesharecouncil.net) and the Timeshare Helpline (☎ UK 0181-296 0900) in the UK. The Timeshare Consumers' Association (Hodsock, Worksop, Notts, S81 0TF, UK, ☎ 01909-591100, 🖳 www.timeshare.org.uk) publishes several useful booklets with advice on timesharing.

INSPECTIONS & SURVEYS

When you've found a property that you like, you should make a close inspection of its condition. Obviously, the nature of the inspection will depend on whether it's a ruin in need of complete restoration, a property that has been partly or totally modernised, or a modern home.

An old property may show signs of damage and decay, such as bulging or cracked walls, rising damp, missing roof tiles and rotten woodwork. Some areas are susceptible to flooding, storms and subsidence, and it's wise to check an old property after a heavy rainfall, when any leaks should come to light.

In the case of a property that has been restored, it's important to ascertain how well the job has been done, particularly if the owner did it himself. Although a vendor must certify that a property is free from 'hidden defects', this provides little assurance as he can usually just plead ignorance and it's usually difficult or expensive to prove otherwise.

The most important thing is to ensure that a property is structurally sound. Although building standards in South Africa are generally high, you should never assume that a building is sound, as even relatively new buildings can have serious faults (although rare). The cost of an inspection is a small price to pay for the peace of mind it affords.

Some lenders might ask for a 'survey' before approving a loan, although this usually consists of a perfunctory valuation to confirm that a property is worth the purchase price. (A master builder will be able to tell you whether the price is too high, given any work that needs to be done.) You can also have a full structural survey carried out. Although this is rare in South Africa, if you'd have a full survey carried out on a similar property in your home country, you should have one done in South Africa.

You may be able to make a satisfactory survey a condition of the preliminary contract, allowing you to withdraw from the purchase and have your deposit returned if serious faults are revealed, although this isn't usual in South Africa and a vendor may refuse or insist that you carry out a survey **before** signing the contract. You may, however, be able to negotiate a satisfactory compromise with the vendor.

If a property needs work to make it habitable, don't accept what you're told regarding the likely cost of repair or restoration unless you have a binding quotation in writing from a local builder. One of the most common mistakes when buying old properties is to underestimate the cost of restoration and modernisation (it bears repeating over and over again!). **You should obtain accurate estimates of renovation and modernisation costs before signing a contract.**

Checks

Always discuss with a surveyor exactly what will be included in a survey and, most importantly, what will be excluded (you may need to pay extra to include certain checks and tests). A general inspection should include the structural condition of buildings (particularly the foundations, roofs, walls and woodwork), plumbing, electricity and heating systems, and (if applicable) a swimming pool and its equipment, e.g. filter system and heating. An electrical inspection is required by law, unless the vendor can supply a valid compliance certificate. You should receive a written report, including anything that could become a problem in the future. Some surveyors will allow you to accompany them and may even produce a video of their findings in addition to a written report.

On the other hand, a home inspection can be limited to a few items or even a single system only, such as the wiring or plumbing in an old house. You may also wish to have a property checked for termites and other pests, which are found in many areas.

Below is a list of items you may want to check or have checked by an expert when inspecting a property. See also **Checks** on page 160.

Description

- Make sure that the property corresponds with the description in the title deeds.
- Check the number of rooms and the area of the property, terraces and the plot.
- In the case of a community property, check the exclusive use areas to which you're entitled (see page 143).
- If there are added rooms (e.g. an extension), terraces, a garage or a swimming pool that aren't mentioned in the property description, ask the owner for proof that planning permission was obtained. Additions or alterations to a property may require new registration for the entire property; if so, enquire whether the current owner will register the change before you buy or pay the costs if they're obtained on completion.

Exterior

- Check for cracks and damp patches on walls.
- On older properties check that the walls are vertical and not bulging.
- Check that all the roof tiles are in place and that there's no sagging. Plants growing on a roof are an indication that it isn't well maintained.

Fittings & Furniture

- Check what's included in the sale (see **Conveyancing** on page 193).
- Check that any appliances included in the sale are in good working order.

Interior

- Check for damp patches throughout a property, including inside cupboards and wardrobes.
- Check for cracks in walls.
- Check that the floor is level and that tiles are in good condition.
- Check the condition of doors and windows and whether they close properly.

- Check the woodwork for rot and signs of wood-boring insects, such as woodworm and termites (termites are difficult to detect unless damage is extensive).

Septic Tank

Many older properties in rural areas aren't connected to mains drainage but must have septic tanks to treat household waste. If a property already has a septic tank, check that it's in good condition. An old-style septic tank takes bathroom waste only, while new all-purpose septic tanks on a soak-away system can cope with a wide range of waste products. The absence of a septic tank or other waste water system isn't usually a problem, provided that the land size and elevation allows for its installation. However, if there's a stream running through a property, it may mean that an expensive system needs to be installed to cope with the effluent, which costs three or four times that of a septic tank. Make sure that a septic tank is large enough for the property in question, e.g. 2,500 litres for two bedrooms and up to 4,000 litres for five bedrooms. Note that you mustn't use cleaning agents such as ammonia in a septic tank, as it will destroy it, and products such as bleach can reduce its effectiveness. Specially formulated cleaners are available, including products that will extend the life of the tank.

Swimming Pool

- Look for cracks in the pool structure or lining and check the condition of paving around the pool.
- Check that the filtration and heating equipment (especially the pump) are in good working order.
- Enquire how much the pool costs to maintain and how much it will cost to refill it, e.g. if it's emptied in winter.
- If a property doesn't have a swimming pool and you want to install one, check that there's sufficient space, that the terrain is suitable and that planning permission can be obtained if necessary.

See also **Swimming Pool** below.

Title

You must obviously check that the vendor is entitled to sell the property and that there are no restrictions on the title you will be buying (see **Conveyancing** on page 193).

Utilities

- Check the reliability of the electricity and water supplies. If the property's water is provided by wells, make sure that there's sufficient for your needs.
- If a property doesn't have electricity or mains water, check the nearest connection point and the cost of extending the service to the property, as it can be **very** expensive in remote rural areas. If there's no mains electricity supply, find out whether you can install alternative means (e.g. solar panels).
- Check that the water/electricity/gas installations are functional, particularly the hot water and central heating systems. Don't take someone's word that these are functional but check them yourself.
- Enquire about the annual cost of heating and air-conditioning systems.
- In the case of a waterside property, you should ensure that it has been designed with floods in mind, e.g. with electrical installations above flood level and tiled floors. Avoid a ground floor property unless you're certain it isn't affected by flooding – check for yourself or ask neighbours in the area.
- If a property has a well or septic tank, have it tested. If it doesn't, check whether one can be installed and how much it will cost (see **Septic Tanks** above).

SWIMMING POOLS

It's common for foreign buyers to install a swimming pool at a home in South Africa, which can greatly increase rental prospects (and the rent that can be charged) and enhance its resale potential. Some self-catering holiday companies won't take on properties without a pool. However, before adding a pool, you need to check whether there's a sufficient water supply. You need planning permission to install a pool and this may be refused in areas with acute water shortages. Pools in some areas may be limited to a certain style and shape and must be finished in natural materials, e.g. marble or stone, so that they blend into the landscape.

There are many swimming pool installation companies in South Africa or you can buy and install one yourself. Above-ground pools are the cheapest but are unsightly. Expect to pay around R20,000 (£1,750) for an 8m x 4m (26ft x 13ft) above-ground pool. A conventional in-ground pool measuring 8m x 4m (with a simple filter unit) can be purchased for between R120,000/£10,400 (with a liner) and R175,000/£15,000 (tiled), including installation and filtration and heating systems. A saline water system costs more but saves on maintenance costs. These prices are guides only: pool prices vary considerably according to size, material used and quality of fittings, etc.

Pools require regular maintenance and cleaning, the cost of which must be added to your budget. If you have a holiday home in South Africa or let a property, you will need to employ someone to maintain your pool (you may be able to get a local family to look after it in return for using it). You might want to employ somebody even if you live in the property year-round in order to save you the time and trouble of maintaining a pool yourself. A typical pool maintenance contract with a professional company includes a weekly or twice-weekly visit to carry out the following tasks:

- Cleaning drains, run-offs, etc.;
- Cleaning the pool bottom and sides or checking the automatic pool cleaner;
- Testing the water and adding chlorine or other chemicals as required;
- Backwashing and rinsing the filter sand;
- Cleaning the salt chlorinator cell (if applicable);
- Checking and re-setting the timer (e.g. at different times of year);
- Assessing when pool equipment needs replacing or repairing.

The additional water consumption you will incur in having a pool will also add to your property taxes (see **Sewerage** on page 218).

If you have a swimming pool, you should take certain safety precautions such as building non-slip steps in the pool and a non-slip surface around it, erecting a fence around it (this is particularly important if children come to the property) and including third-party insurance for the pool (costing from R1,000/£87 per year) in your house insurance policy (see **Household Insurance** on page 231).

SURVIVAL TIP

If you have an outdoor pool, put a plank across it at night so that any animals (or humans) that fall in have a chance to get out again.

RENOVATION & RESTORATION

There are some older properties purchased by foreigners in South Africa that are in need of restoration, renovation and modernisation.

The most common examples are farmhouses that have been neglected since they were built in the 18th and 19th centuries and were abandoned many years ago.

> **SURVIVAL TIP**
> **Before buying a property that needs renovation or restoration, it's vital to obtain accurate estimates of the work involved from one or more reliable local builders. You should budget for costs to be up to 100 per cent higher than quoted, as it isn't unusual for the costs to escalate wildly from original estimates.**

Before buying a property requiring restoration or modernisation, you should consider the alternatives. An extra R200,000 (£17,500) to R400,000 (£35,000) spent on a purchase may represent better value than spending a similar amount on building work. It's often cheaper to buy a restored or partly restored property than a ruin in need of total restoration, unless you're going to do most of the work yourself. See also **Buying An Old Home** on page 142.

⚠ **The price of most restored properties doesn't reflect the cost and amount of work that went into them, and many people who have restored a ruin would never do it again and advise others against it.**

Checks

It's important to ensure that an old property has sound walls. Properties that have walls with serious defects are best avoided, as it's usually cheaper to erect a new building! Almost any other problem can be fixed or overcome at a price. A roof that doesn't leak is desirable and making a building waterproof is the most important priority if funds are scarce. Sound roof timbers are also desirable, as they can be expensive to replace. **Don't believe a vendor or agent who tells you that a roof or anything else can be easily repaired or patched up, but obtain expert advice from a local builder.** Old buildings may also need a damp-proof course, timber treatment, new windows and doors, a modern kitchen and bathroom, re-wiring and central heating. See also **Checks** on page 155.

Regulations

South Africa is governed by National Building Regulations and the Building Standards Act (although planning permission is dealt with locally – see below). You need to ensure that you and your builder (if applicable) are familiar with what can and cannot be done, and comply with the rules. The regulations require three inspections of building work in progress: one of the foundations, one of the open drains and one when construction is completed. There's no mention, however, of the question of privacy: in South Africa, privacy in a built-up area is a privilege rather than a right, and the same applies to a view.

Planning permission must be sought from local town-planning departments and isn't always a straightforward process. To begin with, the rules vary in different parts of the country; secondly, some departments are understaffed and their employees poorly trained; thirdly, some local officials have been found to be boosting their meagre salaries with bribes in exchange for granting approval (referred to by some people as a 'Pretoria handshake'), while politicians have been known taken 'donations' from powerful property developers to smooth the path of planning applications.

In the City of Johannesburg, for example, any new building and any alteration that adds to or changes the structure of an existing building must be approved by the city's Planning Development Management Department. If you build or alter without having obtained approval, a building inspector is entitled to enter your property and order the work to stop. In extreme cases, he can obtain a Court Order to have the building demolished, at your expense (and you must pay the legal costs!). You might also be fined or even sent to prison. Even if you complete a building or alterations without permission and a building inspector doesn't notice, the problem will resurface in the future when you come to try to sell the property and the prospective buyer asks to see approved plans, which you won't have.

To submit a planning application, you complete an application form (obtained from the Planning Department), sign it and attach a copy of the title deed. Local zoning regulations may also require you to attach a site development plan. If structural work is part of the proposed work, you must attach a separate form completed by a professional engineer registered with the Engineering Council of South Africa. There's a fee to pay, which varies with the size and nature of the project and is sometimes calculated as a percentage of the value of the building work or as a fixed rate per square metre of the building. The minimum fee is usually around R325 (£28).

SURVIVAL TIP
It's important to find out exactly what you can and can't do before buying a property for restoration.

DIY Or Builders?

One of the first decisions you need to make regarding restoration or modernisation is whether to do all or most of the work yourself or have it done by professional builders or artisans. You shouldn't tackle jobs by yourself or with friends unless you're sure you're doing it right; cleaning or restoring marble floors or tiles, for example, is a specialist job. It's important to have a sensitive approach to restoration and not to over-modernise an old property in case too much of its natural rustic charm and attraction are lost. In general, you should aim to retain as many of a property's original features as possible and stick to local building materials (wood, stone and tiles). In fact, this may be required by law. When renovations and 'improvements' have been botched, there's often little that can be done except to start again from scratch.

If you decide to go it alone, there's a range of DIY equipment, tools and building supplies in South Africa, although there's less choice than in some European countries (e.g. the UK) and prices are generally higher. There are some DIY markets and stores, which in addition to stocking most DIY materials have a range of tools and machinery for hire. Most DIY stores stock a large selection of goods (and keep most items in stock), accept credit cards and have helpful staff. Always look out for promotions; even if nothing appears to be on offer, it's worth asking, as offers aren't always advertised. Most towns have a hardware store that's handy for tools and small items, and there are building yards that are good for plumbing parts, porcelain, fireplaces and doors. Ask your neighbours about where to buy fittings and materials, as they usually know the best places locally. It's also possible to buy reclaimed materials such as porcelain, tiles, doors and fireplaces from architectural salvage dealers.

Before starting work and while work progresses, most people keep a photographic record of their accomplishments, if only to justify the expense. Also keep all bills (labour and materials) for restoration work, both for legal reasons and to prove to a prospective buyer that the work that has been done and how much it cost.

Finding A Builder

When looking for a builder, it's wise to obtain recommendations from local people you can trust, e.g. an estate agent, mayor or neighbours.

However, estate agents or other professionals aren't always the best people to ask, as they may receive a commission. Always obtain references from previous customers. Any tradesmen you employ should be registered at the local chamber of commerce in the requisite category and in the official list of artisans for their trade.

South African law requires that all builders of domestic property be registered with the National Home Builders' Registration Council (💻 www.nhbrc.org) and must comply with its building quality standards. Before employing a builder, check that he's registered and hasn't been suspended or deregistered (you can do this on the website mentioned above). If you have any problems or disagreements with your builder that cannot easily be resolved, contact the Council for help (it has an office in each province, listed on the website). If your builder goes out of business, the Council has a fund that will pay to have your home finished.

Quotations

You should obtain a written quotation from at least two builders before employing one. It's sensible to obtain a few quotations and offer to pay a fee for a quotation for a large job, which should be reimbursed by the builder who gets the job. Builders usually provide an estimate per square metre, which includes both labour and materials, although where it's difficult or impossible to provide an estimate jobs are done at an hourly or daily rate.

For quotations to be accurate, you must detail exactly the work required; for example, for electrical work this would include the number of lights, points and switches, and the quality of materials to be used. If you have only a vague idea of what you want, you will receive an unreliable quotation.

Make sure that a quotation includes everything you want done and that you fully understand it. Look out for any terms allowing for the price to be increased for inflation or a general rise in prices, and check whether the quote is definitive or provisional, i.e. dependent on further exploratory work. Always ask for start and finish dates in a quotation. You should fix a date for completion and, if you can get a builder to agree to it, include a penalty for failing to meet it. It's difficult to get South African builders to agree to this, but it's worth persevering. A major building contract needs a strict penalty clause, or it can drag on for months (or years) or be left half-finished. After signing a contract, it's usual to pay a deposit, e.g. 10 to 25 per cent, depending on the size of the job.

Supervision

As in many countries, South African artisans never like to turn down work and so tend to take on much more than they can handle and work a day here and a day there to keep all their jobs 'on the boil', thus annoying all their customers. Many building jobs take much longer to complete than the initial estimate, not least because builders often work to 'African time', which makes the Spanish, with their *mañana* syndrome, seem like positive workaholics!

Many unsupervised South African workmen are about as disciplined as South African drivers and it isn't uncommon for artisans to work for a few days and then disappear for weeks!

If you aren't on the spot and able to supervise work, you should hire a 'clerk of works' such an architect to do so on your behalf. He can be employed to oversee an entire project or just one or two aspects of it. The fee is usually a percentage of the total cost, e.g. 10 per cent, and is usually worth every rand. Shop around and compare rates, but beware of expatriate project managers, who have been known to rip off their compatriots. As with builders and artisans, ask for references and seek recommendations. Some South African estate agents will organise renovation and restoration and oversee a project for around 10 per cent of the total cost. Some specialist companies offer complete restoration services, although the major disadvantage of such services is that you have little choice as to how your property is restored. Always obtain references from previous customers.

Be extremely careful who you employ if you have work done in your absence and ensure that your instructions are accurate in every detail. Always make sure that you understand exactly what has been agreed and if necessary get it in writing (with drawings). **It isn't unusual for foreign owners to receive huge bills for work done in their absence that shouldn't have been done at all!**

Cost

All building work, including electrical installation, masonry and plumbing is priced by the square metre (m^2) or metre and prices should include VAT at 14 per cent. The cost of total restoration by professional builders varies according to the type of work involved, the quality of materials used and the region. You should expect to pay a minimum of R1,000 (£87) per m^2 to bring a ruin to a habitable condition and up to

R7,000 (£600) per m² for a top quality job, e.g. insulated roofs, double glazing, full central heating, marble or expensive tiles in kitchens and bathrooms, fully fitted kitchens and an elaborate fireplace. **As a rough guide, you should expect the cost of fully renovating an old 'habitable' building to be at least equal to its purchase price and possibly much more.**

How much you actually spend on restoring a property will depend on your purpose and the depth of your pockets. If you're restoring a property as an investment, it's easy to spend more than you could ever hope to recoup when you sell it. One of the reasons there are so many derelict buildings for sale in some parts of South Africa is that restoration costs are far higher than potential resale costs. **In the last decade some foreigners have spent a lot on renovations, only to find it difficult to recoup their investment. It isn't unusual for buyers to embark on a grandiose renovation scheme, run out of money before it's completed and be forced to sell at a loss.** On the other hand, if you're restoring a property as a holiday or permanent home, you can spend as much as you like (or can afford).

Always keep an eye on your budget (which will inevitably be at least 25 per cent **below** the actual cost but could turn out to be 25 per cent **of** the cost!) and don't be in too much of a hurry. Some people take many years to restore a South African holiday home, particularly when they're doing most of the work themselves.

It's possible to obtain a mortgage that includes the cost of renovation work, but you must obtain detailed written quotations for a lender. It's also possible to obtain a grant to restore a historic property in some regions.

It's important to ensure that you pay for work on time; if you get a reputation as a late payer (or for not paying at all), you will soon find that you cannot get anyone local to work for you. However, you should make sure that a job is completely finished (including repairing any damage done by workmen) and passed by your architect or surveyor before paying bills. **Never pay a builder in advance (apart from a deposit), particularly a large sum, as it's possible that he will disappear with your money (particularly if he's a foreign, non-registered builder).** It's best to pay a month in arrears, which most builders will agree to. On the other hand, if you want a job done while you're away you will need to pay a builder a sum in advance or get someone local to supervise his work and pay him regularly; otherwise he's unlikely to finish the job.

Cash deals are often negotiated without VAT, although it's important to bear in mind that, if you don't have a legitimate bill, you won't be able to offset the cost of work against rental income and won't have a guarantee.

BUILDING YOUR OWN HOME

If you want to be far from the madd(en)ing crowd, you can buy a plot and have a house built to your own design or to a standard design provided by a builder. Although South African builders have a range of standard designs, they will accommodate almost any interior or exterior variation (for a price), provided it's permitted by local building regulations. Costs vary but expect to pay anywhere between around R1,000 (£87) per m^2 for the most basic, low-cost home to R7,500 (£650) per m^2 for a super-luxury home.

If you decide to build your own home, you must ensure that the proposed size and style of house is legal by checking with the local town hall. Don't rely on the builder or developer to do it for you, but check yourself or have your architect or surveyor do it. **If a mistake is made, a building may need to be demolished!** See **Regulations** on page 161.

After building a new house, you must obtain a certificate that building work has been carried out according to the planning application. You will also need a professional valuation of your home for insurance purposes.

SELLING YOUR HOME

Although this book is primarily concerned with buying a home in South Africa, you may wish to sell your South African home at some time in the future. Before offering your South African home for sale, it's wise to investigate the state of the property market. For example, unless you're forced to sell, it definitely isn't wise to try doing so during a property slump. It may be better to let your home long-term and wait until the market has recovered. It's also unwise to sell in the early years after purchase, when you will probably make a loss unless it was an absolute bargain.

Having decided to sell, your first decision will be whether to try to sell it yourself or use the services of an estate agent. Although the majority of properties in South Africa are sold through estate agents, some owners sell their own homes.

If you need to sell a property before buying a new one, this must be included as a conditional clause (see page 193) in the purchase contract for a new home.

Price

It's important to bear in mind that (like everything) property has a market price and the best way of ensuring a quick sale (or any sale) is to ask a realistic price. Some properties remain unsold for ages largely because owners ask absurd prices. If your home is fairly standard for the area, you can find out its value by comparing the prices of other homes on the market or those which have recently been sold. Most agents will provide a free appraisal of a home's value in the hope that you will sell it through them. However, don't believe everything they tell you, as they may over-price it simply to encourage you. You can also hire a professional appraiser to determine the market value.

You should be prepared to drop the price slightly (e.g. 5 or 10 per cent) and should set it accordingly, but shouldn't grossly overprice a home, as this will deter buyers. Don't reject a prospective purchaser who makes a low initial offer, as he may raise it.

You may wish to include furnishings and major appliances in the sale, particularly when selling a relatively inexpensive property with modest furnishings. You should add an appropriate amount to the price to cover the value of the furnishings; alternatively, you can use them as an inducement to a prospective buyer who is undecided.

Presentation

The secret to selling a home quickly lies in its presentation, assuming that it's competitively priced. First impressions (both exterior and interior) are vital when marketing your home, and it's essential to make every effort to present it in its best light and make it as attractive as possible to potential buyers. It may even pay to invest in new interior decoration, new carpets, exterior paint and landscaping. A few plants and flowers can work wonders. However, when decorating a home for resale, it's important to be conservative and not to do anything radical (such as install a red or black bathroom suite); white and the much-maligned magnolia are good neutral colours for walls, woodwork and porcelain.

It may also pay you to do some modernisation such as installing a new kitchen or bathroom, as these are of vital importance (particularly kitchens) when selling a home. Note, however, that although modernisation may be necessary to sell an old home, you shouldn't overdo it, as it's easy to spend more than you could ever hope to recoup on its sale. If you're using an agent, you can ask him what you should do (or need to do) to help sell your home.

If your home is in poor repair, this must be reflected in the asking price and, if major work is needed that you cannot afford, you should obtain a quotation (or two) to show prospective buyers.

Doing Your Own Selling

While certainly not for everyone, selling your own home is a viable option for many people and is particularly recommended when you're selling an attractive home at a realistic price in a favourable market. It may allow you to offer it at a more appealing price, which could be an important factor if you're seeking a quick sale. How you market it will depend on the type of home, the price, and the country or area from which you expect your buyer to come. For example, if your property isn't of a style or in an area desirable to South Africans, it's usually a waste of time advertising it in the local press.

Advertising is the key to selling your home. The first step is to get a professional looking 'For Sale' sign made showing your telephone number and display it in the garden or a window. Do some market research into the best newspapers and magazines for advertising your property, and place an advertisement in those that look most promising. You could also have a leaflet printed (with pictures) extolling the virtues of your property, which you could drop into local letter boxes or have distributed with a local newspaper (many people buy a new home in the vicinity of their present home).

You may also need to have a printed 'fact sheet' if your home's vital statistics aren't included in the leaflet mentioned above, and could offer a finder's fee (e.g. R5,000/£435) to anyone finding you a buyer.

Don't forget to market your home around any local companies, schools and organisations, particularly if they have many itinerant or foreign employees.

Finally, it may help to provide information about local financing sources for potential buyers. With a bit of effort you may even make a better job of marketing your home than an agent! When selling a home yourself, you will need to obtain legal advice regarding contracts and engage a lawyer to complete the sale. Unless you're in a hurry to sell, set yourself a realistic time limit for success, after which you can try an agent.

As when buying a home, you must be very, very careful who you deal with when selling a home. Never agree to accept part of the sale price 'under the table' (which is illegal in any case); if the buyer refuses to pay, there's nothing you can do about it (legally!) – see also **Avoiding**

Problems on page 114. When the buyer has a mortgage, you must usually wait a few weeks after completion to receive payment.

Using An Agent

Many vendors prefer to use the services of an agent, either in South Africa or in their home country, particularly when selling a second home. If you purchased the property through an agent, it's often wise to use the same agent when selling, as he will already be familiar with it and may still have the details on file. You should take particular care when selecting an agent, as they vary considerably in their professionalism, expertise and experience (the best way to investigate agents is by posing as a buyer). Note that many agents cover a relatively small area, so you should take care to choose one who regularly sells properties in your area and price range.

If you own a property in an area popular with foreign buyers, it may be worthwhile using an overseas agent or advertising in foreign newspapers and magazines.

Mandates

An estate agent may not market a property unless given a mandate to do so. There are two types of mandate: sole (given to a single agent) and open (given to more than one agent). A sole mandate must be in writing and you're entitled to a signed copy, but an open mandate can be given orally. The standard duration of a sole mandate is three months, but this is subject to negotiation with the agent. Sole and open mandates both have advantages and disadvantages, although many agents argue that a sole mandate ensures that the property will be marketed more efficiently and thoroughly, and you should bear in mind the following:

- During the period of a sole mandate, you cannot sell your property through another agent. If you sell it yourself during this period or even if you sell it after the end of the mandate period to somebody introduced to you or the property by the estate agent during the mandate period, you may be liable to pay damages (and maybe commission) to the appointed agent.
- Although you cannot be forced to sell your property to a buyer found by an agent, a sole mandate often ties you to the payment of commission if you refuse to sell or if you prevent the agent from concluding a sale.

- If you give open mandates, you run the risk of being asked for the payment of more than one estate agent's commission. This might happen if you sell your property through one agent to a buyer previously introduced to the property by another agent (see below).

You should ensure that you understand the terms of a sole mandate before agreeing to it. Most estate agencies have pre-printed sole mandates, but you're recommended to use the Estate Agency Affairs Board's standard sole mandate form, which is designed to protect the interests of both the seller and the estate agent.

If you decide to approach more than one agent, you should tell every agent that you've also asked other agents to sell the property. To avoid paying more than one commission, before signing a contract of sale, check with the agent whether or not the property has been shown to the buyer by another agent. If the answer is 'yes', you should insist that the buyer and/or the agent through whom the property is sold accepts responsibility for the payment of the second commission.

When giving an estate agent a mandate, whether open or closed, the following matters should be discussed in detail:

- A realistic, market-related selling price;
- The agent's commission and when it's payable. There's no set tariff and commission rates vary with the agent, the area and whether you're granting an open or sole mandate. A commission of 7.5 per cent (plus VAT) is average, although you're free to negotiate a lower rate. In a sluggish property market, however, when sales are few and far between, a seller might be able to negotiate more favourable terms.
- Any defects in the property and how these should be 'presented' to prospective purchasers;
- Which movable items are to be included as part of the property, e.g. wall units and swimming pool equipment;
- Times when the property can be viewed and whether you need to be notified of all viewings;
- The length of the mandate and under what conditions it can be cancelled within that period;
- Any consents (e.g. of a spouse) that have to be obtained before the sale can be made;
- The estate agent's obligations, e.g. to advertise the property in specific publications or to put a 'For Sale' sign on the property.

Offers & Contracts

When an agent receives a written offer from a prospective buyer, he must present this to you for a decision. The offer document must contain the following:

- Your name and address.
- The buyer's name and address.
- The price the buyer is offering to pay.
- Whether the buyer is entitled to a 'cooling-off' period (i.e. if the price is R250,000 or less), during which he can reconsider the offer and cancel it without penalty. A buyer doesn't have the right to a cooling-off period if he's buying on behalf of another person or a company or close corporation, if the property is being sold by auction, or if the selling price is over R250,000.

The offer will probably also contain a list of any fixtures and fittings that you're selling as part of the property and include some or all of the following clauses:

- How the buyer will pay, which is typically 10 per cent on acceptance of the offer, the balance on the transfer of ownership;
- Whether or not the sale is conditional on the buyer obtaining a loan. If so, include the amount of the loan and the date by which it must be secured.
- Whether or not the sale is conditional on the buyer selling another property. If so, include the address and a deadline for selling it.
- The date on which the buyer can occupy the property;
- That you will provide certificates that the property isn't infested by specified insects and that the electrical system complies with relevant safety regulations;
- That you're selling the property '*voetstoots*', i.e. the buyer accepts that there might be defects and not hold you liable (unless you knew about them and didn't tell the buyer).

Your signing the offer document makes it a binding sales contract and renders you liable for damages should you decide not to sell.

Costs

In addition to the agent's commission (if applicable), which is payable by the seller after ownership of the property has officially been transferred into the buyer's name, you're responsible for the cost of an insect inspection (and any repairs that might be necessary) and the cost of the electrical inspection (and any repairs that might be necessary), unless you already have an electrical compliance certificate. If you have a mortgage, you must cancel it, which will involve you paying the balance of the loan, the bank's fee for cancelling it and the Deeds Office registration fee.

4.

MONEY MATTERS

One of the most important aspects of buying a home in South Africa and living there (even for quite short periods) is finance, which includes everything from transferring and changing money to mortgages and taxes (taxes are covered in **Chapter 7**).

If you're planning to invest in a property or business in South Africa financed with imported funds, it's important to consider both the present and possible future exchange rates. On the other hand, if you live and work in South Africa and are paid in rand, this may affect your financial commitments abroad.

If your income is received in a currency other than rand, it can be exposed to risks beyond your control when you live in South Africa, particularly regarding inflation and exchange rate fluctuations.

Foreigners, particularly retirees, often underestimate the cost of living in South Africa (which is no longer the very cheap destination that it used to be) and some are forced to return to their home countries after a few years.

SURVIVAL TIP
If you plan to live in South Africa for long periods, you must ensure that your income is (and will remain) sufficient to live on, bearing in mind devaluations, rises in the cost of living, and unforeseen expenses such as medical bills or anything else that may reduce your income.

Although South Africans sometimes prefer to pay cash rather than use credit or charge cards, it's wise to have at least one credit card when visiting or living in South Africa. Even if you don't like credit cards and shun any form of credit, they have their uses, e.g. no-deposit car rentals, no pre-paying hotel bills (plus guaranteed bookings), obtaining cash 24 hours per day, simple telephone and mail-order payments, greater safety and security than cash and, above all, convenience. However, not all South African businesses accept credit cards, particularly small businesses, and you should check in advance.

If you own a home in South Africa, you can employ a South African accountant or tax adviser to look after your financial affairs there and declare and pay your local taxes. You can also have a representative receive your bank statements, ensure that your bank is paying your standing orders (e.g. for utilities) and that you have sufficient funds to pay them. If you let a home in South Africa through a South African company, it may perform the above tasks for you.

SOUTH AFRICAN CURRENCY

The South African unit of currency is the rand (R), which is divided into 100 cents. Coins are minted in values of 1, 2, 5, 10, 20 and 50 cents, and R1, R2 and R5. Notes are printed in denominations of R10, R20, R50, R100 and R200. The designs of South Africa's currency reflect the country's diverse fauna. The coins depict wildlife, mainly antelope and birds, and the notes have pictures of the 'big five' wild animals (i.e. those that most tourists want to see): a rhino on the R10 note (which is green), an elephant on the R20 note (brown), a lion on the R50 (red), a buffalo on the R100 (blue) and a leopard on the R200 (orange).

There are two types of R2 and R5 coins currently in circulation, as a new design was released in August 2004 to mark ten years of South African democracy. The new R2 coin is virtually identical to the old one, but the new R5, the first bi-metal coin in South Africa, has an edged 'security' groove and is slightly heavier than the old coin.

If possible, it's wise to obtain some rand coins and banknotes before arriving in South Africa and to familiarise yourself with them. Bringing some rand with you will save you having to change money on arrival at a South African airport (where exchange rates are poor). It's sensible not to carry a lot of cash and ideally you should avoid high value notes (R100 and R200), which aren't widely accepted, particularly for small purchases or on public transport (R200 notes are occasionally forged). Beware of short-changing, which is common in some areas (always check your change, particularly when tendering a large note).

IMPORTING & EXPORTING MONEY

There are no exchange controls in South Africa but South African bank notes in excess of R5,000 (£435) per person aren't allowed into the country unless you have the necessary permit from the South African Reserve Bank, 370, Church Street, Pretoria 0002 (write to PO Box 427, Pretoria 0001, ☎ 12-313 3911, 💻 www.reservebank.co.za).

International Bank Transfers

When transferring or sending money to (or from) South Africa, you should be aware of the alternatives, which include the following:

- **Bank Draft** – A bank draft should be sent by registered post. However, in the (unlikely) event that it's lost or stolen, it's impossible to stop payment and you must wait six months before a new draft can be issued.
- **Bank Transfer** – A normal bank transfer should take three to seven days but can take much longer, and an international bank transfer between non-affiliated banks can take weeks! It isn't unusual for transfers to get 'stuck' in the pipeline (which allows the bank to use your money for a period interest free!).
- **SWIFT Transfer** – One of the safest and fastest methods of transferring money is via the Society of Worldwide Interbank Financial Telecommunications (SWIFT) system. A SWIFT transfer should be completed in a few hours, funds being available within 24 hours, although even SWIFT transfers can take five working days, especially from small branches that are unused to dealing with foreign transfers. Australian and UK members of the SWIFT system are listed on the Society's website (💻 www.swift.com). The cost of transfers varies considerably – not only commission and exchange rates, but also transfer charges – but is usually between around R200 (£17.40) and R300 (£26.10).
- **Currency Dealer** – It may be quicker to use a specialist currency dealer to carry out a transfer for you, and you may get a better exchange rate than from a bank. There are many companies specialising in foreign exchange, particularly large sums of money, including the following:
  - Currencies Direct (☎ UK 020-7813 0332, 💻 www.currenciesdirect.com);
  - Currencies For Less (☎ UK 020-7228 7667, 💻 www.currencies4less.com);
  - Halewood (☎ UK 01753-859159, 💻 www.hifx.co.uk);
  - Moneycorp (☎ UK 020-7808 0500, 💻 www.moneycorp.com).

If you routinely transfer large sums of money between currencies, you should investigate Fidelity Money Funds, which operate free of conversion charges and at wholesale rates of exchange.

Always check charges and exchange rates in advance and agree them with your bank (you may be able to negotiate a lower charge or a better exchange rate). Shop around a number of banks and compare fees. Banks are often willing to negotiate on fees and exchange rates when you're transferring a large amount of money. Some foreign banks levy a flat-fee for electronic transfers, irrespective of the amount. British banks charge between £10 and £45 for transfers taking one or more days.

SURVIVAL TIP
If you plan to send a large amount of money to South Africa or abroad for a business transaction such as buying property, you should ensure that you receive the commercial rate of exchange rather than the tourist rate.

When you have money transferred to a bank in South Africa, make sure that you give the account holder's name, the account number, the branch number and the bank code. If money is 'lost' while being transferred to or from a South African bank account, it can take weeks to locate it.

Obtaining Cash

There are various methods of obtaining smaller amounts of money for everyday use. These include the following:

- **Bureaux De Change** – Most banks in major cities have foreign exchange windows, where you can buy and sell foreign currencies, buy and cash travellers' cheques, and obtain a cash advance on credit and charge cards. Banks tend to offer the best exchange rates but may impose charges of R25 (£2.15) or more.

  There are many private exchange bureaux at airports, main railway stations and major cities with longer business hours than banks, particularly at weekends. Most offer competitive exchange rates and low or no commission (but always check). They're easier to deal with than banks and, if you're changing a lot of money, you can usually negotiate a better exchange rate. At airports and in tourist areas in major cities, there are automatic change machines accepting up to 15 currencies, including US$, sterling, euros and Swiss francs. **However, airport bureaux de change and change machines usually offer the worst exchange rates and charge the highest fees (e.g. handling charges).** Never use unofficial money changers, who are likely to short change you.

  The exchange rate against the rand for most European and major international currencies is listed in banks and daily newspapers and on the internet.

- **Cards** – If you need instant cash, you can draw on debit, credit or charge cards (but there's usually a daily limit). Many foreigners living in South Africa (particularly retirees) keep the bulk of their money in a foreign account (perhaps with an offshore bank) and draw on it with a cash or credit card. This is an ideal solution for holidaymakers and holiday homeowners (although homeowners will still need a South African bank account to pay their bills). Exchange rates are better when obtaining cash with a credit or debit card, as you're given the wholesale rate, although there's a 1.5 per cent charge on cash advances and cash machine (ATM) transactions in foreign currencies. Some ATMs may reject foreign cards - if this happens try again and if necessary try another ATM.

- **Telegraphic Transfer** - One of the quickest (it takes around ten minutes) and safest methods of transferring cash is via a telegraphic transfer, e.g. Moneygram (☎ UK 0800-666 3947, 💻 www.moneygram.com). Note that Western Union no longer operates in South Africa, following accusations that the service was being used for money laundering. Money can be sent via American Express offices by Amex cardholders.
- **Travellers' Cheques** - If you're visiting South Africa, it's safer to carry travellers' cheques than cash. However, travellers' cheques aren't as easy to cash in South Africa as in some other countries, e.g. the US, and they're especially difficult to change in rural areas. They aren't usually accepted as cash by businesses, except perhaps in hotels, restaurants and shops in Cape Town and other major cities, which usually offer a poor exchange rate. You can buy travellers' cheques from any South African bank, usually for a fee of 1 per cent of the face value.

  Banks usually offer a better exchange rate for travellers' cheques than for banknotes, but fees and rates vary considerably, so shop around. Buying large denomination cheques saves on per-cheque exchange charges. American Express and Thomas Cook offices don't charge for cashing their own cheques.

  Always keep a separate record of cheque numbers and note where and when they were cashed. American Express provides a free, three-hour replacement service for lost or stolen travellers' cheques at any of its offices worldwide, provided you know the serial numbers of the lost cheques. Without the serial numbers, replacement can take three days or longer. Most companies provide toll-free numbers for reporting lost or stolen travellers' cheques in South Africa.

SURVIVAL TIP

One thing to bear in mind when travelling anywhere is not to rely on one source of funds only.

BANKS

South Africa's banking system is not only the most sophisticated in Africa (which isn't necessarily saying much) but also the equal of that in many western countries. There has been a reduction rather than increase in the number of banks operating in South Africa recently; since 2002, some banks have been taken over, some have given up their banking licence, and others have left the market, including the African Merchant Bank, BoE Bank, Brait Merchant Bank, ING Bank NV and PSG Investment Bank. Surviving banks have had to make fairly drastic staff cuts to contain operating expenses. Nevertheless, according to a 2004 Ernst & Young report, there's a strong demand for banking services, particularly bank loans and mortgages.

According to the central banking authority, the South Africa Reserve Bank (💻 www.reservebank.co.za), South Africa currently has 15 locally-controlled banks, six foreign-controlled banks (which, however, operate in much the same way as South African banks), two registered mutual banks and around 50 registered foreign bank branches and representative offices. The retail market is dominated by the 'big four': Absa (💻 www.absa.co.za), FirstRand Bank (💻 www.firstrand.co.za), Nedcor (💻 www.nedcor.co.za), and Standard Bank (💻 www.standardbank.co.za), who between them have over 15 million customers (including almost 1 million internet customers) and 25 million accounts. As in other countries, internet banking is projected to increase rapidly, although South African customers have so far been wary of banking online, following newspaper stories of hackers stealing large amounts of money.

Despite their sophistication, South African banks are widely accused of the same ills as banks in Australasia, Europe and North America, including high charges, poor levels of customer service, over-regulation (particularly foreign-controlled banks) and generally cartel-like behaviour. As anywhere, you should therefore shop around and compare rates before signing any contracts or taking out a loan (banks must publish their conditions).

Bank opening hours vary but are generally from 9am until 3.30pm, Mondays to Fridays, and 9am until 11am on Saturdays.

Opening An Account

You can open a bank account in South Africa whether you're a resident or a non-resident. It's best to open a South African bank account in person, rather than from abroad. Ask your friends, neighbours or colleagues for their recommendations and just go along to the bank of your choice and introduce yourself. You must be at least 18 and provide proof of identity, e.g. a passport and your address in South Africa (a utility bill usually suffices). Before choosing a bank, it's wise to compare the fees charged for international money transfers and other services, which can be high (a bank's website usually has details of charges, although it can be tedious wading through the long lists of charges for the many services offered).

If you wish to open an account with a South African bank while abroad, you must obtain an application form from a branch of a South African bank (either in South Africa or in your home country). You must select a branch from the list provided. If you open an account by correspondence, you must provide a reference from your bank, including a certified signature (or a signature witnessed by a solicitor or lawyer). You also need a photocopy of the relevant pages of your passport and a rand draft to open the account.

All banks provide credit cards and debit cards to obtain cash throughout South Africa and also abroad, usually via the CIRRUS and NYCE networks. However, it's unwise to rely solely on ATMs to obtain cash, as they often run out of money or are out of operation (and occasionally swallow your card!). Note also that daily withdrawals with an ATM card are generally limited to around R2,000 (£175).

Offshore Banking

If you have a sum of money to invest or wish to protect your inheritance from the tax man, it may be worthwhile looking into the accounts and services (such as pensions and trusts) provided by offshore banking centres in tax havens such as the Channel Islands (Guernsey and Jersey), Gibraltar and the Isle of Man (around 50 locations worldwide are officially classified as tax havens). The big attraction of offshore banking is that money can be deposited in a wide range of currencies, customers are usually guaranteed complete anonymity, there are no double-taxation agreements, no withholding tax is payable, and interest is paid tax-free. Many offshore banks also offer telephone banking (usually seven days a week) and some provide internet banking.

A large number of American, British and other European banks and financial institutions provide offshore banking facilities in one or more locations. Most institutions offer high-interest deposit accounts for long-term savings and investment portfolios, in which funds can be deposited in any major currency. Many people living abroad keep a local account for everyday business and maintain an offshore account for international transactions and investment purposes.

SURVIVAL TIP
Most financial experts advise expatriates not to invest their life savings in an offshore tax haven until they know what their long-term plans are.

Accounts have minimum deposits levels, which usually range from £500 to £10,000 ($750 to $15,000), with some as high as £100,000 ($150,000). In addition to large minimum balances, accounts may also have stringent terms and conditions, such as restrictions on withdrawals or high early withdrawal penalties. You can deposit funds on call (instant access) or for a fixed period, e.g. from 90 days to one year (usually for larger sums). Interest is usually paid monthly or annually. Monthly interest payments are slightly lower than annual payments, although they have the advantage of providing a regular income. There are usually no charges provided that a specified minimum balance is maintained. Many accounts offer a debit card, e.g. MasterCard or Visa, which can be used to obtain cash via ATMs throughout the world.

When selecting a financial institution and offshore banking centre, your first priority should be for the safety of your money. In some offshore banking centres all bank deposits are guaranteed up to a maximum amount under a deposit protection scheme, whereby a maximum sum is guaranteed should a financial institution go to the wall (the Isle of Man, Guernsey and Jersey all have such schemes). Unless you're planning to bank with a major international bank, you should always check the credit rating of a financial institution before depositing any money, particularly if it doesn't provide deposit insurance. All banks have a credit rating (the highest is 'AAA') and a bank with a high rating will be happy to tell you (but get it in writing). You can also check the rating of an international bank or financial organisation with Moody's Investor Service. You should be wary of institutions offering higher than average interest rates; if it looks too good to be true, it probably will be!

Complaints

If you have an unresolved dispute with your bank or a complaint about a banking service or product, you can approach the Banking Adjudicator (☎ 011-838 0035, 💻 www.oba.org.za), an independent body which provides a free, informal, confidential problem-solving service. You can only refer to the Adjudicator after having first approached the bank and the Adjudicator will want your complaint reference number and copies of all correspondence between you and the bank.

If you have a problem concerning a loan, you can approach the Micro Finance Regulatory Council (☎ 0860-100 406, www.mfrc.co.za), a private, non-profit body appointed by the government to regulate the micro-lending industry and protect the interests of customers.

You can check your credit rating (for a small fee) or seek advice about credit problems from either of South Africa's two major credit bureaux: Experian (☎ 089-110 5665, www.experian.co.za) and ITC (☎ Cape Town, 021-401 4200, Durban 031-366 8222, Johannesburg 011-488 2911, www.itc.co.za). If they're unable to solve your credit problem, you next stop is the Credit Information Ombud (☎ 0861-662 837, www.creditombud.org.za), a voluntary, independent association reporting to an industry council.

MORTGAGES

Mortgages or home loans (often called bonds in South Africa) are available from all major South African banks, foreign-controlled banks in South Africa and some banks in other countries, although the last may be reluctant to lend money to buy property in what they see as a potentially unstable part of the world. In the vast majority of cases, non-residents in South Africa may borrow a maximum of 50 per cent of the value of a property, although this percentage is set to increase as the property market develops. Mortgages for residents are limited according to their income: your mortgage repayments, combined with any other monthly outgoings (e.g. credit card payments and maintenance), must not exceed 35 per cent of your gross monthly income. (In South Africa, lenders don't take into consideration any proposed rental income from a property for mortgage purposes.) South African loans can be over a 20-year period, although ten is more common.

South African loans can have a fixed or variable interest rate. Interest rates in South Africa have fallen in recent years and, during 2003, the Reserve Bank cut interest rates 5.5 percentage points, to 8 per cent, bringing the prime lending rate to 11.5 per cent and fuelling demand for homes. Current fixed mortgage rates in South Africa vary between around 10.65 per cent and 12.3 per cent, depending on the size of the loan (larger loans usually attract lower rates), the amount of the loan as a percentage of the value of the property and the length of time that the rate is fixed for. The fixed rate is slightly higher than the variable rate to reflect the increased risk to the lender. The advantage of a fixed rate, however, is that you know exactly how much you must pay over the whole term; with a variable rate, your payments can increase without warning. Many lenders offer low-start mortgages, which are fixed for an initial period e.g. two or three years, after which they may change to a variable rate.

It's unwise to over-stretch your finances when taking out a mortgage, as there will inevitably be added costs that you haven't bargained for. If you default on your mortgage repayments, your property can be repossessed and sold at auction, although most lenders are willing to negotiate and arrange lower repayments if borrowers get into financial difficulties.

If you're buying a new property off plan, where payments are made in stages, a bank will provide a 'staggered' loan, where the loan amount is advanced in instalments as required by the contract. During the period before completion, interest is payable on a monthly basis on the amount advanced by the bank (plus life insurance). When the final payment has been made and the loan is fully drawn, the mortgage enters its amortisation period.

Procedure

There are no non-status (or self-certification) mortgages in South Africa, so all mortgage applications must be backed up with proof of income, e.g. copies of your last three months' pay slips and copies of your past six months' bank statements or, if you're self-employed, copies of your last three years' audited accounts and copies of your last year's business bank statements and last six months' personal bank statements.

It isn't usual to have a survey in South Africa, where a South African lender will value a property, although foreign lenders might insist on one before they will grant a loan.

Fees

There are various fees associated with South African mortgages, including the following:

- An 'initiation' fee for setting up the loan, which is usually between 1 and 1.5 per cent of the loan amount*;
- A mortgage registration fee of around 1 per cent of the loan amount*;
- An inspection fee of 0.2 per cent of the bank's valuation of the property;
- A monthly administration fee – currently around R5.70 (50p).

* Some banks charge only one of these fees.

Second Homes

If you have spare equity in an existing property (either in South Africa or abroad), it may be more cost effective to re-mortgage (or take out a second mortgage) on that property than to take out a new mortgage for a second home; it involves less paperwork and therefore lower legal fees. Depending on the equity in your existing property and the cost of your South African property, doing so may enable you to pay cash for a second home.

Foreign Currency Mortgages

It's also possible to obtain a foreign currency mortgage, e.g. euros, sterling, Swiss francs or US$. However, you should be wary of taking out a foreign currency mortgage, as interest rate gains can be wiped out overnight by currency swings and devaluations.

SURVIVAL TIP
It's generally recognised that you should take out a loan in the currency in which you're paid or in the currency of the country where a home is situated.

In this case, if the foreign currency is devalued, you will have the consolation of knowing that the value of your South African property will have increased by the same percentage when converted back into the foreign currency.

When choosing between a rand loan and a foreign currency loan, be sure to take into account all charges, fees, interest rates and possible currency fluctuations. **However you finance the purchase of a second home in South Africa, you should obtain professional advice from your bank manager and accountant.**

If you have a foreign currency mortgage, you must usually pay commission charges each time you make a transfer to pay your mortgage or remit money to South Africa. However, some lenders will transfer mortgage payments to South Africa each month free of charge or for a nominal amount.

SHARK DIVING

5.

THE PURCHASE PROCEDURE

The procedure for buying a property in South Africa is relatively straightforward and a purchase is usually completed within three months of making an offer. Before committing to a purchase, however, you should consider the type of ownership that best suits your current situation and your plans.

SURVIVAL TIP
It's wise to employ a lawyer before signing any contracts or agreements or paying any money and, if necessary, have him check anything you're concerned about regarding a property you're planning to buy. **See also Avoiding Problems on page 114.**

TYPES OF OWNERSHIP

Non-residents can own property in South Africa in their own names (individual title, which is the most common form of ownership) or through a legal entity, e.g. a close corporation, company or trust. The formation of companies and trusts in South Africa is based on English law and these entities are similar to those found in the UK. A close corporation is a type of company that is more flexible and cheaper to set up and administer than a standard incorporated company.

Buying through a corporation, company or trust can save you tax and transfer duty and protect your assets, although there are many other implications of doing so. **This is a complicated matter and you're recommended to speak to your lawyer and/or an accountant to see which type of ownership best suits your needs and circumstances.**

AGREEMENT OF SALE

Once you've agreed a price with the vendor, you must make an 'agreement of sale', which is normally done through an estate agent. The terms 'agreement of sale' and 'offer to purchase' are sometimes used interchangeably in South Africa, although they aren't quite the same thing. An agreement of sale is a written agreement signed by both the buyer and the seller (and also by the seller's spouse if he's married or subject to the laws of a foreign country), whereas an offer to purchase may be either oral or written. If it's in writing and signed by the buyer and accepted by the seller, an offer to purchase constitutes a binding agreement of sale, whereas an oral offer isn't binding.

Note that the payment of a deposit isn't mandatory in South Africa, but is a gesture of good faith by the buyer and an indication to the seller that he's serious and is in a position to buy the property.

An agreement of sale should include the following:

- The name, address, identity numbers and marital status of the buyer and seller. If a company is buying the property, details of the position or capacity of the signatory must be provided.
- A clear description of the property;
- The selling price and the form of payment. If a deposit is to be paid, the agreement must specify that it be held in trust by the named conveyancer or estate agent.
- When the sale is subject to the buyer obtaining a loan, the amount of the loan, the institution applied to and the date by which the loan must be approved;
- When the sale is subject to the sale of the buyer's property, a description of the property, the amount for which it is to be sold and the date by which it must be sold;
- Confirmation that the buyer must pay all transfer costs, taxes and municipal charges on the property from the date of possession;
- The dates on which the transfer of ownership is to take place and the buyer is to take possession. If occupation is to take place before the transfer of ownership, the buyer must pay interest or rent from that date, in which case the amount and method of payment must be specified.
- That the property is sold '*voetstoots*' (meaning 'as is' or 'in the condition in which the property is found'), i.e. without a guarantee by the seller that it has no defects (although the seller must tell the buyer about any faults that the seller knows about). Property surveys aren't standard in South Africa but they can be carried out and their results included as a condition of purchase. See also **Final Checks** on page 194.
- The name of the conveyancer who will deal with the transfer (see **Conveyancing** below);
- Confirmation that commission is due to a named estate agent and the amount due;
- Whether a certificate has been obtained confirming that all accessible parts of the property are free of infestation by designated beetles (sometimes known as a 'borer-free' certificate), who must pay for the inspection – generally the seller – and details of any work required;

- Who will pay for the electrical certificate confirming that the electrical installation meets statutory safety requirements - generally the seller - and details of any work needed;
- A list of fixtures and fittings included in the sale;
- Confirmation that no amendments to the agreement of sale are valid unless in writing and signed by the buyer and seller.

LEGAL CHECKS

Before buying a property, you or your lawyer should do the following:

- Check that there are no pre-emption rights over the property you're planning to buy and that there are no plans to construct anything (e.g. roads, railway lines, airports, shops, factories) that would adversely affect its value, enjoyment or use.
- Check whether there's a zoning policy in the town or area that may affect the property.
- Check whether the property is subject to a compulsory purchase order.
- Check whether there are any rights of way (e.g. for a neighbour) over the land and, if so, whether these are permanent or renewable.
- Ensure that building permits and planning permissions are in order and that a property was built in accordance with plans and permits (see **Regulations** on page 161). Any modifications, renovations, extensions or additions (such as a swimming pool) must be included on the plans and be authorised. Building plans must be checked against the cadastral plan at the land registry.
- In cases where a property has been inherited, check whether each inheritor has agreed to the sale. Heirs who haven't been contacted may have the right to contest the will.
- If a property was previously owned by a bankrupt company, ensure that the liquidator won't reverse the sale and claim it for the creditors.
- Check that there are no encumbrances, e.g. mortgages or loans, against a property or outstanding debts which you might inherit.
- Enquire at the municipal offices whether there are any unpaid taxes such as property tax (see page 217) or other charges outstanding against a property.
- In the case of a community property or sectional title property (see page 143), check that there are no outstanding levies for the last five

years (it may be possible for a vendor to pay the current year's levy and ignore previous bills) and obtain copies of the scheme rules and the latest accounts of the body corporate (which should state whether there are any impending levies for repairs for which you would be liable).

- Check that all bills for electricity, water, telephone and gas have been paid for the last few years. Receipts should be provided by the vendor for all such services.
- If you're buying land for building or planning to extend an existing building, obtain a certificate from the local town hall stating what can be built on it and what the property and the land can be used for. **It's important to check the size of dwelling that can be built on a plot or how far an existing building can be extended.**
- If the property is a listed building, check that there are no state pre-emption rights or restrictions on use or resale.

You should also ask your lawyer about your rights (e.g. to the return of your deposit and any other funds already paid) if it isn't possible to complete the sale for any reason after an agreement of sale has been signed.

CONVEYANCING

Conveyancing (or conveyance) is the legal term for the process whereby a person, company, close corporation or trust becomes the registered and legal owner of immovable property and ensures that this ownership cannot be challenged. It also covers the process of the registration of mortgages. Conveyancing in South Africa can only be carried out by a licensed conveyancer, i.e. a lawyer (the term attorney is also used in South Africa) who has passed the National Conveyancing Examination.

After an agreement of sale has been made (see above), a conveyancer is appointed (invariably by the seller, who must also pay the fees – see page 138) and instructions are sent to him by the estate agent, including the names of the buyer and seller, a copy of the agreement of sale, and the passport numbers and marital status of the buyer and seller. The conveyancer then drafts the following documents:

- A power of attorney to pass transfer – This must be signed by the seller because it allows the conveyancer to transfer the property on his or her behalf.
- Declaration in respect of marital status, identity number and insolvency – The buyer and the seller must sign an affidavit in which

they confirm their marital status and passport numbers and that they're solvent.

- Transfer duty and value added tax (VAT) declaration – The buyer and seller must sign this to confirm the purchase price, which is conveyed to the Receiver of Revenue for the calculation of transfer duty (normally paid by the vendor). VAT is applicable only if the seller is VAT-registered, in which case he must sign a VAT declaration. If VAT is payable, no transfer duty is payable (see **Chapter 7**).
- Mortgage (bond) documents – If you're obtaining a mortgage from a financial institution, the lender will require you to submit your identity document, marriage certificate and, if applicable, pre-nuptial contract in order for his own conveyancer to draw up the necessary documentation.

The conveyancer should then do the following:

- Contact the seller's mortgage holder (bondholder), if there is one, to request the title deed and mortgage cancellation figures from his attorneys (lawyers) or conveyancers (note that there can be three conveyancers involved in a purchase).
- Obtain written confirmation of the buyer's mortgage from the relevant financial institution;
- Ask the seller to pay any outstanding taxes, utility bills or levies so that a clearance certificate can be obtained from the local municipality (or managing agent in the case of a sectional title scheme - see page 143) and lodged at the Deeds Office. A clearance certificate is usually valid for three months.
- Draft the transfer documents and the new title deed;
- Send the draft deed and guarantee requirements to the buyer's lender (or the lender's lawyer) for him to draw up the title guarantees.

The buyer and seller must then sign the transfer documents and the buyer must pay the transfer costs; the Receiver of Revenue will issue a receipt for the transfer duty. The seller must consent to the cancellation of his mortgage (if applicable), the new deed is lodged at the Deeds Office, where it's registered 8 to 14 days later, the seller's mortgage is cancelled and the balance repaid (less any commission and penalties that apply)

Final Checks

Property is sold subject to the condition that it's accepted in the state it's in ('*voetstoots*') at the time of completion, so you should be aware of anything that occurs between signing the agreement of sale and the transfer of ownership. Before signing the transfer documents, it's **imperative** to check that the property hasn't fallen down or been damaged or altered in any way, e.g. by a storm or the vendor. If you've employed a lawyer or are buying through an agent, he should accompany you on a final inspection visit.

You should also take an inventory immediately before the transfer of ownership (the vendor should already have vacated the property) to ensure that the vendor hasn't absconded with anything that was included in the price or purchased separately, e.g. carpets, light fittings, curtains or kitchen appliances, and that any appliances you've bought are in good working order where applicable. You should also check that expensive or valuable items (such as kitchen apparatus or antique fittings) haven't been substituted by inferior (possibly secondhand) items. Any garden ornaments, plants and shrubs present in a garden when you viewed it should still be there when you take possession, unless otherwise stated in the contract.

Some vendors will go to amazing extremes, for example removing not just light bulbs, but bulb-holders, wiring (flex) and even ceiling roses as well as bulbs, plants, shrubs and trees from the garden!

If you find that anything is missing, damaged or isn't in working order, you should make a note and insist on immediate restitution such as an appropriate reduction in the amount to be paid.

Although you or your lawyer should already have checked that there are no encumbrances, e.g. mortgages or loans, against a property or outstanding debts (see **Legal Checks** on page 192), **it's important for you or your lawyer to go to the land registry and check ALL entries up to the day of the completion** (this could be done a few days earlier and then you need only examine entries since the last check on the day of the transfer of ownership).

SURVIVAL TIP

You should refuse to go through with a purchase if you aren't completely satisfied, as it will be very difficult or impossible to obtain redress later.

6.

Moving House

Moving into your new South African home is the culmination of your dreams, but it can also be a highly stressful experience. It's possible to limit the strain on your mental and physical health by careful planning and preparation. This chapter contains checklists that should help to ensure that you don't forget anything important - provided you don't leave everything till the last minute!

SHIPPING YOUR BELONGINGS

It usually takes around four weeks to have your belongings shipped to South Africa from within continental Europe or from the east coast of the US, six weeks from the US west coast or the Far East, and around eight weeks from Australasia. It's usually wise to use a major shipping company with a good reputation and it's best to use a company that's a member of the International Federation of Furniture Removers (FIDI) or the Overseas Moving Network International (OMNI), with experience in South Africa. Members of FIDI and OMNI usually subscribe to an advance payment scheme providing a guarantee: if a member company fails to fulfil its commitments, the removal is completed at the agreed cost by another company or your money is refunded. Some removal companies have subsidiaries or affiliates in South Africa, which may be more convenient if you encounter problems or need to make an insurance claim.

You should obtain at least three written quotations before choosing a company, as costs vary considerably. Moving companies should send a representative to provide a detailed quotation. Most companies will pack your belongings and provide packing cases and special containers, although this is naturally more expensive than packing them yourself. Ask a company how they pack fragile and valuable items, and whether the cost of packing cases, materials and insurance (see below) is included in a quotation. If you're doing your own packing, most shipping companies provide packing crates and boxes.

Shipments are charged by volume, e.g. the cubic metre in Europe and the cubic foot in the US. If you're flexible about the delivery date, shipping companies will quote a lower fee based on a 'part load', where the cost is shared with other deliveries (sometimes called a 'groupage' service). This can result in savings of 50 per cent or more compared with an individual delivery. A large shipping container is loaded with different clients' goods. When there are enough goods to fill the container, it's booked on a vessel. The period of consolidation of shipments (i.e. the time taken to fill the container) naturally varies and depends largely on the amount of business the shipper has, but it usually takes between one and four weeks. This means that groupage shipment times from Europe to South Africa are between five and nine weeks, and there might be an additional period to wait before the goods are delivered to your home address in South Africa, usually around 8 to 12 days, perhaps longer to remote, inland destinations.

SURVIVAL TIP
Whether you have an individual or shared delivery, obtain the maximum transit period in writing, or you may be made to wait months for delivery!

Be sure fully to insure your belongings during removal with a well established insurance company. Don't insure with a shipping company that carries its own insurance, as it may fight every rand of a claim. Insurance premiums are usually 1 to 2 per cent of the declared value of your goods, depending on the type of cover chosen. It's prudent to make a photographic or video record of valuables for insurance purposes. Most insurance policies cover for 'all risks' on a replacement value basis. Note that china, glass and other breakables can usually only be included in an all-risks policy when they're packed by the removal company. Insurance usually covers total loss or the loss of a particular crate, rather than that of individual items (unless they were packed by the shipping company).

If there are any breakages or damaged items, they should be noted and listed before you sign the delivery bill; it's obviously impractical to check everything on delivery, but most (reputable) companies allow damage to be reported up to 48 hours after delivery. If you need to make a claim, be sure to read the small print, as some companies require clients to make a claim within a few days, although seven is usual. Send a claim by registered post. Some insurance companies apply an excess (deductible) of around 1 per cent of the total shipment value when assessing claims. This means that, if your shipment is valued at R300,000 (£26,000) and you make a claim for less than R3,000 (£260), you won't receive anything.

If you're unable to ship your belongings directly to South Africa, most shipping companies will put them into storage and some allow a limited free storage period prior to shipment, e.g. 14 days.

SURVIVAL TIP
If you need to put your household effects into storage, it's wise to have them fully insured, as warehouses have been known to burn down!

Make a list of everything to be moved and give a copy to the removal company. Don't include anything illegal (see **Prohibited & Restricted Goods** on page 202) with your belongings, as customs checks can be rigorous and penalties severe. Provide the shipping company with **detailed** instructions how to find your South African home from the nearest main road and a telephone number where you can be contacted. **If your South African home has poor or impossible access for a large truck you must inform the shipping company (the ground must also be firm enough to support a heavy vehicle).** In these cases, or if furniture needs to be taken in through an upstairs window, you may need to pay extra.

First-Time Immigrants

First-time immigrants may import the following household and personal effects without the payment of customs duty or VAT, provided that they're the *bona fide* property of the person and members of his family, imported into South Africa for their own use:

- Household furniture and other household effects, including curtains, linen, crockery, computer and electrical appliances such as stoves, kettles, radios, television sets, video recorders, DVD players etc (see below);
- Other household effects (see below);
- Other removable effects, including trailers, boats and caravans (but excludes ocean-going yachts) and equipment necessary for the exercise of the calling, trade or profession of the importer ('tools of the trade'), other than industrial, commercial or agricultural plant (see below).

Other household effects includes goods which are normally necessary to equip a self-contained home; you're generally allowed a maximum of two articles each of items such as television sets and hi-fi equipment. Tools of the trade normally include items such as cameras imported by a press photographer or tools imported by an artisan. The following items are excluded:

- Industrial, commercial and industrial plant;
- Motor vehicles;
- Alcoholic beverages and tobacco products.

Goods must be for your own use only and may not be sold or disposed of in any other way for at least six months from the date of clearance.

At least a month before shipping, you must obtain an import permit from the Director of Import and Export Control, Department of Trade and Industry, Private Bag X84, Pretoria 0001, South Africa (☎ 012-310 9791). When you go to the port to collect the goods, you must sign a declaration (form DA304) and form PI160 (obtainable from the Controller of Customs and Excise at the port) and present the import permit and a full inventory of the goods so that they can be cleared through customs.

After considering the costs, you may decide to ship only selected items of furniture and personal effects, and buy new furniture in South Africa. Bear in mind when moving home that everything that can go wrong often does, so allow plenty of time and try not to arrange your move from your old home on the same day as the new owner is moving in. That's just asking for fate to intervene! See also **Customs** on page 202 and the **Checklists** on page 206.

PRE-DEPARTURE HEALTH CHECK

If you're planning to take up residence in South Africa, even for part of the year only, it's sensible to have a health check before your arrival, particularly if you have a record of poor health or are elderly. If you're taking regular medication, you should ask your doctor for the generic name, as the brand names of medicines vary from country to country. If you wish to match medication prescribed abroad, you will need a current prescription with the medication's trade name, the manufacturer's name, the chemical name and the dosage. Most medicines have an equivalent in other countries, although particular brands may be difficult or impossible to obtain in South Africa.

It's possible to have medication sent from abroad, when no import duty or value added tax is usually payable. If you're visiting a holiday home in South Africa for a short period, you should take sufficient medication to cover your stay. In an emergency, a local doctor will write a prescription that can be filled at a local chemist's, or a hospital may refill a prescription at its own pharmacy. It's also wise to take some of your favourite non-prescription medicines (e.g. aspirins, cold and flu remedies and lotions), as they may be difficult or impossible to obtain in South Africa or may be much more expensive. If applicable, take a spare pair of spectacles, contact lenses, dentures or a hearing aid with you. See also **Prohibited & Restricted Goods** below and **Health** on page 44.

CUSTOMS

Foreign visitors to South Africa, residents who have been on holiday abroad and South African citizens are entitled to bring certain goods, including gifts and souvenirs, into the country duty-free. The following are the current per person duty-free allowances (children under 18 don't qualify for the alcohol, cigarette and tobacco allowances):

- 1 litre of spirits and other alcoholic beverages;
- 2 litres of wine;
- 200 cigarettes;
- 250g of cigarette or pipe tobacco;
- 50 cigars;
- 50ml perfumery;
- 250ml toilet water.

Duty for additional goods, new or used (except firearms - see below), up to a value of R12,000 (£1,043) is charged at a flat rate of 20 per cent. Goods carried on behalf of third parties or which are for commercial or trading purposes are subject to full duty and may require an import permit.

Personal effects, sporting and recreational equipment belonging to tourists are allowed into South Africa, free of customs duty and VAT, if imported as accompanied or unaccompanied passenger baggage, for their own use during their stay.

At customs, choose the green channel if you're sure that the goods in your possession fall within the duty free allowance. Don't try to conceal any goods or mislead a customs officer; anything that isn't correctly declared may be detained or seized, and this can result in criminal prosecution or the imposition of fines up to three times the value of the goods.

Prohibited & Restricted Goods

Certain goods are subject to special regulations and in some cases their import and export is prohibited or restricted in order to protect South Africa's citizens, their health and the environment. The amount of rand bank notes that can be imported is restricted to R5,000 (£435) per person. For further information about this matter and details of how to obtain a permit to bring in higher amounts, contact the South African Reserve Bank (☎ 012-313 3911).

Medicine

The importation of medicines by private individuals is generally prohibited, but immigrants and tourists may bring with them for their own personal use one month's supply, provided that they have a prescription for such medicine or a certificate from a chemist confirming that the medicine was prescribed by a doctor. These restrictions don't apply to small amounts of patent medicines for personal use, e.g. aspirin.

Pornography & Drugs

The importation of all pornography involving children or bestiality is prohibited, as is the importation of all narcotic and habit-forming drugs.

Firearms

The South African Police Service (💻 www.saps.org.za) controls the importation of firearms as accompanied passenger baggage and they issue temporary import permits. You can only import firearms on a temporary basis (unless you secure a South African import permit and firearm licence), so no duty or VAT is payable. Upon arrival in South Africa, inform the ground handling staff that you have a firearm, which they will deliver to the Police Service; you will then be escorted to the Police Office to finalise the process and collect your firearm. You must have your home country's Firearm Certificate or Licence. When the Police Service has issued the permit, you can pass through customs. **You're strongly recommended to contact the airline with which you're travelling to check its policy regarding firearms.**

Animals, Plants & Food

Live animals may only be imported with a permit issued by the Director, Division of Veterinary Services, Private Bag X138, Pretoria 0001, South Africa (see page 52). The importation of meat is prohibited unless you have a health permit issued by the Director of Veterinary Services, as above. You can bring in cheese if you have a permit from the Department of Agriculture (☎ 012-325 8087). South Africa is a signatory to the convention on international trade in endangered wild fauna and flora species (CITES), according to which strict control is exercised over the import and export and also re-export of all endangered wildlife, live or dead, including all parts thereof and articles manufactured from them. You need a permit to engage in any such import and export, obtainable from the South African National Parks, PO Box 787, Pretoria 0001, South Africa (☎ 012-428 9111, 🖳 www.parks-sa.co.za). Honey and all honey products or preparations are prohibited from being imported into South Africa.

Plants, seeds, bulbs, etc. may only be imported with a permit issued by the Department of Agriculture, Division Plant and Seed Control, Private Bag X258, Pretoria 0001, South Africa, as well as a Phytosanitary Certificate issued by the authority concerned in the country of export, e.g. the Department for the Environment, Food and Rural Affairs (DEFRA) in the UK (☎ 020-7216 6808).

EMBASSY REGISTRATION

Nationals of some countries are required to register with their local embassy or consulate after taking up residence in South Africa, and most embassies like to keep a record of their country's citizens resident in South Africa (it helps to justify their existence). It also makes it easier for them to find you in an emergency, e.g. when someone is urgently trying to contact you. For a list of embassies see **Appendix A**.

FINDING HELP

One of the most important tasks facing new arrivals in South Africa is how and where to obtain help with everyday tasks such as buying a car, obtaining medical help and taking out insurance. How successful you are at finding local help depends on your employer (if applicable), the town or area where you live (those who live in major cities are usually better served than those who inhabit small towns), your nationality, English proficiency and sex (women are usually better served than men, through numerous women's clubs). Some companies may have a department or staff whose job is to help new arrivals settle in, or they may contract this task out to a relocation company. Unfortunately, some employers in South Africa seem totally unaware of (or uninterested in) the problems and difficulties faced by their foreign employees.

There's an abundance of information available in English, but little in other foreign languages. An additional problem is that much of the available information isn't intended for foreigners and their particular needs. You may find that your friends and colleagues can help, as they can often offer advice based on their own experiences and mistakes. **But take care!** Although they mean well, you're likely to receive as much useless as useful information (it may not be wrong, but it may be invalid for your particular situation). Your local community is usually an excellent source of reliable information, but you need to speak the local language to benefit from it.

If a woman lives in or near a major town, she's able to turn to many English-speaking women's clubs and organisations for help. The single foreign male must usually fend for himself, although there are men's expatriate clubs in some areas and mixed social clubs throughout the country. If you ask around among your neighbours or colleagues, it's possible to find various Anglo-South African 'friendship' clubs or English-speaking organisations. Finally, don't neglect to check the internet, where local newspapers, government offices, clubs and organisations often have their own websites. Many businesses (particularly large multi-national companies) produce booklets and leaflets containing useful information about clubs or activities in the area. Bookshops may have some interesting publications about the local region, and tourist and information offices are also useful sources of information. Most embassies and consulates (see page 294) in South Africa also provide their nationals with local information, including the names of lawyers, interpreters, doctors, dentists, schools, and social and expatriate organisations.

MOVING IN

One of the most important tasks to perform after moving into a new home is to make an inventory of the fixtures and fittings and, if applicable, the furniture and furnishings. When you've purchased a property, you should check that the previous owner hasn't absconded with any fixtures and fittings that were included in the price or anything which you specifically paid for, e.g. carpets, light fittings, curtains, furniture, kitchen cupboards and appliances, garden ornaments, plants or doors (see **Conveyancing** on page 193).

When moving into a long-term rental property, it's necessary to complete an inventory of its contents and a report on its condition. This includes the condition of fixtures and fittings, the state of furniture and furnishings, the cleanliness and state of the decoration, and anything that's damaged, missing or in need of repair. An inventory should be provided by your landlord or agent and may include every single item in a furnished property (down to the number of teaspoons). The inventory check should be carried out in your presence, both when taking over and when terminating a rental agreement. If an inventory isn't provided, you should insist on one being prepared and annexed to the lease. If you find a serious fault after signing the inventory, send a registered letter to your landlord and ask for it to be attached to the inventory.

If the inventory made when you moved in doesn't correspond with the one made when you move out, you must make good any damages or deficiencies or the landlord can do so and deduct the cost from your deposit. Although South African landlords are generally no worse than those in most other countries, some will do almost anything to avoid repaying a deposit.

Note the reading on your utility meters (e.g. electricity, water and gas, if applicable) and check that you aren't overcharged on your first bill. The meters should be read by utility companies before you move in, although you may need to organise it yourself.

It's wise to obtain written instructions from the previous owner concerning the operation of appliances and heating and air-conditioning systems, maintenance of grounds, gardens and lawns, care of special surfaces such as wooden, marble or tiled floors, and the names of reliable local maintenance men who know a property and are familiar with its quirks. Check with your local authorities regarding local regulations about such things as rubbish collection, recycling and on-road parking.

CHECKLISTS

Before Arrival

The following checklist contains a summary of the tasks that should (if possible) be completed before your arrival in South Africa:

- Check that your family's passports are valid!
- Obtain a visa, if necessary, for you and all your family members (see page 31). Obviously this **must** be done **before** your arrival in South Africa.
- If possible, visit South Africa before your move (preferably a few times, at different times of the year) to prepare yourself for all the changes you will have to make. You might be surprised at the amount of people who decide to live in another country without ever having visited it!
- Arrange schooling for your children.
- Find temporary or permanent accommodation and buy a car if you will need one. If you purchase a car in South Africa, you need to license it and arrange insurance.
- Arrange the shipment of your personal effects to South Africa (see page 198).

- Arrange health (and travel) insurance for your family. This is essential if you aren't already covered by a private insurance policy and won't be covered by the South African health service (see **Chapter 8**).
- Open a bank account in South Africa and transfer funds (see **Chapter 4**). You may also find it more convenient to obtain some rand before you arrive, which will save you having to change money immediately on arrival.
- Obtain an international driving permit, if necessary.
- Obtain an international credit or charge card, which will prove invaluable during your first few months in South Africa.
- Obtain as many credit references as possible, e.g. from banks, mortgage companies, credit card companies, credit agencies, companies with which you've had accounts, and references from professionals such as lawyers and accountants. These will help you to establish a credit rating in South Africa.

If you're planning to become a permanent resident, you should take all your family's official documents with you. These may include birth certificates, driving licences, marriage certificate, divorce papers or death certificate (if a widow or widower), educational diplomas and professional certificates, employment references and curricula vitae, school records and student ID cards, medical and dental records, bank account and credit card details, insurance policies (plus records of no-claims allowances) and receipts for any valuables. You also need the documents necessary to obtain a residence permit (see page 36) plus certified copies, official translations and numerous passport-size photographs (students should take around a dozen).

After Arrival

The following checklist contains a summary of the tasks to be completed after arrival in South Africa (if not done before):

- Have your visa cancelled and your passport stamped, as applicable, at the airport, port or border post.
- If you aren't taking a car with you (as the majority of people don't), you may wish to rent or buy one locally. **Note that it's practically impossible to get around in rural areas without a vehicle.**
- Register with your local social security office.
- Register with your local embassy or consulate (see page 294).

- Open a bank account (see page 181) and give the details to your employer and any companies that you plan to pay by direct debit or standing order (such as utility companies).
- Register with a local doctor.
- Arrange whatever insurance is necessary (see **Chapter 8**).

SAFE
SAFARIS

7.

TAXATION

An important consideration for anyone (even for non-residents) buying a home in South Africa is taxation, including property tax, income tax (for example, if you earn an income from a home) and possibly capital gains tax. It's important to check tax information with an accountant or tax office (but get it in writing) in order to establish that it's correct, including the information contained in this book.

Direct taxes in South Africa include the following: income tax; capital gains tax; donations tax; estate duty; company tax and a secondary tax on companies; and a tax on certain dividends from foreign registered or incorporated companies.

Indirect taxes include the following: value added tax; excise and customs duties; stamp duties; transfer duty; property taxes; regional levies; unemployment insurance contributions and a skills development levy.

Most South African taxes are levied by the national government, although the provincial authorities impose some - mainly assessment rates and other taxes on immovable property. The central tax authority is the South African Revenue Service (usually known by its initials, SARS, which are also the initials of a potentially fatal flu-like illness; some will regard this as a not inappropriate coincidence!). Its website contains a list of all its offices in the country (💻 www.sars.gov.za - click on 'contact us').

SURVIVAL TIP

Before you decide to settle in South Africa permanently, you should obtain expert advice regarding South African taxes. This will (hopefully) ensure that you take maximum advantage of your current tax status and that you don't make any mistakes that you will regret later.

DOUBLE-TAXATION TREATIES

The following is the status in June 2004 of agreements to avoid double-taxation of income accruing to South African taxpayers from foreign sources and to foreign taxpayers from South African sources.

- Comprehensive agreements are in place with Algeria, Australia, Austria, Belarus, Belgium, Botswana, Canada, Croatia, Cyprus, the Czech Republic, Denmark, Egypt, Finland, France, Germany, Greece, Hungary, India, Indonesia, Iran, Ireland, Israel, Italy, Japan, Korea, Lesotho, Luxembourg, Malawi, Malta, Mauritius, Namibia, the

Netherlands, Norway, Oman, Pakistan, the People's Republic of China, Poland, Romania, the Russian Federation, the Seychelles, Singapore, the Slovak Republic, Swaziland, Sweden, Switzerland, Thailand, Tunisia, Uganda, the United Kingdom (newly updated and also extending to Grenada and Sierra Leone), the United States of America, Zambia and Zimbabwe.

- Comprehensive agreements have been ratified in South Africa with Brazil, Nigeria, New Zealand and Rwanda.
- New or updated comprehensive agreements have been signed, but not ratified, with Ethiopia, Kuwait, Swaziland and Ukraine.
- Comprehensive agreements have been negotiated or renegotiated, but not signed, with Bulgaria, the Democratic Republic of Congo, Estonia, Gabon, Germany, Ghana, Kuwait, Latvia, Lithuania, Malawi, Malaysia, Morocco, Mozambique, Namibia, the Netherlands, Portugal, Qatar, Saudi Arabia, Spain, Sri Lanka, Tanzania, Turkey, the United Arab Emirates, Zambia and Zimbabwe.
- Comprehensive agreements are being negotiated or renegotiated, but not finalised, with Bangladesh and Cuba.
- Limited sea and air transport agreements exist with Brazil, Portugal and Spain.

INCOME TAX

Until 1st January 2001, a 'source-based' tax system was in use, meaning that tax was payable only on income from (or deemed to be from) a South African source. Since then, however, South African residents have been taxed on their worldwide income. This includes the income of a foreign-controlled company. Certain types of income from outside South Africa are exempt and credit is allotted for foreign taxes paid. Non-South African residents, however, are still taxed only on South African-source income.

Individuals are deemed to be resident in South Africa for tax purposes if they normally live in the country or are in South Africa for more than 183 days a year.

Each individual is taxed separately in South Africa, with no distinction between male and female, or between married and single people.

The tax year is 1st March to 28th (or 29th) February. Tax is payable in instalments by companies, close corporations and those individuals who are classified as provisional taxpayers (e.g. directors of companies and members of close corporations). Individuals make two provisional payments based on estimated tax liability (in relation to previous years' payments): the first due six months after the beginning of the assessment year (i.e. by the end of August), the second at the end of the assessment year (by the end of February). Late payment results in a penalty and interest is payable. If the total paid is less than the amount due, a final payment must be made within seven months of the end of the assessment year (i.e. by the end of September). Interest (non-deductible) is due on the shortfall at a decreed rate (currently 11.5 per cent). If the amount paid exceeds the amount due, the overpaid amount is refunded and interest on is paid to the taxpayer - but at a considerably lower rate (currently 7.5 per cent) - and the interest is taxable for resident taxpayers!

Employees' tax is deducted at source ('pay-as-you-earn') and paid by employers the tax to the authorities monthly. The tax thus deducted is a credit against the employee's total tax liability as assessed by his or her annual tax return. Under the SITE system (Standard Income Tax on Employees), people earning under R74,000 (£6,435) per year aren't required to file an annual income tax return, and the tax deducted from their salaries constitutes their total and only liability for tax.

Income Tax Rates

Income tax rates for the assessment year ending February 2005 are as follows:

Taxable Income (R)	Tax Rate (%)	Cumulative Tax (R)
Up to 74,000	18	13,320
74,001 - 115,000	25	23,570
115,001 - 155,000	30	35,570
155,001 - 195,000	35	49,570
195,001 - 270,000	38	78,070
Over 270,000	40	

A primary rebate of R5,800 (£504) is available to all individuals for the tax year ending in February 2005, and a secondary rebate of R3,200 (£278) is available to those over 64. The rebates aren't available to trusts.

Dividends & Interest

Local dividends from all companies and distributions from all close corporations are exempt from tax. Foreign dividends received by South

African residents with a holding of less than 25 per cent in the company declaring dividends are usually taxable. The first R11,000 (£956) of interest and non-exempt foreign dividends received by individual resident taxpayers under the age of 65 is exempt from tax. The exemption rises to R16,000 (£1,391) for resident taxpayers aged 65 or over. The first R1,000 (£86.95) of the exemption applies to foreign dividends.

Foreign dividends qualify for tax exemption in the following circumstances:

- If dividends were received by shareholders holding certain minimum holdings, currently 25 per cent;
- If dividends were declared by listed companies in which South African residents have at least a 10 per cent holding;
- If dividends were declared out of profits already subject to South African tax.

Interest paid to non-residents (other than those who are residents of Lesotho, Namibia and Swaziland) is generally exempt from tax. In order to qualify, a non-resident must be absent from South Africa for not less than 183 days during the assessment year.

Tax is levied at 18 per cent on monthly gross interest, non-exempt foreign dividends and net rental received by or accrued to pension, provident and retirement annuity funds.

Temporary Residents

Foreign nationals temporarily living and working in South Africa are taxable on their remuneration, irrespective of where their employer lives or where payment is made. This income may, however, be exempted under one of South Africa's double-taxation agreements (see page 212).

CAPITAL GAINS TAX

Capital gains tax (CGT) applies to the disposal of assets by the following:

- South African residents (CGT applies to worldwide assets);
- Non-South African residents for immovable property in South Africa (including immovable property held through a company) and assets of a branch or agency in South Africa.

The portion of the gain (inclusion rate) included in taxable income is 25 per cent for an individual, special trust or an insurer's individual policyholder fund, and 50 per cent for other taxpayers, e.g. a company, close corporation, business or family trust. Capital losses can be deducted from capital gains or carried forward to future assessment years, but they cannot be offset against revenue income.

The first R1 million (£86,956) of the gain on a primary owner-occupied residence is exempt from CGT, as are the following:

- Transfers of property from a deceased spouse;
- Transfers between spouses;
- An individual's belongings;
- Private motor vehicles;
- Small business assets;
- Transactions subject to income tax;
- Gambling proceeds.

DONATIONS TAX

Tax is payable on the donation of property by South African residents (other than public companies) at a rate of 20 per cent, with the following exemptions:

- If the donation is between spouses;
- If the donation is by a public company or a trust;
- If the donation only comes into effect on the donor's death (in which case estate duty applies - see below);
- If the property was acquired from non-residents or derived from trade outside South Africa.

On all other donations, an exemption of R30,000 (£2,608) per year for an individual donor and R10,000 (£869.56) per year for a non-public company applies.

ESTATE DUTY

Estate duty is charged on inheritances at 20 per cent, with the following exemptions:

- The first R1.5 million (£130,435) of an estate;
- Bequests to a surviving spouse;
- Overseas property that the deceased acquired by inheritance or held before taking up residence in South Africa.

VALUE ADDED TAX

Value added tax (VAT) was introduced to South Africa in 1991 and is an invoice-based tax, similar to those found in western Europe and New Zealand. Most transactions involving goods and services attract VAT, which is currently applied at a single rate of 14 per cent. The transfer of immovable property is subject to VAT when the seller is VAT-registered (in which case he's exempt from transfer duty – see below), unless the buyer is also VAT-registered and the sale is part of a business that's a going concern.

EXCISE & CUSTOMS DUTIES

Excise duty is imposed on the local production of some commodities, e.g. automobiles, jewellery, beer and wine. Clothing, basic foods, medicine, rent, some utilities and professional services are exempt from excise duty.

Imported goods are subject to customs duty at various rates (up to 45 per cent), which aren't always the same as the rates for excise duty. You can obtain a rebate on customs duty if the imported goods are to be used in manufacturing for export.

STAMP DUTIES

Stamp duties apply to a number of types of document. Some stamp duties are at a fixed amount, others are related to the value of the transaction. The government plans to remove stamp duties, which currently apply to property rentals, bank withdrawals, credit card and Postbank accounts, and instalment credit agreements.

TRANSFER DUTY

If you buy a home in South Africa, you must pay transfer duty on the value of the property above R150,000 (£3,000) unless you or the vendor is VAT-registered, in which case VAT is due instead (see page 217).

PROPERTY TAXES

Property-related taxes include municipal rates (sometimes confusingly referred to as 'property taxes') and charges for refuse and sewerage, although the latter apply mainly to those in urban areas; there are no refuse or sewerage services in some rural areas!

Municipal Rates

Most South African property owners must pay municipal rates, based on the 'market value' of their property; some rural properties are exempt, although there are government plans to include them. The calculation of municipal rates was controversially changed in March 2004, when the Local Government: Municipal Property Rates Bill became law. Previously, poor areas were charged a higher percentage than wealthy ones, so lower income households effectively subsidised wealthier ones, but rates are now levied at a common percentage (around 1 per cent) irrespective of property values, although municipalities may levy different rates for different types of property, e.g. residential, industrial, commercial, business, agricultural and commercial. In the case of sectional title schemes, rates are applied to the whole scheme and divided among individual owners according to their Participation Quota (see **Community Properties** on page 143).

Your municipality will send you a valuation notice, stating the official value of your property. From this, you should subtract the specified 'rate-free' amount (usually around R50,000). Then multiply the net figure by the municipal rates percentage (e.g. 0.98 per cent in Cape Town) to calculate the annual amount payable. Divide this by 12 to arrive at your monthly payment. For example, if the value of your house is R1 million (£87,000), you will pay rates on R950,000 at 0.98 per cent (in Cape Town), which gives an annual municipal rates bill of R9,310 or a monthly rate of R776 (£67.50).

Refuse

Like municipal rates, refuse charges vary from place to place. In Cape Town, for example, there are two parts to the refuse charge: the first is calculated by subtracting R50,000 from the valuation of your property (as with municipal rates) and multiplying the result by 0.038 per cent (R360/£31 on a property valued at R1 million/£87,000); the second part is a charge of R38.60 (£3.35) per month for a 240-litre 'wheelie' bin, or R33.60 (£2.90) if one isn't available (and you use plastic refuse bags) – half these amounts if your property is valued at less than R100,000 (if it's worth less than R50,000, you get a free bin!).

Sewerage

Sewerage is also usually charged in two parts: a fixed charge of up to R38 (£3.30), depending on the value of your property, and a variable charge according to your water consumption, as follows:

Annual Consumption	**Charge Per '000 Litres**
0 - 4,200 litres	0
4,201 - 14,000 litres	R2.04
14,001 - 35,000 litres	R3.25

So, if you consumed 200,000 litres in a year (average for a couple or small family), you would pay R650 (£43) plus the fixed charge.

REGIONAL LEVIES

Regional services councils, metropolitan councils and joint services boards are responsible for supplying basic services in their regions. To pay for these, a regional establishment levy is payable by businesses to these councils and a regional services levy is made on employees' salaries. The amount of these levies varies from region to region but is usually modest; for example, in Johannesburg, the regional establishment levy is 0.14 per cent and the regional services levy is 0.35 per cent. VAT is added to these amounts.

UNEMPLOYMENT INSURANCE

Employers are liable to pay unemployment insurance fund contributions to a maximum of 1 per cent of salaries (limited to a maximum monthly salary of R8,836/£768) and a skills development levy of 1 per cent of pay. Some of the levy may be reclaimed, provided that staff training is deemed 'appropriate'.

8.

INSURANCE

An important aspect of owning a home in South Africa is insurance, principally home and contents insurance and health insurance for your family when visiting South Africa. You should also ensure that you have the necessary (and adequate - not necessarily the same thing) car insurance (which is expensive in South Africa), including breakdown insurance, and third-party liability insurance (usually included in household insurance - see page 231).

It's unnecessary to spend half your income insuring yourself against every eventuality, from the common cold to cutting your finger, although it's important to insure against any event that could precipitate a major financial disaster, such as a serious accident or your house being demolished by a storm. The cost of being uninsured or under-insured can be astronomical.

You're responsible for ensuring that you and your family are legally insured in South Africa. The law in South Africa may differ considerably from that in your home country or your previous country of residence, and you should never assume that it's the same.

As with anything connected with finance, it's important to shop around when buying insurance. Simply collecting a few brochures from insurance agents or companies (listed in the yellow pages) or making a few telephone calls could save you a lot of money. The global insurance industry has been going through a crisis in recent years and (at long last) is becoming more consumer-driven. One major change has been the advent of telephone and internet insurers, which allow you to obtain and compare estimates in minutes. Some internet brokers allow you to compare rates online.

South Africa is served by a wide range of insurance companies, both local and international, including Gerling (www.gerling.com), Liberty Group (www.liberty.co.za), Mutual & Federal (www.mf.co.za), Old Mutual Assurance (www.oldmutual.co.za), SA Eagle (www.saeagle.co.za), Sanlam (www.sanlam.co.za), which dubs itself 'the market leader in short-term insurance in South Africa', and SASRIA (www.sasria.co.za). The three largest (by market share) are Sanlam, Mutual & Federal and SA Eagle, with around 26 per cent, 18 per cent and 9.5 per cent respectively.

Not all insurance companies are equally reliable or have the same financial stability and it may be better to insure with a large international company with a good reputation than with a small (e.g. South African) company, even if this means paying higher premiums. In recent years, there have been a number of company failures in the short-term insurance sector (motor, home, fire, etc.) and policy holders have suffered as a result. Read insurance contracts carefully and make sure that you understand the terms and the cover provided before signing them. Some insurance companies will do almost anything to avoid paying claims and will exploit any available legal loophole.

If you wish to make a claim on an insurance policy, you may be required to report an incident to the police within 24 hours. If you're unsure of your rights, you're recommended to obtain legal advice for anything other than a minor claim.

Before choosing an insurance company, it's well worth taking advice from friends and colleagues regarding the efficiency, reliability and competitiveness of different insurance companies and brokers. You should also consult the regulatory authority, The Financial Services Board (FSB), which is an independent institution established by statute to oversee the South African non-banking financial services industry in the public interest. Insurance companies must be registered and authorised by the FSB in order to provide cover. Until recently, short-term insurance brokers weren't subject to statutory control, but the Financial Advisory and Intermediary Services Act (FAIS) passed at the end of 2002 applies to all financial advisory and intermediary services. Nevertheless, you must still be vigilant when choosing a broker to deal with your insurance needs. There are representative bodies for brokers which apply a strict code of conduct and you're recommended to choose a broker who's a member of such an organisation, e.g. the Insurance Brokers' Council and The South African Financial Services Intermediaries Association.

The FSB makes a number of recommendations for people arranging short-term insurance, including the following:

- Check whether the insurer's name appear frequently in the documents? It should. If not, ask the name of the company that will pay in the event of a claim and check whether it's registered. If you're in any doubt, check with the FSB.
- Compare the quoted premium with that from other insurers but remember that, as with most things, the cheapest insurance product isn't necessarily the best.
- Ask about excesses (deductibles).
- If somebody else fills in your insurance application, check that it's correct and meets your needs.
- Be careful not to underinsure or a claim will probably be scaled down by the percentage that you're underinsured (sometimes called the principle of average).

- Insist on receiving a full policy document within around 30 days of the start of the insurance, not simply a policy schedule and/or insurance certificate/cover note.
- Ensure that the name of the registered insurer appears on the policy document.
- Insist that your broker confirms in writing that he won't switch to another insurer without your permission.
- If your insurance is to be placed with Lloyd's of London, check that your broker is an authorised Lloyd's agent. Ask the FSB if there's any doubt.
- Only use a broker who's a member of a representative body with a code of conduct and check that the broker has professional indemnity cover.
- If you use a broker, insist that he doesn't act as a sub-broker but has direct communication with the insurance company.
- Check whether the insurer requires the installation of any security devices (a usual requirement in South Africa).

For a full list of registered insurers, go to the FSB website (💻 www.fsb.co.za) and click on 'Departments' and then on 'Insurance'. Other useful sources of insurance information and advice include the Insurance Brokers' Council (💻 www.ibcsa.org.za), the Long-term Ombudsman (💻 www.ombud.co.za), the Short-term Ombudsman (💻 www.osti.co.za) and the South African Insurance Association (💻 www.sainsurance.co.za).

HEALTH INSURANCE

If you're visiting or living or working in South Africa, it's extremely risky not to have health insurance for your family; if you're uninsured or under-insured, you could be faced with some high medical bills. When deciding on the type and extent of health insurance, make sure that it covers **all** your family's present and future health requirements in South Africa **before** you receive a large bill. A health insurance policy should cover you for **all** essential health care, whatever the reason, including accidents (e.g. sports accidents) and injuries, whether they occur in your home, at your place of work or while travelling. Don't take anything for granted, but check in advance. **When travelling in South Africa, you should carry proof of your health insurance with you at all times.**

You should avoid a company that reserves the right to cancel a policy unilaterally when you have a serious illness or when you reach a certain age (maximum insurable age), as it will prove difficult or impossible to find alternative cover. You should also steer clear of a one-year contract, which a company can refuse to renew. Policies often have a period (e.g. five years) during which the insurance company cannot exclude you from cover, even if you have a serious illness costing the insurance company a lot of money.

Visitors

Visitors spending short periods in South Africa (up to a month or so) should have a travel health insurance policy (see page 229), particularly if they aren't covered by an international health policy. If you plan to spend up to six months in South Africa, you should either take out a long-stay policy or an international health policy (see **Foreign Companies** on page 227). **There are no reciprocal health agreements between South Africa and Australia, European countries or the US.**

Residents

If you're planning to take up residence in South Africa, your family will be entitled to subsidised or free medical treatment under the national health service (see page 49). In theory, this provides hospital accommodation and treatment (including tests, surgery and medication during hospitalisation), visits to family doctors (GPs), specialist medical assistance provided by paediatricians, obstetricians and other specialists, discounted medicines, laboratory services, appliances, ambulance services and free or subsidised services at a local health unit.

In practice, the South African public health system is badly underfunded, overstretched and often inefficient, meaning that receiving proper treatment can be a difficult, time-consuming procedure. For this reason, **almost everybody in South Africa who can afford it has some form of private medical insurance, covering at least major treatment, and you're strongly recommended to do the same.**

Private Health Insurance

When buying private health insurance, you should consider South African as well as international companies. When comparing policies, carefully check the extent of cover and exactly what's included and excluded from a policy (often indicated only in the **very** small print), in addition to premiums and excess charges. In some countries, premium increases are limited by law, although this may apply only to residents in the country where a company is registered.

Although there may be significant differences in premiums, generally you get what you pay for and can tailor premiums to your requirements. The most important questions to ask yourself are: does the policy provide the cover required and is it good value? If you're in good health and are able to pay for your own outpatient treatment, such as visits to your family doctor and prescriptions, the best value is usually a policy covering only specialist and hospital treatment.

SURVIVAL TIP

If you aren't covered by South African social security and need comprehensive private health insurance to obtain a residence permit, you must ensure that your health policy will be accepted by the authorities.

South African Companies

The South African healthcare sector has been facing challenges in the early 21st century: sharply rising medical costs and legislation to enforce 25 per cent solvency reserves on providers have led to some collapses and many mergers in this constantly evolving sector. In order to survive, South African healthcare providers have had to be innovative and devise schemes that people can actually afford; the choice is bewildering and includes clever, managed healthcare schemes and savings plans offering comprehensive, partial and limited cover.

Younger, fitter people often buy limited coverage, for serious conditions (a list of over 50 chronic conditions is specified in some policies), and pay for minor treatment themselves. In other schemes, your insurance covers only a percentage (e.g. 80 per cent) of claims and you must pay the balance yourself (in effect an excess or deductible), for which you pay a lower premium than for 100 per cent coverage.

Private policies vary considerably in price, depending on their scope and the percentage coverage, but generally cost from R1,000 (£85) to R2,000 (£175) per month for a family of four, although costs are higher for comprehensive cover and the elderly. Many companies, retirement groups and other organisations offer lower rates and some South African employers pay 50 per cent of key employees' health insurance costs.

The largest medical insurer in South Africa is Discovery Health (💻 www.discoveryworld.co.za), with over 1.5 million members – at least twice as many as any of its competitors. Its website tells potential customers that its claim-paying record has received an AA rating, the highest in the industry. However, the website also states that Discovery Health's annual price increases 'have consistently been contained to 12 per cent to 15 per cent over the past seven years', which indicates how much private healthcare costs have been rising in South Africa.

Smaller healthcare providers include Multimed (🖳 www.multimed.co.za) and Selfmed (🖳 www.selfmed.co.za). The latter claims that 'whilst small enough to ensure that members receive the personalised, individual attention they deserve, Selfmed is still big enough to ensure members have peace of mind about all their healthcare needs.' A full list of costs for various schemes can be found on 🖳 www.discoveryworld.co.za/dhealth/rate_tables_2004.jhtml.

Shop around and compare policies, which vary considerably: some have particularly murky small print that entitles the insurer to avoid paying almost any claim! It's well worth seeking out and speaking to people who have used various medical insurance schemes, to discover which ones actually live up to the promises made on their websites and in their promotional literature.

As in many countries, South African insurance companies are loath to pay claims (one of the reasons they don't insist on a medical examination is so that they can refuse to pay a claim because you omitted to tell them you'd had a heavy cold three years previously!). So, when completing the questionnaire, be sure to list **all** previous illnesses, hospitalisation, current ailments and treatment. However, South African companies are usually no worse (or better) in this respect than those in other countries.

Foreign Companies

There are a number of foreign health insurance companies with agents or offices in South Africa or offering cover for people living in South Africa, including AXA PPP Healthcare (🖳 www.axappphealthcare.com), BUPA International (🖳 www.bupa-intl.com), the Exeter Friendly Society (🖳 www.exeterfriendly.co.uk) and HealthCare International (🖳 www.healthcareinternational.com). These companies offer special policies for expatriates, and most international health policies include repatriation or evacuation (although it may be optional), sometimes including shipment (by air) of the body of a person who dies abroad to his home country for burial. An international policy may also allow you to choose (within limits) the country in which you have non-urgent medical treatment.

Most international insurance companies offer health policies for different areas, e.g. Africa, Europe, worldwide excluding the US, and worldwide including the US. Most companies also offer different levels of cover, e.g. basic, standard, comprehensive and 'prestige'. Each level has a different limit on the total annual medical costs, the minimum usually being R2 million/£175,000 (although you're recommended to have much more cover and many companies provide cover of up to R7.5 million/£650,000) and some companies limit the charges for specific treatment or care such as specialists' fees, operations and hospital accommodation.

A medical examination isn't usually required for international health policies, although 'pre-existing' health problems are excluded for a period, e.g. two years.

Claims are usually settled in major currencies and large claims are usually settled directly with the hospital or doctor by insurance companies. Always check whether an insurance company will settle large medical bills directly; if you're required to pay bills and claim reimbursement from an insurance company, it can take several months before you receive your money (some companies are slow to pay).

It isn't usually necessary to translate bills into English or another language, although you should check a company's policy. Most international health insurance companies provide emergency telephone assistance.

The cost of international health insurance varies considerably with your age and the extent of cover. With most international policies, you must enrol before you reach a certain age (usually between 60 and 80) to be guaranteed continuous cover in your old age. Premiums can sometimes be paid monthly, quarterly or annually, although some companies insist on payment annually in advance.

If you already have private health insurance in country other than South Africa, you may be able to extend it to include South Africa rather than taking out a new policy.

Changing Employers Or Insurance Companies

When changing employers or leaving South Africa, you should ensure that you have continuous health insurance. If your family is covered by a company health scheme, your insurance will probably cease after your last official day of employment. If you're planning to change your health insurance company, however, you should ensure that important benefits aren't lost; for example, existing medical conditions won't usually be covered by a new insurer for a period. When changing health insurance companies, it's wise to inform your old company if you have any outstanding bills for which they're liable.

▲ *Malachite Kingfisher, Mpumalanga Province*

▲ *Inland Lake, Ceres, Western Cape*

▼ *Johannesburg, Gauteng Province*

◀ *Howick Falls, KwaZulu-Natal*

▼ *Hout Bay, Western Cape*

Zulu Woman, KwaZulu-Natal

Mossel Bay, Western Cape

Clifton, Cape Town,
Western Cape

Long Street, Cape Town, Western Cape

Diamonds, Northern Cape

Steam Train, Bethleham, Free State

Simonsberg Mountains, Stellenbosch, Western Cape

Ladismith, Klein Karoo, Western Cape

All photographs
© South Africa Tourism
www.southafrica.net

Strech's Court, Graaff-Reinet, Eastern Cape

Namaqualand, Northern Cape

▲ *Beach, Western Cape*

▲ *Sun City, North Western Province*

▲ *Table Mountain, Cape Town, Western Cape*

▲ *Amsterdamhoek, Eastern Cape*

▼ *Surfing, KwaZulu-Natal*

TRAVEL INSURANCE

Holiday or travel insurance is recommended for everyone, irrespective of whether you have an international health policy. As you probably know, anything can and often does go wrong with a holiday, sometimes before you even get started (particularly when you **don't** have insurance). The following information applies equally to residents and non-residents, whether you're travelling to or from South Africa or within South Africa. **Nobody should visit South Africa without travel (and health) insurance.**

Travel insurance is available from many sources, including travel agents, insurance companies and brokers, banks, motoring organisations and transport companies (airline, rail and bus). Package holiday companies and tour operators also offer insurance policies, some of which are compulsory, overpriced **and don't provide adequate cover.** You can also buy 24-hour accident and flight insurance at major airports, although it's expensive and doesn't offer the best cover.

Before taking out travel insurance, you should carefully consider the range and level of cover you require and compare policies. Short-term holiday and travel insurance policies may include cover for holiday cancellation or interruption, missed flights, departure delay at both the start and the end of a holiday (a common occurrence), delayed, lost or damaged baggage, lost belongings and money, medical expenses and accidents (including evacuation home), personal liability and legal expenses, and default or bankruptcy, e.g. a tour operator or airline going bust. You may also need cover for transport strikes in South Africa!

Always check any exclusion clauses in contracts by obtaining a copy of the full policy document, as all relevant information won't be included in an insurance leaflet. High-risk sports and pursuits should be specifically covered and **listed** in a policy (there's usually an additional premium). Winter sports policies are available, although they're obviously more expensive than normal holiday insurance (dangerous sports are excluded from most standard policies, although the definition of 'dangerous' varies from company to company). Third-party liability cover should be at least R20 million (£1.8 million) in the US and R10 million (£870,000) in the rest of the world.

Third-party liability cover doesn't usually cover you when you're driving a car or other mechanically propelled vehicle, for which you will normally require specific insurance.

Health Cover

Medical expenses are an important aspect of travel insurance and you shouldn't rely on insurance provided by reciprocal health agreements (of which South Africa has none!), charge or credit card companies, household policies or private medical insurance (unless it's an international policy), none of which usually provide adequate cover, although you should take advantage of what they do offer. The minimum medical insurance recommended by experts is R5 million (£435,000) for South Africa and R10 million (£870,000) for the rest of the world (many policies have limits of between R15 million/£1.3 million and R50/£4.3 million, which is particularly recommended if you're visiting the US).

If applicable, check whether pregnancy-related claims are covered and whether there are any restrictions for those over a certain age, e.g. 65 or 70 (travel insurance is becoming increasingly expensive for those over 65, although they don't usually need to worry about pregnancy - particularly the men!).

Visitors

Travel insurance for visitors to South Africa should include personal liability and repatriation expenses. If your travel insurance expires while you're visiting South Africa, you can buy further insurance from a local insurance agent, although this won't include repatriation expenses. Flight and comprehensive travel insurance are available from insurance desks at most airports, including travel accident, personal accident, worldwide medical expenses and in-transit baggage.

Cost

The cost of travel insurance varies considerably according to where you buy it, how long you intend to stay in South Africa and your age. Generally, the longer the period covered, the cheaper the daily cost, although the maximum period covered is usually limited, e.g. to six months. With some policies, an excess must be paid for each claim; with others, the excess applies only to certain items, such as luggage, money and medical expenses. As a rough guide, travel insurance for South Africa costs from around R250 (£22) for one week, R375 (£33) for two weeks and R700 (£61) for a month for a family of four (two adults and two children under 16). Premiums may be higher for people over 65 or 70.

Annual Policies

For people who travel abroad frequently, whether on business or on pleasure, an annual travel policy usually provides the best value. Many insurance companies offer annual travel policies for around R1,000 (£85) to R2,000 (£175) per year for an individual (the equivalent of around two to three months' insurance with a standard travel insurance policy), which are excellent value for frequent travellers.

The cost of an annual policy may depend on the area covered, e.g. Africa, Europe, worldwide excluding the US and worldwide including the US, although it doesn't usually cover travel within your country of residence. There's also a limit on the number of trips per year and the duration of each trip, e.g. 90 or 120 days. Some insurance companies offer an 'emergency travel policy' for holiday homeowners who need to travel abroad at short notice to inspect a property, e.g. after a severe storm or burglary.

Carefully check exactly what's covered (or omitted), as an annual holiday and travel insurance policy may not provide adequate cover.

Claims

If you need to make a claim, you should provide as much documentary evidence as possible to support it. Travel insurance companies gladly take your money, but they aren't always so keen to pay claims and you may need to persevere before they pay up. Always be persistent and make a claim **irrespective** of any small print, as this may be unreasonable and therefore invalid in law. Insurance companies usually require you to report a loss (or any incident for which you intend to make a claim) to the local police or carriers within 24 hours and obtain a written report. Failure to do so may mean that a claim won't be considered.

HOUSEHOLD INSURANCE

There's no requirement to have cover for your home or belongings and some South Africans don't bother to insure their home or its contents, although if you have a mortgage, your lender will require you to have building insurance. Nevertheless, it's highly recommended to take out insurance covering damage to the building due to fire, water, explosion, wind, freezing, snow, theft, vandalism and natural catastrophes.

Household insurance generally constitutes a multi-risk policy for buildings and contents, although some companies require separate policies for fire and theft and for liability and others offer fire and damage with an extra premium for theft and liability. Special conditions apply to holiday homes (see below).

It's possible (and legal) to take out building and contents insurance in another country for a property in South Africa, although the policy may still be subject to South African law (so always check). The advantage is that you have a policy in a format you can understand (you may also be more likely to be paid or be paid earlier). This may seem like a good option for a holiday home in South Africa, although it may be more expensive than insuring with a South African company and can lead to conflicts if the building is insured with a South African company and the contents with a foreign company.

Building Insurance

It's important to have insurance against storm damage in South Africa, which can be severe in some areas, although the country is generally free of tidal waves, severe floods, typhoons, monsoons and other natural perils. Earthquakes are rare (but rockfalls and subsidence are common in mining areas) and there are no active volcanoes. Read the small print and check that you're covered for natural disasters such as floods. However, if you live in an area that's hit by a succession of natural disasters, your insurance may be cancelled. Note also the following:

- Water damage caused by burst pipes due to old age or freezing may be excluded.
- If you use bottled gas, you must inform your insurance company, as there might be an extra premium to pay.
- You must specifically insure electrical systems and major apparatus against risk such as lightning strikes, or an insurance company won't pay.

An item to consider including in your building and contents insurance in South Africa that you might not have insured in your home country (especially if it has a cooler climate and lower crime rate) is cover for accidental damage to the machinery of swimming pools, Jacuzzis, boreholes, irrigation systems and electrical gates.

> **SURVIVAL TIP**
> **In the event of total loss, building insurance payments are based on the cost of rebuilding your home, so make sure that you insure your property for the true cost of rebuilding. Add an extra 10 or 15 per cent of the rebuilding cost to cover the professional fees associated with rebuilding.**

If you have a property restored or modernised, you must obtain a professional valuation on completion for insurance purposes.

Apartments

If you own an apartment or a property that shares common elements with other properties, building insurance is included in your service charges, although you should check exactly what's covered. You must, however, still be insured for third-party risks in the event that you cause damage to neighbouring apartments, e.g. through flood or fire. Having insurance also helps you to claim against a neighbour if they cause damage to your apartment.

Rented Property

Your landlord might insist that you have third-party liability insurance, as detailed in the rental contract. A lease might require you to insure against 'tenants' risks', including damage you may make to the rental property and to other properties if you live in an apartment, e.g. by causing a flood, fire or explosion.

Contents Insurance

Contents are usually insured for the same risks as a building (see above) and are insured for their replacement value. Contents polices are restrictive with regard to security, including locks, window shutters or grilles (all windows less than 3m/10ft from the ground must be barred), armoured doors, guard dogs, alarms connected to a central station, etc. All security requirements must be adhered to or claims are reduced or won't be paid.

You cannot usually insure valuables (e.g. antiques, jewellery and other precious objects) unless they've been valued by an approved South African expert (valuations can be expensive) and they generally need to be stored in a safe, which must be approved by your insurance company.

You should insist on a certificate being issued to verify that a safe has been approved. Valuables are usually covered only in the home, rather than abroad or on holiday. Due to the many loopholes, you may be better off keeping your valuables in a bank safety deposit box.

When claiming for contents, you should produce the original bills (keep bills for expensive items) and bear in mind that imported items may be much more expensive in South Africa.

Holiday Homes

Premiums are generally higher for holiday homes due to their vulnerability (particularly to burglaries) and are usually based on the number of days per year a property is inhabited and the interval between periods of occupancy. **Cover for theft, storm, flood and malicious damage may be suspended when a property is left empty for more than three weeks at a time.** In areas with a high risk of theft (e.g. most major cities and resort areas), you may be required to fit extra locks and other security measures. Some companies may not even insure holiday homes in high risk areas.

If you're absent from your property for long periods, e.g. more than 60 days per year, you may be required to pay an excess on a claim arising from an occurrence that takes place during your absence (and theft may be excluded). It's unwise to leave valuable or irreplaceable items in a holiday home or a home that's vacant for long periods. Always check carefully the small print of a policy.

SURVIVAL TIP
Where applicable, it's important to ensure that a policy specifies a holiday home and not a principal home.

Premiums

Contents insurance premiums vary with the area but are generally high. Premiums are usually calculated on the age and size of the property (either the habitable area in square metres or the number of rooms) rather than its value. Usually the sum insured is unlimited, provided the property doesn't exceed a certain size and is under a certain age. The cost of multi-risk contents insurance in a medium-risk area is around R4,000 (£350) per year for a property with one or two bedrooms, R7,000 (£600) for three or four bedrooms and around R10,000 (£875) per year for five or six bedrooms. Premiums can be higher in high-risk areas. If you have an index-linked policy, cover is increased each year in line with inflation.

There's usually an excess of between R750 (£65) and R2,500 (£215) for each claim. Note also that it's standard on South African policies to limit cover for the contents of fridges and freezers. For example, Sanlam limits cover to a meagre R1,000 (£87). On the other hand, under Sanlam's house contents and buildings cover, the insured amount for contents is increased annually by 10 per cent from 15th December to 31st January to give extra cover over the festive period!

Claims

If you wish to make a claim, you must usually inform your insurance company in writing (by registered letter) within two to five days of an incident or 24 hours in the case of theft. Thefts should also be reported to the local police within 24 hours, as the police statement, of which you receive a copy for your insurance company, usually constitutes irrefutable evidence of your claim.

SURVIVAL TIP

Check whether you're covered for damage or thefts that occur while you're away from the property and are therefore unable to inform your insurance company immediately.

9.

LETTING

Many people planning to buy a holiday home are interested in owning a property that will provide them with an income, e.g. from letting, to cover the running costs and help with the mortgage payments. Letting a home for a few weeks or months in the summer can more than recoup your running costs and pay for holidays. However, if you're planning to let a property, it's important not to overestimate the income, particularly if you're relying on it to help pay the mortgage and running costs.

If you're planning on holiday lets, don't overestimate the length of the high season, which varies with the region, or even assume that you'll be able to rent the property throughout the high season – owners rarely achieve full occupancy with holiday lets. Apartments in major tourist cities (especially Cape Town and Durban) have year-round letting potential, but rates vary considerably between high, medium and low season and you shouldn't make the mistake of assuming that you can charge high season rates all year. You may be unable to meet all your mortgage payments and running costs from rental income, even if a property is available to let year-round.

Most experts recommend that you don't purchase a home in South Africa if you need to rely on rental income to pay for it. The holiday rental market is extremely volatile and subject to unpredictable highs and lows; a good rental season can easily be followed by a poor one.

In most areas, it's difficult to make a living providing holiday accommodation, as the high season is too short and there's often too much competition.

RULES & REGULATIONS

If you let a property in South Africa, you're required by law to pay tax on your rental income in South Africa and not in the country where the income is received (see page 213). You should have third party insurance (costing at least R1,250/£115 per year) covering accidents and injuries to guests (or anyone) using your property. If you're planning to buy a community property (see page 143), you must check whether there are any rules that prohibit or restrict short-term letting. You may also be required to notify your insurance company.

Short-Term Letting

Most people who do holiday letting have a simple agreement form that includes a property description, the names of the clients, and the dates of arrival and departure. However, if you do regular letting, you may wish to check with a lawyer that your agreement is legal and contains all the necessary safeguards. If you plan to let to non-English speaking clients (South Africa is attracting visitors from all over the world), you must have a letting agreement in other languages. If you use an agent, he will provide a standard contract.

Long-Term Letting

Owners who will be away from South Africa for much of the year or for long periods might consider a long-term let while they're absent. Unless your property is rent-controlled (and very few in South Africa are) you can set any rent you decide. It must be realistic, of course, or nobody will rent the property. The best way to gauge the current rental level is to investigate rents being charged for other properties in the area; pose as a potential tenant if necessary or enquire at local estate agents.

If you're away from South Africa for long periods, you might decide to let your property through an estate agent who, as well as finding a tenant, will mange the property while you're absent. If you use an agent, you will have to pay him commission. There's no fixed rental commission in South Africa, but expect to pay at least 10 per cent (probably more), the amount depending on the type of service provided, i.e. partial or full management of the property.

If somebody wants to rent your property, he must make the offer in writing. If an agent is handling the letting, he will probably draw up a document for the applicant to sign. You should ask for and check an applicant's credit references and/or proof of income.

Lease

Since August 2000, residential leases have been governed by the Rental Housing Act, which stipulates that a lease must contain the following:

- The landlord's name and address;
- The tenant's name and address;
- A description of the property, e.g. its address;
- A list of any existing defects to the property (see **Obligations** below);
- The amount of rent and any periodic increases;
- Any other expenses that the tenant must pay;
- When the rent must be paid (usually the beginning of each calendar month);

- How much deposit must be paid by the tenant as insurance against any damage he might cause (at least six to eight weeks' rent is usual);
- The period of the lease unless it's 'open-ended', and details of the notice required by the landlord and tenant to terminate it;
- The landlord's and tenant's obligations towards each other (see below);
- Any 'house rules' that the tenant must comply with (which usually include restrictions on noise, particularly between around 11pm and 8am, keeping pets and sub-letting);
- A list of furniture and fittings, if the property is let furnished (see page 243).

Strangely, a lease can be oral, but you're strongly recommended to draft a written lease; in any case, if a tenant requests a written lease, a landlord must provide one.

Obligations: The law requires the following obligations from landlords and tenants:

- The landlord must issue a detailed written receipt for every payment received from the tenant.
- If the tenant pays a deposit, the landlord must invest it in an interest-bearing bank account and must give the tenant a written statement of the interest earned whenever he asks for one.
- Before the tenant moves in, he and the landlord must inspect the property and draw up a list of defects, which must be attached to the lease.
- When the tenant moves out, he and the landlord must inspect the property again to see if the tenant has caused any damage.
- If there's no damage, the landlord must refund the deposit and the interest within seven days.
- If there's damage, the landlord can pay for repairs out of the deposit and must refund the balance and the interest within 14 days.
- If the tenant owes money to the landlord, the landlord can deduct it from the deposit before refunding it.

If any disputes arise between landlords and tenants, they can be referred to the Rental Housing Tribunal of the province in which the property is located. Contact a provincial government office for details.

Bed & Breakfast

The number of bed and breakfast (B&B) establishments in South Africa has rocketed over the last decade. In the mid-'90s, there were barely 300, but now there are well over 10,000. Some people, foreigners included, imagine that running a B&B is easy and probably even fun. But be warned: it involves long hours, hard work, and patience and grace under pressure, often for modest rewards.

Before you can turn your South African home into a B&B, your plans must be agreed by the Town Planning Department of your local council. If they approve them, you must register the business and secure a trading licence from the Licensing Department. You must also register with the regional Services Board and the tax authorities, as a business sole proprietor, close corporation (cc) or private company (pty).

If you're still tempted to run a B&B in South Africa, further information and advice can be obtained from the following: the Bed and Breakfast Association of South Africa (BABASA), PO Box 2005, Groenkloof, 0027 (☎ 012-480 2041, 💻 www.babasa.co.za) and the Guest House Association of Southern Africa (GHASA), 27 Tennant Road, Kenilworth, Cape Town, 7800 (☎ 021-762 0880).

LOCATION

If income from a South African home has a high priority, its location should be one of your main considerations when buying (see also page 92). When considering the location for a property you plan to let, you should bear in mind the following factors.

Accessibility

A property should be situated within easy reach of a major airport, as some holidaymakers won't consider travelling more than an hour to their destination after arriving at an airport. Choose an airport with frequent flights from your home country and preferably one with a range of scheduled flights. It isn't wise to rely on an airport served only by budget airlines, as they may alter or cancel routes at short notice. See **Airline Services** on page 100.

It's an advantage if a property is served by public transport or is situated in a town where a car is unnecessary. If a property is located in a town or village within a maze of streets, you should provide a detailed map. If it's in the country where signposts are all but non-existent, you will not only need to provide a detailed map with plenty of landmarks, but you may also need to erect signs; holidaymakers who spend hours driving around trying to find a place are unlikely to return or recommend it! Maps are also helpful for taxi drivers, who may not know the area.

Attractions

The property should be close to tourist attractions and/or a good beach, depending on the sort of clientele you wish to attract. If you want to let to families, a property should be close to leisure facilities such as theme parks, water parks, sports grounds and nightlife. If you're planning to let a property in a rural area, it should be somewhere with good walking possibilities and preferably near one of South Africa's many wildlife parks.

Climate

Properties in areas with a pleasant year-round climate, especially the coasts to the north and south of Durban, have a greater rental potential, particularly outside high season. This is also important should you wish to use the property yourself outside the high season; for example, you could let a property during school holiday periods, when rental income is at its highest, and use it yourself at other times and still enjoy fine weather.

SWIMMING POOL

If you're planning to let your property, a swimming pool is a major advantage, as properties with pools are much easier to let to certain types of client than those without (some private letting agencies won't handle properties without a pool), unless a property is situated on a beach, lake or river. It's usually necessary to have a private pool with a single-family home (e.g. a detached villa), although a shared pool is adequate for an apartment. If you plan to let mainly to families, it's wise to choose an apartment with a 'child-friendly' communal pool, e.g. with a separate paddling pool or a pool with a shallow area. You can charge a higher rent for a property with a private pool and it may be possible to extend the letting season even further by installing a heated or indoor pool, although the cost of heating a pool may be higher than the rental return.

LETTING RATES

Letting rates vary considerably with the time of year, area and size and quality of a property but are generally low compared with those in countries such as France and Spain. A modest property sleeping two to four people in an average area can be let for only around R3,000 (£260) per week even in high season, which generally includes the months of December and January, and possibly school holiday times; on the other hand, a luxury property in a popular area (for example, the much sought-after Camp's Bay on the Cape Peninsular – see page 83) with a pool and accommodation for 8 to 12 can be let for several tens of thousands of rand per week in high season. The mid-season usually comprises October, November, March and April (except Easter, which is often counted as high season), when rents are around 20 to 25 per cent lower than the high season; the rest of the year is the low season, although parts of South Africa are popular all year and don't have a low season.

FURNISHINGS

If you let a property, it's wise not to fill it with expensive furnishings or valuable belongings. While theft is rare, items will eventually get damaged or broken. When furnishing a property that you plan to let, you should choose hard-wearing, dark-coloured carpets or rugs which won't show stains (although most properties have tiled or marble floors rather than carpets) and buy durable furniture and furnishings. Simple, inexpensive furniture is best in a modest home, as it will need to stand up to hard wear.

Small, two-bedroom properties usually have a sofa bed in the living room. You may also need a cot and/or high chair. Properties should be well equipped with cooking utensils, crockery and cutlery (including a kitchen knife that cuts!), and it's usual to provide bed linen and towels (some agents provide a linen hire service). Make sure the bed linen and towels are of good quality and replace them before they wear out. You can buy good quality, inexpensive household linen at some supermarkets in South Africa, particularly during the sales, which take place in mid-winter (July/August) and after Christmas.

Appliances should include a washing machine and microwave, and possibly a dishwasher and tumble-dryer. Depending on the rent and the quality of the property, your guests may also expect central heating, air-conditioning, covered parking, a barbecue and garden furniture (including loungers). Heating is essential in southern and central South Africa if you want winter lets, while air-conditioning is an advantage when letting property in summer (particularly around Durban, where it becomes very humid), although it's considered mandatory only when letting a luxury property. Some owners provide bicycles and badminton and table tennis equipment. It isn't usual to have a telephone, although you could install a credit card phone or one that just receives incoming calls.

KEYS

You will need several sets of spare keys (plus spare remote controls for electric gates, etc.), which will probably get lost at some time. If you employ a management company, its address and not the address of the house should be on the key fob. If you lose keys or if they can easily be copied, you should change the lock barrels regularly (at least annually). You don't need to provide guests with keys to all the external doors, only the front door (the others can be left in your home). If you arrange your own lets, you can send keys to guests in your home country or they can be collected in South Africa. It's possible to install a security key-pad entry system, the code of which can be changed after each let.

CLEANING

It goes without saying that a property should always be spotlessly clean when holidaymakers arrive and you should provide basic cleaning equipment. You will need to arrange for cleaning between lets and also at regular intervals, e.g. weekly or twice-weekly, for lets of more than a week. If you use a local agent, he will usually arrange cleaning, which should cost you little more than R20 (£1.75) per hour. If applicable, you must also arrange pool cleaning and a gardener (see **Maintenance** on page 248).

LETTING AGENTS

If you use an agent, ask the following:

- When the letting income is paid;
- What extras are levied and what for;
- Whether he provides detailed accounts of income and expenses (ask to see samples);
- Who he lets to (e.g. what nationalities and whether families, children or singles, etc.);
- How he markets properties;
- Whether you're expected to contribute towards marketing costs;
- Whether you're free to let the property yourself and use it when you wish.

The larger agencies market homes via newspapers, magazines, overseas agents and colour brochures, and have representatives in many countries. Management contracts usually run for a year. A management company's services should include arranging routine and emergency repairs, reading meters (if electricity is charged separately), routine maintenance of house and garden, including lawn cutting and pool cleaning, arranging cleaning and linen changes between lets, advising guests on the use of equipment, and providing guest information and advice (24 hours per day in the case of emergencies).

Agents may also provide someone to meet and greet clients, hand over the keys and check that everything is in order. A letting agent's representative should also make periodic checks when a property is empty to ensure that it's secure and that everything is in order. The services provided usually depend on whether a property is a basic cottage or a luxury villa costing tens of thousands of rand per week.

Before buying a community property, you should check that letting is permitted. You may need to notify the property's administrator and your insurance company if a property is to be let (see **Rules & Regulations** on page 238).

DOING YOUR OWN LETTING

Some owners prefer to let a property to family, friends, colleagues and acquaintances, which allows them more control – and with luck the property will also be better looked after. In fact, the best way to get a high volume of lets is usually to do it yourself, although many owners use a letting agency in addition to doing their own marketing in their home country. You will need to decide whether you want to let to smokers and whether you will accept pets and young children – some people won't let to families with children under five due to the risk of bed-wetting and the propensity for young children to wreak havoc. Some owners also prefer not to let to young, single groups. Note, however, that this reduces your letting prospects.

Advertising

If you wish to let a property yourself, there's a wide range of South African and foreign newspapers and magazines in which you can advertise, e.g. *Daltons Weekly* (☎ UK 020-8329 0100, 💻 www.daltons.co.uk) and newspapers, such as the *Sunday Times* in the UK. However, it can be prohibitively expensive to advertise a single property in a national newspaper or magazine. You will need to experiment to find the best publications and days of the week or months to advertise.

A cheaper and better method is to advertise in property directories such as *Private Villas* (☎ UK 020-8329 0170, 💻 www.privatevillas.co.uk) or on websites such as those of Holiday Rentals (☎ UK 020-8743 5577, 💻 www.holiday-rentals.co.uk) and Owners Direct (☎ UK 01372-722708, 💻 www.ownersdirect.co.uk), where you pay for the advertisement and handle the bookings yourself.

You can advertise among friends and colleagues, in company and club magazines (which may even be free), and on notice boards in offices, shops and public places. The more marketing you do, the more income you're likely to earn, although you should ensure that you provide a quick and efficient response to any enquiries. It pays to work with local people in the same business and send surplus guests to competitors (they will usually reciprocate). In addition to advertising locally and in your home country, you can extend your marketing abroad (or advertise via the internet). Note that it's usually necessary to have an answering machine and preferably also a fax machine.

Internet

Advertising on the internet is an increasingly popular option for property owners. There are many tourism websites where you can advertise. Typical arrangements include posting your property's details (in up to four languages), photos and prices, and links from major search engines. Some companies will even provide you with your own website.

Your own website is an excellent advertisement and can include photographs, booking forms and maps, as well as comprehensive information about your property. You can also provide information about flights, car rental, local attractions, sports facilities and links to other websites. A good website should be easy to navigate (avoid complicated page links or indexes) and must include contact details, ideally an email address. It's wise to subscribe to a company that will submit your website to the main search engines, such as Google and Yahoo. You can also exchange links with other websites.

Brochures & Leaflets

If you don't have a website containing photographs and information, you should produce a coloured brochure or leaflet. This should contain external and internal pictures, comprehensive details of the property, the exact location, and a list of local attractions and details of how to get to them (with a map if necessary). You should enclose a stamped addressed envelope when sending out details and follow up within a week if you don't hear anything. It's necessary to make a home look as attractive as possible in a brochure or leaflet without distorting the facts – advertise honestly and don't over-sell the property, which will be counter-productive in the long term.

Handling Enquiries

If you plan to let a home yourself, you must decide how to handle enquiries about flights and car rentals. It's easier to let clients make bookings themselves, but you should be able to offer advice and put them in touch with airlines, ferry companies, travel agents and car rental companies.

INFORMATION PACKS

Pre-Arrival

After accepting a booking, you should provide guests with a pre-arrival information pack containing:

- A map of the local area and instructions for finding the property;
- Information about local attractions and the local area (available free from tourist offices);
- Emergency contact numbers in your home country (e.g. the UK) and South Africa if guests have any problems or plan to arrive late;
- The keys or instructions on where to collect them on arrival.

It's ideal if someone can welcome your guests when they arrive, explain how things work, and deal with any special requests or problems.

Post-Arrival

You should also provide an information pack in your home for guests explaining:

- How things work. e.g. kitchen appliances, TV/video player, heating and air-conditioning;
- Security measures (see page 249);
- What not to do (for example, if you allow young children and pets, you should make a point of emphasising dangers such as falling into the pool);
- Local emergency numbers and health services such as a doctor, dentist and hospital/clinic;

- Numbers of useful services such as a general repairman, plumber, electrician and pool maintenance company (you may prefer to leave the telephone number of a local caretaker, who can handle any problems);
- Recommended shops, restaurants and attractions.

Many people provide a visitors' book for guests to write their comments and suggestions, and some send out questionnaires. If you want to impress your guests, you can arrange for fresh flowers, fruit, a bottle of wine and a grocery pack to greet them on their arrival. It's personal touches that ensure repeat business and recommendations; you may even find after the first year or two that you rarely need to advertise. Many people return to the same property year after year. Simply do an annual mail-shot to previous clients. **Word-of-mouth advertising is the cheapest and always the best.**

MAINTENANCE

If you do your own letting, you will need to arrange for cleaning and maintenance, including pool cleaning and a gardener if applicable. Ideally you should have someone on call seven days per week.

Caretaker

If you own a second home in South Africa, you will find it beneficial or even essential to employ a local caretaker, irrespective of whether you let it. You can have your caretaker prepare the house for your family and guests, as well as looking after it when it isn't in use. If it's a holiday home, have your caretaker check it periodically (e.g. weekly) and allow him to authorise minor repairs. If you let a property yourself, your caretaker can arrange for (or do) cleaning, linen changes, maintenance, repairs and gardening and pay bills. If you employ a caretaker in South Africa, where domestic wages are low, you probably won't have to pay more than around R2,000 (£170) per month.

Closing A Property For The Winter

Before closing a property for the winter, you should turn off the water at the mains (required by insurance companies), empty food cupboards and the fridge/freezer, disconnect gas cylinders and turn off mains gas (if applicable), and empty bins. You should leave interior doors and a few small windows (with grilles or secure shutters), as well as wardrobes, open to provide ventilation. Lock main doors, windows and shutters, and secure anything of value or leave it with a neighbour or friend. Check whether any work needs to be done before you leave and if necessary arrange for it to be done in your absence. Most important, leave a set of keys with a neighbour or friend and arrange for them (or a caretaker) to check your property periodically.

SECURITY

Most people aren't security conscious when on holiday and you should therefore provide detailed instructions for guests regarding security measures and emphasise the need to secure the property when they're out, which is particularly important in South Africa. It's also important for them to be security conscious when in the property, particularly when having a party or in the garden, as it isn't unusual for valuables to be stolen while guests are outside.

When leaving a property unattended, it's important to employ all the security measures available, including:

- Storing valuables in a safe (if applicable) – hiding them isn't a good idea, as thieves know ALL the hiding places;
- Closing and locking all doors and windows;
- Locking grilles on patio and other doors;
- Closing shutters and securing any bolts or locks;
- Setting the alarm and notifying the alarm company when you're absent for a long period;
- Making it appear as if a property is occupied by the use of timers and leaving lights and a TV/radio on.

Bear in mind that prevention is always better than cure, as stolen possessions are rarely recovered. If you have a robbery, you should report it to your local police station, where you must make a statement. You will receive a copy, which is required by your insurance company if you make a claim. See also **Home Security** on page 259.

INCREASING RENTAL INCOME

Rental income can be increased outside high season by offering special interest or package holidays – which can be organised in conjunction with local businesses or tour operators – to broaden the property's appeal and cater for larger parties. These include:

- Sporting activities such as golf, tennis, cycling or hiking;
- Visits to sporting events, notably international cricket and rugby matches (and the soccer World Cup, which will be held in South Africa in 2010 - plan ahead!);
- Cooking, gastronomy and wine tours/tasting;
- Arts and crafts such as painting, sculpture, photography and writing courses;
- Wildlife spotting, e.g. visits to game parks and reserves, and whale-watching.

You don't need to be an expert or conduct courses yourself but can employ someone to do it for you.

10.

MISCELLANEOUS MATTERS

This chapter contains miscellaneous - but nevertheless important - information for homeowners in South Africa, including information about crime, heating and air-conditioning, postal services, security, shopping, telephone, television and radio services, and utilities.

CRIME

Many people are put off visiting South Africa, let alone buying a home there, by stories of its supposedly runaway crime problem, so it's important to set out some facts and figures and to put them in perspective.

The task facing the first post-apartheid government in 1994 was daunting: an Interpol survey of 80 countries put South Africa fourth in the number of murders, first in the number of rapes and 13th for vehicle theft. The overall crime rate was double the international average, and the police force was prey to low morale, absenteeism, resignation and early retirement, and corruption. Prisons had 25 per cent overcapacity, the courts were trying to cope with far too many cases, and only 8 out of every 1,000 crimes committed were punished by a jail sentence of two years or more.

In 2000, the government embarked on a ten-year programme to reduce crime and improve crime-fighting efficiency and capacity. The aim was to bring South African crime rates down to the international average by the end of the period. According to police figures, by autumn 2003, South Africa's murder rate had decreased by almost 30 per cent since 1994, thanks to the introduction of child protection units, specialised courts, the recruitment and deployment of more police officers, and countrywide anti-crime operations.

Other crimes were also down: rape decreased by 5.7 per cent between 2001/2002 and 2002/2003, vehicle hijackings by over 20 per cent and bank robberies by more than 15 per cent over the same period. The seizure of illegal firearms has contributed to the reduction in crime: Operation Sethunya was launched in April 2003 and between 1st April and 31st July 2003, 15,340 firearms were confiscated.

South Africa's crime problem is far from being solved - crime and HIV/AIDS are invariably cited as the major challenges facing the country - but it closely follows demographic patterns, most violent crime being confined to the country's poorest areas: mainly the townships and parts of Johannesburg. Most foreign visitors and property buyers don't even visit these areas, let alone buy property there.

You must be careful in South Africa (see below) but not paranoid. Crime rates vary wildly in different parts of South Africa and different areas of its cities. Don't be put off by the widespread manifestations of an obsession with security: the barred or buzzer entrances to most shops outside guarded shopping malls, the high walls topped with razor wire, the firearm shops (many citizens carry guns), the guard dogs, security bars, burglar alarms, electronic gates and fast-response security firm signs. See also **Household Insurance** on page 231 and **Home Security** on page 259.

Crime Avoidance

Wherever you are in the country, seek advice from locals, hotel staff, security guards or the police about where it is and isn't safe to go. Always know where you're going (and look as if you know, i.e. don't appear lost or nervous, and don't brandish maps or guidebooks), especially at night. Avoid gangs of children ('street kids', responsible for a lot of petty crime and some more serious crime) by crossing the road if necessary.

Don't carry a camera, camcorder or personal stereo or wear ostentatious jewellery, designer sunglasses or expensive clothes. Keep the amount of cash and the number of credit cards and other valuables that you carry to a minimum. Wear bags sideways across the body rather than on one shoulder (which makes them much harder to grab) and keep mobile phones (cellphones) out of sight.

Local public transport in South Africa attracts a lot of criminals and, subject to local advice, is often best avoided. If you're unlucky enough to be mugged, never resist. There are a lot of poor and desperate people in South Africa who won't think twice about using violence if they feel threatened when committing a crime.

Never hitchhike or pick up hitchhikers. Drivers need to be aware of the risk of 'carjacking' (car hold-ups and hijackings), which is high in some parts of South Africa. Always be on the alert when you stop at traffic lights (known as 'robots' or 'robbos' in South Africa) or stop signs or arrive at or depart from a premises. Keep doors and windows locked at all times, and plan your trip in advance so that you don't become lost and have to stop to ask for help from strangers. Keep valuables in the car out of sight. When parking the vehicle at night, only park in well lit or security-controlled parking areas. There are numerous street security guards in South Africa who will watch over your car for a few rand.

Cash dispensing machines (ATMs) have become targets for thieves in South Africa in recent years. If possible, go with somebody else when withdrawing money from an ATM and never allow strangers to 'help' you with your transaction. Try to make sure that the person behind you in the queue stands well back from you. Concentrate on what you're doing throughout the transaction and don't allow yourself to be distracted. If your card becomes stuck in the machine, enter the PIN number three times incorrectly, meaning that the machine will retain your card and it won't fall into a criminal's hands. If you lose a card or it's retained by a machine, notify the bank as soon as possible.

Finally, the South African National Police (SANP) do their best but are understaffed and underfunded, so don't rely on them turning up to help if you encounter trouble (see **Security Services** on page 261).

HEATING & AIR-CONDITIONING

Although most of South Africa is warm or hot for much of the year, heating is necessary, at least in the winter months (July and August), as winter nights can be cold in much of the country. Heating requirements in winter vary from six hours per day for around 14 weeks per year in parts of the north to up to 14 hours per day for six months in parts of the centre and south. Summer temperatures often exceed 40°C (104°F) in some areas, and air-conditioning is desirable (and may be necessary if you wish to let a property).

Heating

Heating systems in South Africa may be powered by oil, gas, electricity, solid fuel (usually wood) or even solar power. Whatever form of heating you use, it's essential to have good insulation, without which up to 60 per cent of heating is lost through the walls and roof. Not many South African homes have central heating, but you may wish to install it if you buy a home in a cooler area or plan to spend winters there.

The currently available fuel options are described below. South Africa is investigating the feasibility of wind power generation, and areas around Cape Town and Durban have been identified as having the country's best potential, but wind power isn't available yet.

Electric

Electric central heating isn't common in South Africa. However, some people with well insulated modern homes and a permanent system of ventilation use electric storage heaters. Electric central heating isn't recommended for old properties with poor insulation. If you install an electric central heating system, you may need to increase your electricity rating to cope with the extra demand (see **Power Supply** on page 283).

Stand-alone electric (e.g. halogen) heaters are relatively expensive to run and are best suited to holiday homes.

Gas

Mains gas central heating is rare in South Africa, but its use should increase over the coming decade. Gas is clean, economical and efficient, and the boiler is usually fairly small and can be wall-mounted. In rural areas where there's no mains gas, you can sometimes have a gas tank installed on your property.

Liquid Fuels

South Africa's wealth of cheap coal has meant that it has been slow to develop its reserves of petroleum and natural gas. Liquid fuels, which include diesel, ethanol, gasoline, hydrogen and methanol, are available, although mainly in the Johannesburg area and their use is largely industrial rather than domestic; together they provide around 20 per cent of the country's energy requirements.

Solar Power

Most areas of South Africa average over 2,500 hours of sunshine per year (compared with 1,645 in Copenhagen, 1,535 in Cologne, 1,500 in London, 1,375 in Dublin and 1,350 in Edinburgh), and the country's annual 24-hour solar radiation average is around 220 watts per m^2, compared with around 150 in much of the US and around 100 in Europe – all of which means that South Africa is well suited to solar energy generation.

A solar power system can be used to supply all your energy needs, although it's usually combined with an electric or gas heating system, as solar power cannot be relied upon year-round for lighting, heating and hot water. A solar power system can be used to provide electricity in a remote rural home, where the cost of extending electricity is prohibitive. Solar power can also be used to heat a swimming pool.

The main drawback is the high cost of installation, which varies considerably according to the region and how much energy you require. You should pay between R15,000 (£1,300) and R35,000 (£3,000) for an installation sufficient to operate basic lighting and a couple of appliances (a solar power system must be installed by an expert). Costs are likely to come down, however, as studies are being undertaken into the feasibility of large-scale solar energy systems. Continuous advances in solar cell and battery technology are expected to dramatically increase the efficiency and reduce the cost of solar power, which is forecast to become the main source of energy worldwide in this century.

The advantages are no running costs, silent operation, low maintenance and no electricity bills. A system should last 30 years (it's usually guaranteed for ten years) and can be uprated to provide more power in the future.

Solid Fuel

Many people (up to a third of South Africa's population) rely solely on wood-burning stoves or fireplaces for their heating and hot water, particularly in rural areas. Stoves come in a huge variety of sizes and styles and may also heat radiators throughout a house and provide hot water. Most people burn wood (which should have been seasoned for at least two years, but often isn't), which is relatively inexpensive, rather than coal or coke. You can have it delivered cut and dried or can collect it free if you live in the country, as many people do.

The main disadvantages are the chores of collecting and chopping wood, cleaning the grate and lighting fires. Smoke can also be a problem. Open fireplaces can be wasteful of heat and fuel; an enclosed hearth with a glass door is more efficient and often has the advantages of a hot-air chamber that warms other parts of a home, a reduced fire risk, and less ash and dust.

Air-Conditioning

Few older homes in South Africa have built-in air-conditioning, which is more common in newer homes, particularly in Kwazulu-Natal. Although properties are built to withstand the heat, you may find it beneficial to install some air-conditioning, although there can be negative effects if you suffer from asthma or respiratory problems. You can choose from a huge variety of air-conditioners: fixed or moveable, indoor or outdoor installation, and high or low power. Air-conditioning units cost from around R4,000 (£350), plus installation, for a unit that's sufficient to cool an average-size room. An air-conditioning system with a heat pump provides cooling in summer and heating in winter. For extra cooling in the summer, many people fit ceiling fans (costing from around R400/£35), which are standard fixtures in some new homes.

Humidifiers & De-Humidifiers

Central heating dries the air and may cause your family to develop coughs. Those who find dry air unpleasant (and much of South Africa is dry for most of the year, particularly away from the coasts) can purchase a humidifier to add moisture to the air. Humidifiers that don't generate steam should be disinfected occasionally with a special liquid available from chemists (to prevent nasty diseases). Humidifiers range from simple water containers hanging from radiators to expensive electric or battery-operated devices.

If you're going to be using a holiday home only occasionally, it's worthwhile installing de-humidifiers, especially in the bedrooms, to prevent clothes and linen going mouldy.

HOME SECURITY

Security is of paramount importance when buying a home in South Africa, particularly if it will be left empty for long periods. Obtain advice from local security companies and neighbours. Bear in mind, however, that no matter how good its security, a property is rarely impregnable, so you should never leave valuables in an unattended home unless they're kept in a safe.

When moving into a new home, it's often wise to replace the locks (or lock barrels) as soon as possible, as you have no idea how many keys are in circulation for the existing locks. This is true even for new homes, as builders often give keys to sub-contractors. In any case, it's wise to change the external locks or lock barrels regularly, e.g. annually, particularly if you let a home. If not already fitted, it's best to fit high security (double cylinder or dead bolt) locks. Modern properties may be fitted with high security locks that are individually numbered. Extra keys for these locks cannot be cut at a local hardware store and you will need to obtain details from the previous owner or your landlord.

In areas with a high risk of theft (e.g. most major cities and coastal resorts) and if you have an isolated country home, your insurance company will insist on extra security measures such as two locks on external doors, internal locking shutters, security bars on windows less than 3m (10ft) from the ground and grilles on patio doors. An external door must usually be armoured, with a steel rod locking mechanism. An insurance policy may specify that all forms of protection must be employed when a property is unoccupied. If security precautions aren't taken, a claim may be reduced by half or rejected altogether. It's usually necessary to have a safe for any insured valuables, which must be approved by your insurance company.

You may wish to have a security alarm fitted (your insurers may insist), which is usually the best way to deter thieves and may also reduce your household insurance (see page 231). It should cover all external doors and windows and be connected to internal infra-red security beams; it may also be linked to a coded entry keypad (which can be frequently changed and is useful for clients if you let a home) and 24-hour monitoring (with some systems it's even possible to monitor properties remotely from another country). With a monitored system, when a sensor (e.g. smoke or forced entry) detects an emergency or a panic button is pushed, a signal is sent automatically to a 24-hour monitoring station. The duty monitor will telephone to check whether it's a genuine alarm and, if he cannot contact you, will send someone to investigate.

You can deter thieves by ensuring that your house is well lit and not conspicuously unoccupied. External security 'motion detector' lights (that switch on automatically when someone approaches), random timed switches for internal lights, radios and televisions, dummy security cameras, and tapes that play barking dogs (etc.) triggered by a light or heat detector may all help deter burglars.

You can fit UPVC (toughened clear plastic) security windows and doors, which can survive an attack with a sledge-hammer without damage, and external steel security blinds (which can be electrically operated), although these are expensive. A dog can be useful to deter intruders, although it should be kept inside where it cannot be given poisoned food. (Irrespective of whether you actually have a dog, a warning sign with a picture of a fierce dog may act as a deterrent.) If not already present, you should have the front door of an apartment fitted with a spy-hole and a chain so that you can check the identity of a visitor before opening the door. **Remember, prevention is better than cure, as stolen property is rarely recovered.**

Holiday homes are particularly vulnerable to thieves and in some areas they are regularly ransacked. No matter how secure your door and window locks, a thief can usually obtain entry if he's sufficiently determined, often by smashing a window or even by breaking in through the roof or knocking a hole in a wall! In isolated areas thieves can strip a house bare at their leisure and an unmonitored alarm won't be a deterrent if there's nobody around to hear it. If you have a holiday home in South Africa, it isn't wise to leave anything of great value (monetary or sentimental) there.

If you vacate your home for a long period, it may be obligatory to notify your caretaker, landlord or insurance company, and to leave a key with the caretaker or landlord in case of emergencies. If you have a robbery, you should report it immediately to your local police station, where you must make a statement. You will receive a copy, which is required by your insurance company if you make a claim.

When closing up a property for a long period, e.g. over the winter, you should ensure that everything is switched off and that it's secure (see **Closing A Property For The Winter** on page 248).

Another important aspect of home security is ensuring that you have early warning of a fire, which is easily accomplished by installing smoke detectors. Battery-operated smoke detectors can be purchased for around R200 (£17) (they should be tested regularly to ensure that the batteries aren't exhausted, although some emit a beep when the batteries are low). If you have gas appliances, you can fit an electric-powered gas detector that activates an alarm when a gas leak is detected.

There are many specialists who will inspect your home and offer free advice on security, in the hope of selling you security equipment (see below), although you should always shop around and obtain at least two quotations before having any work done.

Security Services

Many homes and businesses in South Africa use the services of private security companies. Private security has become a huge business in the country and there are currently around 4,500 security companies, although the sector is dominated by a few giant operations, some foreign-owned. It's estimated that there are over 500,000 security guards in South Africa, half of them employed in-house by firms and private individuals, the other half by security companies.

Chubb (💻 www.chubb.co.za), Securicor (💻 www.securicor.com/za.htm) and ADT Security (💻 www.adt.co.za) are three of the big players. ADT Fire & Security is the world's largest provider of electronic security services, with over 7.5 million customers, and ADT Security in South Africa protects over 200,000 residential and commercial properties.

Security companies may provide the following services for homes:

- Alarm installation, maintenance and upgrades;
- 24-hour armed response and alarm monitoring;
- A private ambulance service, such as that provided by Netcare 911;
- Closed circuit television (CCTV) and other monitoring systems;
- Domestic and community guarding;
- Fire detection services;
- Localised security services (see below).

Localised Security Services

A localised security service consists of security staff manning access points (e.g. to an estate), patrolling on foot or by bicycle (in vehicles in larger developments). Access points are usually fitted with booms and everyone entering and leaving is monitored. Patrol staff periodically check quieter areas where intruders can hide, and keep suspicious-looking people away from the area. They're in 24-hour, two-way radio or mobile telephone contact with response vehicles.

Prices for security services vary widely between different companies and for different types and levels of service but start at around R400 (£35) per month for a general service covering a residential area. Some companies offering security services have only entered the business to make money and have little or no experience in the field. A company that offers a low price may be undermanned, and staff may not turn up when required - even if they do, they may have little idea how to deal with a situation. Ask for advice from neighbours, colleagues and friends about which security companies are reliable and offer value. (Security is one of the most popular dinner table topics of conversation in South Africa and you will have no trouble finding people who are more than willing to talk about the subject.)

For further information about the industry, consult the website of the Private Security Industry Regulatory Authority, which calls itself SIRA (💻 http://sira-sa.co.za).

POSTAL SERVICES

The South African Post Office (SAPO) isn't one of the country's strengths and doesn't enjoy a good reputation. This is because of its often snail-like, unreliable service and the amount of money and valuables that 'disappear' while in the system (despite the SAPO's proud claim, 'we deliver, whatever it takes', which appears on the front of the booklet listing rates and services, available from post offices). For important or valuable items, many South Africans use a courier company such as Federal Express, which is much more expensive than the post office but also much more reliable. In any case, you should never send cash by post but should send postal orders instead.

The majority of South African towns have a post office (there are around 2,760 postal outlets and 30 mail processing centres in the country), with opening hours usually 8.30am to 4.30pm Mondays to Fridays, and 8 to 11.30am on Saturdays, although hours are shorter at some offices. Australian, British and US visitors will feel at home in a South African post office, because they have a similar feel to post offices in those countries.

Unfortunately, this contentment rarely extends to the service: it takes around a week for a letter to be delivered from one South African city to another; if you're sending something to a rural town, it can take even longer. And if you send a letter or package from South Africa to Europe, for example, it can six weeks to arrive! The SAPO intends to restructure, become more efficient and make a profit, in anticipation of a proposed privatisation – it can only get better!

The South African post office has a range of services. As well as post, it offers 'faxmail' (post offices can supply details and rates), franking machines, a business reply service and bulk mail arrangements, money transfer services, a bill paying service, laminating and photocopying, and the sale of philatelic products.

The standard postal service is known as ordinary mail and rates for sending a small, medium or large letter or postcard (sizes are specified in the post office services booklet) within South Africa are currently R1.70 (15p), R3.45 (30p) and R4.35 (38p) respectively, while small and large cylinders/rolled items cost R4.35 (38p) and R7.55 (66p) respectively.

You can send items by the more expensive Fastmail service, which supposedly offers a two-day letter delivery service within South Africa between major towns and cities, and a three-day delivery to other destinations. The rates for sending a small, medium or large letter or postcard by Fastmail are R2.80 (24p), R6.65 (58p) and R8 (69p) respectively, while small and large cylinders/rolled items cost R6.80 (59p) and R8.30 (72p) respectively.

Other postal services offered by the SAPO include Speed Services Couriers, a domestic overnight courier service, and Parcelplus, an economical parcel post.

South African post offices sell postage-included envelopes, in various sizes and for ordinary and Fastmail delivery. Prices range from R1.90 (16p) to R8.90 (77p). The post office also offers modest discounts (around 2 to 5 per cent) for bulk purchases of stamps and postage-included envelopes.

The SAPO has a registered letter service, with an insurance option. The fee varies according to the size of the letter and the level of insurance required, up to a maximum of R2,000 (£175) of cover (on which the insurance costs R69/£6). The insurance option applies only to domestic mail and it cannot be used in conjunction with Fastmail, Speed Services Couriers or Parcelplus.

International postal rates include the following: a postcard sent by surface mail costs R2.10 (18p) or R3.45 (30p) by airmail; a small letter costs R3.35 (29p) by surface mail or R4 (35p) by airmail. Rates for sending parcels are split over six zones (A to F) and between surface mail and airmail. The post office rate booklet contains a full list of all the costs and conditions.

An alternative to the SAPO is offered by Postnet, an independent postal service found in some shopping malls. Rates are similar to the SAPO's but there are seldom the long queues found in some post offices.

Information about all SAPO postal services is available from its website (🖳 www.sapo.co.za). For information about fax see page 273.

SHOPPING

Shopping is one of the most popular pastimes in South Africa's cities, with both locals and tourists. The country has warmly welcomed the shopping mall and many shops are now located in one of these retail therapy temples, which are sometimes outside town centres and offer shops selling everything you could ever want (and a lot that you probably wouldn't even dream of buying), as well as cafés, bars, cinemas, banks, fast-food outlets and restaurants - a complete day out, in fact. Parking facilities and security services are usually top-notch at South Africa's shopping malls, which is an additional attraction in such a security-conscious country. The biggest and best malls are in and around Cape Town, Durban, Johannesburg and Pretoria. Cape Town's V & A Waterfront shopping area is probably the country's premier shopping destination.

One of South Africa's chainstores is the famous Woolworths, which sells a wide selection of items and has some of the country's best food halls. Others include OK Bazaars (general items and food), Checkers and Pick 'n Pay (supermarkets and hypermarkets, the former part of South Africa's largest food retailing group, Shoprite), Clicks (primarily household items) and Edgars, Foschini and Truworths (clothes). Most South African chains are the equal of their counterparts in Australia, Europe and North America, although some of the food halls and supermarkets have rather dated décor and limited product ranges (but this is changing). South Africa also has large cash and carry stores, including Makro and Game, which are often used by smaller shops as their source of inexpensive goods, as well as by individual customers (an access card is required for Makro, but anyone can obtain one free).

Markets are common throughout South Africa and include general markets selling the kind of inexpensive clothes, jewellery, ornaments and general goods found the world over, as well as farmers' markets, flea markets, arts and crafts markets, wooden carvings markets and others. The most famous is probably the Grand Parade in Cape Town, selling everything from fruit to books and 'antiques' (it also acts as Cape Town's equivalent of London's Speaker's Corner, allowing zealots to express their ideas about the subject of their choosing, usually religion). Another notable South African market is the Indian market in Durban (sometimes called the Victoria Street Market), with a huge range of spices as well as Indian and African art and curios.

People wanting to buy books, magazines, etc. in South Africa are well served, particularly by the CNA (Central News Agency) Chain and Exclusive Books. Indigenous crafts and carvings are for sale throughout South Africa, although their quality varies enormously and quite many are made in other African countries. Haggling is expected by most sellers of craft items and is part of the enjoyment. Never buy anything made of ivory (it's illegal to trade in it in South Africa) and beware of buying coral and sea shells, which may be endangered species or have been collected illegally. South Africa is famous as a producer of gold and diamonds, and both are widely for sale throughout the country. Johannesburg, the centre of the mining industry, is the best place to buy them.

You should try to avoid offering a shopkeeper a large-denomination rand note when you're buying a low-cost item and should also avoid using a credit card to pay for items costing less than around R100 (£8.70); you may not be permitted to do so anyway. In Cape Town and other major cities and resorts, where there are lots of tourists, you must be wary of pickpockets and bag-snatchers. **Never** tempt fate with an exposed wallet or purse or by flashing your money around.

Opening Hours

Shopping hours vary in South Africa according to the region, city or town and the type of shop. However, in general, shops open Mondays to Fridays from around 8.30 or 9am to between 5 and 7pm, although in some cities shops may remain open until 9pm. Saturday hours are 8.30am to 1pm. Shops in malls and large supermarkets are usually open on Saturday afternoons too, and between around 10am and 2pm on Sundays.

Furniture & Furnishings

A wide range of modern, traditional and tribal furniture is available in South Africa. Modern furniture is popular and is sold in furniture shops, some hypermarkets and cash and carry outlets (Makro and Game are good sources of inexpensive furniture and household items) throughout the country. Department stores also sell some furniture. Exclusive modern and traditional furniture is also available in the major cities, although not everyone can afford the exclusive prices.

There are a limited number of nationwide chains of furniture shops. OK Furniture (🖳 www.okfurniture.co.uk), which is part of the Shoprite Group, has 140 outlets in South Africa, Botswana, Lesotho, Namibia and Swaziland, selling local and imported furniture at competitive prices. You can completely refurbish a property in one go because the chain sells accessories, home entertainment systems, bedding, bedroom suites, dining furniture, furnishings, home appliances, home offices, kitchenware, linen, loose carpeting, lounge furniture and outdoor and patio furniture. Also part of the Shoprite Group, House & Home (🖳 www.shoprite.co.za, click on House & Home) has 21 outlets across South Africa and is more upmarket than OK Furniture. It positions itself between general furniture shops and small, specialist design companies. Wetherlys (🖳 www.wetherlys.co.za) has 12 branches in various parts of the country.

A number of South Africa's furniture stores are local or regional rather than national but will often deliver nationally. Glick's (🖳 www.glicks.co.za), for example, has 14 branches in Gauteng and Kwazulu-Natal and calls itself 'one of the finest premier furniture retailers' in South Africa. Pine Connection (🖳 www.pineconnection.co.za) has two branches in the Cape Town area and promises furniture that is 'functional and elegant with smooth organic lines'. Woodcraft Furniture (🖳 www.woodcraftfurniture.co.za) serves the Eastern Cape, while Griffiths & Griffiths (🖳 www.griffithsandgriffiths.co.za) serves the Johannesburg area with 'solid mahogany English replica furniture'.

Most stores make deliveries or loan or rent (at reasonable rates) self-drive vans.

South African furniture and furnishing shops often offer design services (which may be free to customers) and stock a wide range of beautiful fabrics and materials in patterns and colours ideally suited to South African homes and the climate and conditions, although designs tend to be ethnic and animal-themed, which may not be to your taste.

If you're spending a lot of money, don't be reluctant to ask for a reduction, as most stores will give you a discount. Most furniture shops offer special deals on furniture packages for a complete room or home. The best time to buy furniture and furnishings is during the summer and winter sales (particularly the latter), when the prices of many items are slashed. It's possible for residents to pay for furniture (and large household appliances) interest-free over a year or with interest over a longer period, e.g. five years.

If you're looking for old furniture at affordable prices, you may find a few bargains at antique fairs and flea markets, although genuine antiques are expensive and difficult to find. Many second-hand furniture sellers and dealers advertise in the local and regional press. If you do come across anything worthwhile, you must usually drive a hard bargain, as the asking prices are generally high, particularly in popular tourist areas during the summer. Markets are, however, good places to buy fabric (e.g. for curtains), bed linen and wallpaper, and charity shops are an Aladdin's cave of household goods and furniture (and they hold periodic sales).

The kind of furniture you buy depends on a number of factors, including how long you're planning to stay, whether you plan to take it with you when you leave, the style and size of your home, your budget, the local climate, whether you intend to let the property and, not least, your taste. If you intend to furnish a second home with antiques or expensive modern furniture, bear in mind that you need adequate security and insurance.

Newsagents' shelves groan with a plethora of the type of home decoration, interiors and house makeover magazines familiar to many Australians, Europeans and Americans. As well as providing ideas and inspiration for what to do with your South African home, they contain page after page of advertisements, which are a useful resource for people in search of everything from slate flooring to light fittings, cappuccino machines and bamboo screens. Magazines include the monthly *Conde Nast House & Garden South Africa*, which costs R25.95 (£2.25) and *South African Home Owner*, which is bi-monthly and costs R28.95 (£2.50).

Household Goods

Household goods sold in South Africa are generally of good quality and there's a large choice. Prices compare favourably with European countries, and bargains can be found at supermarkets and hypermarkets, such as Dion's, Electrical City, Hi-fi Warehouse, Hyperama and Stax, and cash and carry stores such as Game and Makro (see page 264). The magazines listed under **Furniture & Furnishings** above include advertisements for a range of household goods.

SURVIVAL TIP
When you buy anything electrical, buy a plug too, as they aren't usually supplied with the item.

DIY Shops

DIY isn't as popular in South Africa as in some other countries (particularly the UK) because the low cost of labour means that many people opt for PSE: pay-somebody-else! Nevertheless, there are do-it-yourself (DIY) retailers in some areas, selling everything for the home, including furniture (beware of buying complicated home-assembled furniture with indecipherable instructions and too few screws), bathroom and kitchen units, decorating materials and lighting, plus services such as tool rental and wood-cutting. Many are located in shopping centres on the outskirts of large cities. Dion's, Hyperama and Mica shops sell a wide range of items as well as general DIY materials.

There are salvage and second-hand companies selling old doors, window frames, fireplaces, tiles and other materials that are invaluable when restoring an older home or to add a special touch to a modern home.

Newspapers & Magazines

South Africa has 17 daily newspapers, seven Sunday papers and 24 weeklies, mostly based on the British model, and total newspaper readership is around 13.4 million. There are also over 90 free newspapers, usually distributed in a local area and often called 'freebies' or 'knock-and-drops', with 3.5 million distributed per week.

South Africa's size and diversity have helped to preclude the development of national dailies. The only truly national newspapers are four of the Sunday newspapers: *Sunday Times* (💻 www.suntimes.co.za), *Rapport* (💻 www.news24.com/Rapport/Home), *Sunday Independent* and *Sunday Sun*, and the weekly newspaper *City Press* (💻 www.news24.com/City_Press/Home).

South Africa's newsagents are supplied with numerous magazines, both local and international, including (in descending order of claimed circulation figures) *Huisgenoot, You, Sarie, Rooi Rose, True Love, Reader's Digest, TV Plus, People, The Motorist* and *Cosmopolitan*. Around 300 consumer magazines and over 500 trade, technical and professional magazines are registered in South Africa.

VAT Refunds

Non-resident foreign passport holders over the age of seven who are on temporary visits to South Africa and departing by air or sea (there are different rules for exports via land border posts) can claim a VAT refund on some items purchased in South Africa provided that the supplier is VAT registered. South African citizens and residents aren't entitled to claim a refund, and diplomats posted to South Africa should contact their embassy for details of the applicable refund scheme.

You can only claim on individual purchases valued at R250 (£22) or more, and only on goods which can be removed from South Africa, e.g. clothing, books, artwork and jewellery, nor goods consumed or services rendered within South Africa, e.g. restaurant meals or tour-group or taxi bills. The items bought must be exported within 90 days of the date of issue of the tax invoice. An administration fee of 1.5 per cent of the value of the claim is charged, subject to a minimum fee of R10 (87p) and a maximum of R250 (£22). Special rules apply to second-hand goods, for which you will receive a postal refund when the amount refundable has been determined.

In order to claim a refund, when buying something costing over R250 (£22), identify yourself as a non-resident and ask for a tax invoice, usually simply an amended version of a standard till receipt. The shop assistant will often ask if you want one. A tax invoice must contain the following:

- The words 'Tax Invoice';
- The seller's name and address;
- The seller's VAT registration number;
- The date of issue;
- A tax invoice number;
- A full description of the goods purchased;
- The cost of the goods in rand;
- The amount of VAT charged, or a statement that VAT at the rate of 14 per cent is included in the cost of the goods;
- In the case of purchases over R1,000 (£87), the purchaser's name and address and the quantity or volume of the goods must appear on the tax invoice.

If you leave from Cape Town, Durban or Johannesburg International Airports, you must present your tax invoice(s) and show the goods purchased to a VAT refund official for inspection. You should therefore keep the goods readily accessible. (If they're in a suitcase, you must obviously claim your refund before checking in!)

If you leave from one of the following airports or harbours, you must present your purchases and tax invoices to a South African customs official there: Bloemfontein, Gateway, Lanseria, Nelspruit, Pilanesberg, Port Elizabeth or Upington airport; Cape Town, Durban, East London, Mossel Bay, Port Elizabeth, Richards Bay or Saldanha port.

Refunds are paid by rand cheque, which most people cash in their home currency at an airport or port bank. However, to avoid queuing at Cape Town or Johannesburg International Airport, for example, you can go to one of the VAT refund offices in resort areas to have your invoices checked and the paperwork completed, so that at the airport or harbour you only have to have the goods themselves checked before obtaining a refund. Ask at local tourist information to see if there's a VAT office in the area where you're staying. To have your invoices checked you must present the following:

- Your passport;
- The tax invoice(s);
- Your flight ticket or confirmation of flight details.

Claims can only be processed within seven days of your departure.

TELEPHONE SERVICES

Telecommunications is the fastest-growing industry in South Africa. The country ranks 23rd in the world in terms of telecommunications development and 17th in internet use. South Africa's efficient telephone system is run by the public utility Telkom (💻 www.telkom.co.za), whose monopoly officially ended in May 2002, although the competition isn't yet up and running! Telkom is Africa's largest provider of telephone services (as well as offering a range of other telecommunications services and products) and employs around 45,000 people. The government intends to privatise the company (the plans are being held up by the global economic slowdown as well as by objections from some unions and political groups) and, in a tentative initial step, has sold 30 per cent of Telkom to Malaysian Telecom and the US company Southwestern Bell; another 20 per cent will soon be available to the public. Telkom's monopoly is expected to be ended by the formation a second telecommunications company, 51 per cent owned by independent investors, after which prices should come down.

Installation & Registration

To apply for a telephone, you can visit a Telkom Customer Service Branch and fill in the appropriate form, telephone the company (☎ 10219 for residential, ☎ 10217 for businesses) or apply online (💻 www.telkom.co.za/business/porder.jsp) and ask a Telkom representative to contact you.

The fee for installing a new line in a property is R274.35 (£24), or R225.70 (£20) for customers over 69. The transfer of a telephone number to another location within the same code area is free of charge, as is changing the name of the user of an existing telephone line (i.e. taking over an existing line); the new renter must contact Telkom's Service Activation department (☎ 10219), and both the previous and new renter must agree to a 'Transfer of Service'. You may also have to pay a security deposit.

If you're considering bringing a telephone from abroad, contact the Independent Communications Authority of South Africa (ICASA, ☎ 011-321 8200) to discover whether it will work. Any equipment used in South Africa must be licensed by the ICASA before it will be connected.

Using The Telephone

Dialling a local number in South Africa used to involve dialling seven digits, but the ICASA has proposed the introduction of ten-digit dialling, which should have been implemented by September 2004 but may not have been in all areas. For the time being, Telkom caters for both seven and ten-digit dialling, the latter being required for all non-local calls. Ten-digit dialling involves adding the three-digit area code to the subscriber's number. There are some 68 codes in South Africa; those for the major cities are as follows:

Bloemfontein	051
Cape Town	021
Durban	031
East London	043
Johannesburg	011
Pretoria	012
Port Elizabeth	041

Many businesses and organisations have numbers beginning with an 08 code, e.g. 0800, 0860, 0861 (but not 082, 083 or 084, which belong to the mobile networks – see page 274). These can be dialled from anywhere in South Africa (but not from outside the country); charges are as follows:

- 080 numbers (usually 0800) – free;
- 0860 numbers – local call rate;
- 0861 numbers – various flat rates.

Telkom provides an international telephone service to 234. Making international calls to these countries is straightforward: simply dial the international access code, 09, followed by the country code of the country you're calling (e.g. 44 for the UK, 1 for the US), dial the area code in the country you're calling, omitting the initial 0 if applicable, and finally dial the individual number that you want. Calls to other countries must be made via the operator.

Charges

Line rental is charged in advance (usually at R81.90/£7 per month) but calls are charged in arrears (bills list 'calls up to and including' a certain date). The Telkom website contains an extensive (and sometimes bewildering) list of charges for its many services and types of call, the basic call charges currently being as follows:

- Local calls (those that are within 50km/31mi) during 'standard time' (Mondays to Fridays, 7am to 7pm) cost 0.631 cents (0.054p) per second, subject to a minimum charge of 56.3 cents (4.89p).
- Local calls at all other times ('callmore time' in Telkom-speak) are charged at just 0.253 cents (0.022p) per second, but the same minimum charge applies.
- Long-distance calls (those over 50km/31mi) during 'standard time' are charged at a rate of 1.65 cents (0.14p) per second, subject to a minimum charge of 99 cents (8.60p).
- Long-distance calls during 'callmore time' cost 0.825 cents (0.071p) per second, subject to the same minimum charge.
- International calls have two charge periods: 'standard time' (8am to 8pm, Mondays to Fridays) and 'global off-peak time' (all other times). A list of charges to all countries is available on the Telkom website but, as an example, the rates for a call to the UK were 5.2 cents (0.45 pence) per second in standard time and 4.68 cents (0.41 pence) per second off-peak.

Telkom also offers a range of packages designed to 'save the customer money' (i.e. encourage him to use the telephone more often!), including Telkom BestFriends, where you select up to five national fixed line telephone numbers and get a 10 per cent discount when you call them. There's an 'activation' charge of R10 (86p) and a monthly fee of R9.85 (85p) for this service.

Payment

Telkom is keen to take its customers' money and offers them a wide choice of payment methods:

- By post;
- By direct debit (debit order);
- Via a cash dispenser (ATM);
- At a Telkom Customer Service Branch (including via a SMARTEC terminal within a branch);
- At a post office;
- At Compu-pay kiosks (bill-paying terminals found in some shops and supermarkets);
- At EASYPAY terminals in Checkers or Pick 'n Pay supermarkets;
- Via your bank's website.

Emergency Numbers

There are two emergency numbers in South Africa:

- 1011 for the police or fire service;
- 10177 for an ambulance.

Fax

Fax services are widely available in South Africa, where messages can be sent and received from some Telkom and Postnet offices (see page 264) and privately run telephone centres. Faxes sent nationally and internationally from a post office cost around R7 (60p) per page, although rates vary according to when the fax is sent and to where.

There are no special rules for fax machines except that they should conform to the international G3 standard. The cost of a fax machine varies according to the make, the kind of paper used (e.g. rolls or sheets of paper) and the features (such as an answerphone). For example, some fax machines can be used as a scanner and colour printer when connected to a computer. An average price for a middle-of-the-range machine is around R1,500 (£130). If you bring your own fax machine to South Africa, it should work provided it operates on a 220V power supply, although some machines will need modifying.

Public Telephones

Public telephones can be found in many places in South Africa, including bus depots, railway stations, airports, bars, cafés and restaurants, main road rest areas, various business premises, main post offices, and in streets in cities and towns. All public telephones allow International Direct Dialling (IDD) and international calls can also be made via the operator. Some public telephones are coin operated but these are now being phased out and replaced by green 'cardphones' accepting only accept Telkom phonecards, which are fixed value microchip cards available in denominations of R20, R50, R100 and R200. These can be used to make local, national and international calls, and calls to mobile phones. They're available at over 15,000 retail outlets in South Africa, including Telkom Customer Service Branches, post offices, Shoprite Checkers, some Pick 'n Pay shops, most service stations, vending machines in some shopping centres, major airports and some corner shops, travel agents, chemists', supermarkets and even schools.

Mobile Telephones

South Africa is the fourth-fastest growing mobile communications market in the world, with three major operators: CellC (💻 www.cellc.co.za), MTN (💻 www.mtn.co.za) and Vodacom (💻 www.vodacom.co.za). Vodacom is the largest of the three, with around 61 per cent of the market, and Telkom is its major shareholder, with a 50 per cent interest. By the end of 2003, there were over 15 million cellular users in the country, a number expected to grow to 21 million (half the population) by 2006. The mobile telephone (cellular) network covers most of South Africa's densely populated areas and its main roads. It operates on the GSM digital system.

As in other countries, the cost of phones and calls varies enormously. To give just a few examples, in September 2004 MTN offered some phones free of charge, others at competitive prices, e.g. a Motorola C115 for R700 (£60) and a Sony Ericsson T105 for R850 (£75). In order to take out a contract with MTN, you must provide an identity document, proof of income, a bank statement, postal address and credit references.

A bewildering variety of payment plans are available from the mobile telephone operators. For example, in autumn 2004, MTN was offering a MyCall 100 plan, which includes 100 free minutes of calls per month, 85 of them at off-peak and 15 at peak times. There's a one-off connection charge of R99 (£8.60) and a monthly subscription of R129 (£11.20). Calls are charged at between R1.85 (16p) and R2.70 (23p) per minute, depending on the time and type of call.

All mobile phone numbers begin 082 (Vodacom), 083 (MTN) or 084 (Cell C), followed by seven digits.

Internet

Internet use is popular in South Africa and the country ranks 17th in the world in terms of internet usage. Internet cafés are common in South Africa's cities and towns, and most large and medium-size companies quote an email address and many a website in their advertising. Private customers have also 'hooked up' in droves. (Internet use grew by an estimated 29 per cent between 2000 and 2004, when there were approximately 3.5 million registered users.)

As in other areas of the telecommunications market, Telkom is a prominent player, and its website has extensive details of its wide and ever-changing range of internet services and products. It offers the sort of internet 'packages' that will be familiar to users from Australia, Europe and North America. The six Telkom SurfMore Packages have monthly prices varying from R154 (£13.40) to R470 (£41). Packages often include a modem, email address(es) and various amounts of internet access, at both off-peak and peak times.

Telkom is the only supplier of Asymmetric Digital Subscriber Lines (ADSL), which provide fast Internet access: you pay a monthly fee and aren't charged for the time spent online. Installation costs R404 (£35) and monthly charges are between R450 (£40) and R680 (£60) for most home users. Some business services cost more.

One drawback to the offer of free services at off-peak times is that the networks can be busy during the evenings and weekends; sometimes you cannot connect at all. Furthermore, the telephone support available is of variable quality and availability and may be charged at extortionate rates. You may therefore be better off choosing a subscription service.

There are dozens of internet service providers (ISPs) in South Africa, where some areas are well covered by local ISPs and others not at all, although these are mostly remote rural areas with few inhabitants. The major ISPs include ABSA (💻 www.absa.co.za), AT&T SA (💻 www.attbusiness.net), M-Web (💻 www.mweb.co.za) and World Online (💻 www.worldonline.co.za). Most computer shops have agreements with local ISPs and act as agents for them. They will sell you a software kit and provide you with access numbers, and the service is usually activated within a few hours. The cost is reasonable at around R700 (£60) per year, which usually includes one email address and unlimited access to the internet.

If you just want an email address (or want a 'portable' one), you can sign up with one of the free web-based email services such as Yahoo Mail (www.yahoo.com) or Microsoft Network's Hotmail (www.hotmail.com); with these, you can send and receive emails using any computer with internet access, e.g. at a library or internet café. Note, however, that mail sent to and from such services isn't necessarily secure.

The website of the Internet Service Providers' Association (ISPA), which represents around 50 ISPs in South Africa, including those listed above, includes a list of ISPs and their addresses and telephone numbers (www.ispa.org.za).

TELEVISION & RADIO

There are several English-language television (TV) and radio channels in South Africa, and the quality of programmes is generally high. Before taking TV sets, video cassette recorders (VCRs) and DVD players to South Africa, you should consider both costs and compatibility (see **TV Standards** below and **Video & DVD** on page 279). For video, the latter should be PAL VHS, like the UK; for DVD, Region 2, again like the UK.

Television

South Africa's terrestrial TV network dates from only 1976. The official television broadcaster is the SABC (www.sabc.co.za), its network comprising four terrestrial channels, two satellite pay-TV channels aimed at audiences in Africa and the snappily-titled BOP-TV, which is a regional network located in Bophuthatswana (in the North West province). Around 50 per cent of all programmes transmitted are produced in South Africa. The terrestrial channels broadcast in 11 languages and reach a daily adult audience of nearly 17 million, which is by far the largest TV audience in Africa.

M-Net (www.mnet.co.za), South Africa's first private subscription TV service, was launched in 1986. It now has over 1.23 million subscribers, spread over 49 African countries. The main M-Net channel focuses on films and sport but also offers general entertainment. It has a two-hour 'open window' when unencrypted programmes (available to viewers without decoders) are screened, including the country's longest-running local soap opera, Egoli Place of Gold.

TV Standards

South African TV uses the PAL I system. TVs and video recorders from the UK (which also operates on PAL I) should work in South Africa, but those from many other countries won't, for example the French (SECAM) and North American (NTSC) systems won't function in South Africa, and neither will those from most other continental European countries, which use the PAL-BG standard (different types of PAL use different video and audio carrier specifications). Some foreign equipment can be modified, although check that this is definitely the case before undertaking the expense of shipping it to South Africa.

TV Licence

Anybody who has one or more TV sets in South Africa, whether in use or not, needs a TV licence. There are six categories of licence: domestic, business, dealer, lessor, mobile TV and concessionary. The first five types of licence each cost R225 (£19.50) per year; a concessionary licence, which is available to those on social security and people over 69, costs R65 (£5.65).

When first applying for a TV licence in South Africa, you must pay the full fee at once. Thereafter, for the first five categories of licence above, you can pay in monthly instalments of R23 (£2). You can pay your licence at a wide range of outlets, including banks (ABSA, FNB, Nedbank and Standard Bank), post offices and some supermarkets, or via your bank's website. The SABC sends out licence renewal notices around two months in advance, but not receiving the notice isn't deemed to be a valid reason for not paying. The penalty for non-payment of your TV licence is a fine of R500 (£43.50) or imprisonment for up to six months or both. for further details visit the South African TV Licence website (💻 www.tvlic.co.za/payments.htm).

Satellite TV

Satellite TV isn't as prevalent in South Africa as in much of North America and Europe, but choice is increasing all the time (cable is little used in South Africa). Current satellite television service providers include the following: Deukon Television (💻 www.deukon.co.za), which offers five German channels and some German radio stations; DStv MultiChoice (💻 www.dstv.co.za), offering 40 English channels and five foreign (Italian, Greek, Portuguese, Chinese and Hindi); Multichoice Africa (💻 www.multichoice.co.za), offering 30 English channels, two

French and one Chinese; and Vivid (Sentech Direct-To-Home, www.sentech.co.za), offering the three SABC channels, BOP TV, eTV and 15 radio channels (for which subscription is free).

You must rent or buy a decoder and pay a monthly or annual subscription to receive satellite programmes. The cost of decoders varies: some companies offer them 'free' (they cover the cost by higher installation and subscription charges); to hire one costs around R60 (£5.20) per month (plus a deposit of around R700/£60); to buy one can cost up to R3,000 (£260). In recent years some broadcasters have changed their decoders in an effort to thwart 'pirates', although so far they've had little success. Until the situation is resolved, you would be better off renting a decoder than buying an expensive one.

You can sign up for a satellite subscription by telephone, via the internet or at a TV store. Subscription costs vary greatly according to the provider and the channel package but are generally from around R175 (£15) to R425 (£37) per month.

BBC World Television: The BBC's commercial subsidiary, BBC World Television (formerly BBC Worldwide Television) broadcasts two 24-hour channels: BBC Prime (general entertainment) and BBC World (24-hour news and information). BBC World is free-to-view, while BBC Prime is encrypted. Both channels are available via satellite in South Africa through the local distributor MultiChoice, MultiChoice Building, 75 Republic Road, Randburg 2125, South Africa (☎ 11-289 2222, www.multichoice.co.za).

For more information and a programming guide, contact BBC World Television, PO Box 5054, London W12 0ZY, UK (☎ 020-8433 2221). The BBC publishes a monthly magazine, *BBC On Air*, giving comprehensive information about BBC World Television programmes. A programme guide is also listed on the internet (www.bbc.co.uk/worldservice/programmes) and both BBC World and BBC Prime have their own websites (www.bbcworld.com and www.bbcprime.com). When accessing them, you need to enter the name of the country (in this case, South Africa), so that schedules are displayed in local time.

Equipment: A satellite receiver should have a built-in Videocrypt decoder and be capable of receiving satellite stereo radio. A system with an 85cm dish costs from around R2,500 (£215) plus the cost of installation, which may be included in the price. Shop around, as prices vary considerably. With a 1.2 or 1.5m motorised dish, you can receive hundreds of stations in a multitude of languages from around the world. If you wish to receive satellite TV on two or more TVs, you can buy a satellite system with two or more receivers. To receive stations from two or more satellites simultaneously, you need a motorised dish or a dish with a double feed antenna (dual LNBs).

Location: To receive programmes from any satellite, there must be no obstacles between the satellite and your dish, i.e. no trees, buildings or mountains must obstruct the signal, so check before renting or buying a home. Before buying or erecting a satellite dish, check whether you need permission from your landlord or the local municipality. Some towns and buildings (such as apartment blocks) have regulations regarding the positioning of antennae, although generally owners may mount a dish almost anywhere. Dishes can usually be mounted in a variety of unobtrusive positions to avoid offending the eye (and neighbours) and can also be painted or patterned to blend in with the background. Individual dishes are being removed from some apartment buildings and substituted with a single communal antenna with a cable connection to apartments.

Video & DVD

Video cassettes are widely available to rent or buy from video shops in all main towns and cities, which are listed in yellow pages. To rent videos you usually need to join a club and pay a small annual fee. Rental costs from R15 (£1.30) per night (for an old 'classic') to R50 (£4.35) per night for the latest Hollywood blockbuster. Videos to buy cost from R70 (£6) to R300 (£26). In some places you may be offered pirate tapes of new films that haven't yet been released on video, which should be avoided, as the quality is usually terrible; they're also illegal!

You may be able to buy or swap English-language and TV videos with other foreigners through expatriate clubs, and you can buy English-language videos via the internet and through mail-order video catalogues. BBC Television produces three-hour videos of its best programmes (including entertainment, humour, sport, natural history, news and current affairs), available on subscription from Video World, Subscription Dept, 680 Romford Road, London E12, UK. Choices Direct, 19–24 Manasty Road, Orton Southgate, Peterborough, PE2 6UP, UK (☎ 01733-236800, 💻 www.choicesdirect.co.uk), which is licensed by the BBC to sell their videos, will search for anything you request if you don't find it in their catalogue; if you order from their website, you don't pay postage.

DVDs are becoming increasingly popular in South Africa. Although they're still considerably more expensive than videos, they often offer additional features such as extra scenes, multiple language soundtracks and subtitling. Be particularly careful, however, to buy DVDs for the correct 'zone', as films intended for an American audience (Zone 1) won't play back in a South African DVD player (Zone 2, like the UK) unless it has been modified, and Zone 1 versions often don't contain the alternate soundtracks and subtitling. There are multi-zone DVD players available and it's also possible to modify many single-zone players to read multiple-zone DVDs.

Radio

Radio is very popular in South Africa and has a long history. The first radio broadcast in the country took place in 1923 and the first radio station, JB Calling, went on air in 1924. South Africa's numerous radio stations now have a huge audience and are an important source of news, information and entertainment, especially in the country's vast hinterland. It's estimated that almost 90 per cent of the rural population listens to the radio at least once a week.

The SABC (💻 www.sabc.co.za) is now South Africa's public broadcaster, its network comprising 18 stations and reaching an average daily audience of 20 million. It operates a public broadcast service radio station in each of the country's 11 official languages (frequencies are listed in local newspapers), broadcasting a range of programmes, including news, discussion, music and light entertainment. The SABC also runs an external service, which is similar in approach to the BBC World Service and The Voice of America; originally called Radio South Africa but now known as Channel Africa, it reaches millions of listeners throughout Africa and broadcasts in four languages: English, French, Kiswahili and Portuguese.

A number of private radio stations have been granted licences by the Independent Communications Authority of South Africa (ICASA, 💻 www.icasa.org.za). The following can be received anywhere in South Africa:

- East Coast Radio (💻 www.ecr.co.za);
- Highveld Stereo;
- Radio Algoa (💻 www.radioalgoa.co.za);
- Radio Jacaranda (💻 www.jacarandafm.co.za);
- Radio KFM (💻 www.kfm.co.za);
- Radio Oranje (💻 www.ofm.co.za).

The following stations can be received only in certain areas (as stated):

- Cape Talk MW (💻 www.capetalk.co.za) in the Western Cape;

- Classic FM (🖳 www.classicfm.co.za) in Gauteng;
- Kaya FM (🖳 www.kayafm.co.za) in Gauteng;
- P4, a jazz station, in Cape Town and Durban;
- Radio 702 (🖳 www.702.co.za) in Gauteng;
- Y-FM (🖳 www.yfm.co.za) in Johannesburg.

There are also almost 100 community radio stations.

English-Language Stations

The BBC World Service is broadcast on short wave on several frequencies (e.g. short wave 12095, 9760, 9410, 7325, 6195, 5975 and 3955 KhZ) simultaneously and you can usually receive a good signal on one of them. The signal strength varies according to where you live in South Africa, the time of day and year, the power and positioning of your receiver, and atmospheric conditions. For a free BBC World Service programme guide and frequency information write to BBC World Service, BBC Worldwide, PO Box 76, Bush House, Strand, London WC2B 4PH, UK (☎ 020-8752 5040). The BBC publishes a monthly magazine, *BBC On Air*, containing comprehensive programme listings for BBC World Service radio, BBC Prime TV and BBC World TV. It's available on subscription from the BBC, On Air Magazine, Room 207 NW, Bush House, Strand, London WC2B 4PH, UK (☎ 020-7240 4899, ✉ on.air.magazine@bbc.co.uk) and from some newsagents in South Africa.

Satellite Radio

If you have satellite TV, you can receive many radio stations via your satellite link, for example, BBC Radio 1, 2, 3, 4 and 5, BBC World Service, Sky Radio, Virgin 1215 and many foreign-language stations. Satellite radio stations are listed in British satellite TV magazines such as *Satellite Times*. If you're interested in receiving radio stations from further afield, you should obtain a copy of the *World Radio TV Handbook* (Watson-Guptil Publications).

UTILITIES

Immediately after buying or renting a property (unless utilities are included in the rent), you should arrange for your meters (if applicable) to be read, contracts (e.g. electricity, water and gas) to be registered in your name and services switched on. Always check in advance that all bills have been paid by the previous owner, or you will be liable for any debts outstanding (see **Conveyancing** on page 193). Registration usually entails a visit to the company's office, although some companies offer the possibility of registering online or by telephone.

If you go to the utility company's office, you must take with you some identification (passport or residence permit) and the contract and bills paid by the previous owner. If you've purchased a home in South Africa, the estate agent may arrange for the utilities to be transferred to your name or go with you to the offices (no charge should be made for this service). Make sure all previous bills have been paid and that the contract is transferred to your name from the day you take over. If you're a non-resident owner, you should also give your foreign address in case there are any problems requiring your attention, such as a bank failing to pay the bills. You may need to pay a deposit.

See also **Heating & Air-Conditioning** on page 256.

Electricity

Eskom supplies over 95 per cent of South Africa's electricity and over 50 per cent of the African continent's electricity. The company has been in existence for over 80 years and has a number of joint ventures in Africa, the Middle East and South America. Eskom has 24 power stations in South Africa and relies on the coal-fired power stations to produce around 90 per cent of its electricity, using over 90 million tons of coal per year. A long-awaited second operator, SNO, was due to receive its licence in September 2004 and provide competition for Eskom.

After buying or renting a property (unless utilities are included in the rent) - and until SNO becomes operational - you must apply to become an Eskom customer. This is done by telephoning your nearest Eskom Contact Centre (there are seven, manned 24 hours per day), by visiting your nearest Eskon Customer Service Office, or via the Eskom website (💻 www.eskom.co.za).

Eskom will then provide you with a quotation. Depending on the type and location of the supply you require, they may need to carry out an investigation of the cost of the labour and materials involved before providing a quotation, which will affect the length of time you need to wait. For transfers and new supplies in already electrified areas where standard tariffs apply and no additional infrastructure is required, quotations should be immediate; for minor projects, quotations should be issued within 17 days of receipt of your application; for major projects, you may have to wait 43 days.

When you accept a quotation, you must pay the connection fees, deposits and any other charges/guarantees that may be required, depending on the size and type of the supply. An account is then opened for you in Eskom's Customer Information and Billing system before any necessary work is undertaken. Transfers of supply involving no new infrastructure should be effected within 24 hours; transfers of supply involving new infrastructure can take up to 30 days, new connections involving minor work up to three months and new connections involving major work an average of 77 days (in which case you should ensure that you have a good supply of matches and candles!).

The electricity industry in South Africa is well regulated in all areas, including wiring standards, appliances, distribution, billing, meters and transformers. The National Electricity Regulator (NER, ☎ 012-401 4600, 💻 www.ner.org.za) regulates the electricity supply industry, while Standards South Africa (💻 www.stansa.co.za), which is a division of the South Africa Bureau of Standards (SABS, 💻 www.sabs.co.za), sets the standards for electrical installations, which were updated in 2003. All properties must have an electrical compliance certificate, and most modern properties (e.g. less than 20 years old) have good electrical installations. If you have any problems with your electricity supplier, contact the NER.

Power Supply

The electricity supply in urban South Africa is generally 220/230 volts AC with a frequency of 50 hertz (cycles), although there are variations, including Port Elizabeth at 220/250 volts and Pretoria at 250 volts. Plugs are mostly 15 amp three-pin (round pin), although 5 amp two-pin plugs are used for some low-voltage appliances.

If you have electrical equipment rated at 110 volts AC (for example, from the US) you will require a converter or a step-down transformer to convert it to 220 or 250 volts. However, some electrical appliances are fitted with a 110/220-volt switch. Check for the switch, which may be inside the casing, and make sure it's switched to 220 or 250 volts **before** connecting the appliance to the power supply. Converters can be used for heating appliances, but transformers are required for motorised appliances. Add up the wattage of the devices you intend to connect to a transformer and make sure that its power rating **exceeds** this sum.

Generally, small high-wattage electrical appliances, such as kettles, toasters, heaters, and irons need large transformers. Motors in large appliances such as cookers, refrigerators, washing machines, dryers and dishwashers will need replacing or fitting with a large transformer. In most cases it's simpler to buy new appliances in South Africa, which are of good quality and reasonably priced (see page 267), and sell them when you leave if you cannot take them with you. Note also that the dimensions of cookers, microwave ovens, refrigerators, washing machines, dryers and dishwashers purchased abroad may differ from those in South Africa, so they may not fit into a South African kitchen.

An additional problem with some electrical equipment is the frequency rating, which, in some countries, e.g. the US, is 60 hertz (hz) and not South Africa's 50hz. Electrical equipment **without** a motor is generally unaffected by the drop in frequency to 50hz (except televisions). Equipment with a motor may run with a 20 per cent drop in speed, but automatic washing machines, cookers, electric clocks, record players and tape recorders must be converted to 50hz. To find out, look at the label on the back of the equipment. If it says 50/60hz, it should work properly; if it says 60hz, you can try it, **but first ensure that the voltage is correct as outlined above.** Bear in mind that the transformers and motors of electrical devices designed to run at 60hz will run hotter at 50hz, so make sure that apparatus has sufficient space around it to allow for cooling.

Power cuts (many lasting just a few micro-seconds – long enough to crash a computer!) are frequent in many areas of South Africa, particularly in rural parts but also in the major cities: for example, Johannesburg was plagued by power cuts in the winter of 2004. The electricity supply can also be unstable, with power surges commonplace. If you use a computer, you should have an uninterrupted power supply (UPS) with a battery backup, which allows you time to shut down your computer and save your work after a power failure. If you live in an area where cuts are frequent and rely on electricity for your livelihood, e.g. for operating a computer, fax machine and other equipment, you may need to install a back-up generator.

SURVIVAL TIP

Even more important than a battery back-up is a power surge protector for appliances such as TVs, computers and fax machines, without which you risk equipment being damaged or destroyed.

In remote areas you must install a generator or solar power system (see page 257) if you want electricity, as there's no mains electricity, although some people make do with gas and oil lamps (and without TV and other modern conveniences).

Tariffs

Connection fees vary widely according to your intended consumption (known as your 'notified maximum demand' or NMD): you might pay as little as R1,000 (£87) for a small summer holiday home with just a few power points but as much as R7,700 (£670) for a mansion chock full of electrical appliances. You pay 27.95 cents (2.43p) per kWh for the electricity you consume (among the lowest rates in the world) but must also pay a monthly 'service' charge of R40.80 (£3.50) plus a monthly 'network' charge of R63.63 (£5.50), R134.51 (£11.70), R270.96 (£23.50) or R310.82 (£27), depending on your consumption, plus 'administration' charges for the privilege of being an Eskom customer!

If you have an NMD of at least 25 kilovolt-amperes (kVA) and use at least part of your electricity during Eskom's off-peak periods (10pm to 6am on weekdays, weekends and public holidays), you might qualify for a reduced tariff called 'Nightsave (Urban)'.

Payment

There are many different ways to pay your electricity bill: by direct debit, cheque, credit card (only up to payments of R5,000/£435), via the internet, or in person at any of the thousands of payment points throughout the country, including Eskom Walk-In, banks (ABSA, FNB, Nedbank and Standard Bank), Pick 'n Pay shops and post offices.

There are two payment systems: a monthly billed system (which is most likely to apply to you) and via a prepayment meter. The latter method was introduced for the benefit of poor people and those living in slum and rural areas. You must buy tokens to insert into your electricity meter. Tokens can be of any value, as they're coded when you buy them. There are over 3,000 outlets in South Africa selling tokens, including Eskom offices.

Monthly billed customers can choose from a wide range of schemes according to their electricity use. Details are provided on the Eskom website (under 'tariffs').

Gas

Natural gas is of minimal importance in South Africa, currently accounting for a mere 2 per cent of the total energy supply. For example, one of the major providers, Egoli Gas (💻 www.egoligas.co.za), currently has only around 12,500 customers in the Greater Johannesburg area. But gas's position as a poor relation is set to change because the country has recently initiated a project to develop the gas industry, based on a supply from natural gasfields in Mozambique. The first phase, due to take place in 2004, is the opening of an 860km (534mi) transmission pipeline from the Pande gasfields to north-eastern South Africa. By around 2012, natural gas is intended to supply between 5 and 7 per cent of South Africa's energy needs from a transmission net of 2,300km (1,429mi), including a pipeline from Namibia's offshore gasfields to Cape Town and Port Elizabeth. The gas will be supplied by private companies, subject to state regulation.

Liquefied petroleum gas (LPG) is sold in bottles but isn't widely available owing to limited demand. Most poor households (the vast majority in South Africa) cannot afford the bottles and appliances: a large bottle costs R300 (£26) plus a deposit of R85 (£7.40). Bottled gas is mostly used for cooking but can also be used to provide hot water and heating. A bottle used just for cooking lasts an average family around six weeks. Some people keep their gas bottles outside, often under a lean-to. If you do, you must buy propane gas rather than butane, as it can withstand a greater range of temperatures than butane, which is for internal use only. Although bottled gas is very safe, if you use it you must inform your household insurance company, as there's an extra premium to pay.

Water

South Africa is a dry country subject to periodic droughts, and water supply is a contentious issue in the country, both because of potential, serious shortages in the near future and because of the many much-publicised incidents in recent years when people who haven't paid their bills were cut off. Despite these problems, water in South Africa is inexpensive compared with many countries - slightly cheaper than in Australia and the US and around a third of the price of water in the UK. for example - but the situation is changing.

There isn't a central water provider in South Africa, where 15 water boards control the water in their area. These invariably rely on private companies for their supplies, which is a contentious issue, as the privatisation of the water supply is seen as an obstacle to the provision of reliable, free or inexpensive water to the country's poor. For example, Johannesburg's water board, Johannesburg Water (🖳 www.johannesburgwater.co.za), is supplied by Rand Water (🖳 www.randwater.co.za), a large operation, supplying water in five provinces: Free State, Gauteng, Limpopo (Northern Province), Mpumalanga and North West; it also supplies around 60 per cent of South African industry. In 2000, the French company Suez Lyonnaise Des Eaux signed one of the largest water contracts in the world, taking over a large section of South Africa's water utilities, and other companies have followed: Biwater, Vivendi and Saur, for example, all now own part of South Africa's water supply.

Since the end of apartheid in 1994, pipes that used to supply the poorer regions of Johannesburg with free, clean water have been slowly replaced with prepaid pumps, installed by private companies. Each water pump has a counter that deducts units from a pre-paid card, eliminating the difficulty and expense of issuing bills and collecting payment, and trials of similar meters are now taking place in other areas.

Since the private companies have begun to take over, prices have gone up, water quality has deteriorated and the poor have suffered. In the city of Nelspruit, for example, prices rose by over 400 per cent in the five years following Biwater's appointment as supplier in 1995. Since 1996, over 10 million South Africans have had their water cut off after being unable to pay their bills. This has led to the rise of the 'struggle plumber', who knows how to bypass or unblock pipes leading from the main supply to individual homes. And water prices are set to increase further (at least 6 per cent) in much of South Africa following drought, particularly in the north of the country.

The consequences of these price increases and the consequent cut-offs have been severe. For example, in 2000, when many people in Kwazulu-Natal had their water cut off after failing to pay bills, they resorted to drinking untreated water from rivers, ponds and even puddles. By the end of 2001, over 100,000 people had been infected with cholera, which had been almost non-existent in South Africa for decades.

Connection procedures, pricing and billing of water supplies vary according to the local utility and supplier, but the following is an example of 2004/05 tariffs (from the above-mentioned Johannesburg Water):

Litres ('000)	Rand Per 1,000 Litres
0 – 6	0
7 – 10	3.60
11 – 15	4.80
16 – 20	6.00
21 – 40	7.19
Over 40	8.50

Wells

When buying a property in South Africa, always confirm that it has a reliable water source. A well or spring may be quaint, but they can dry up, particularly in parts of central South Africa. Subject to availability, well water is usually excellent (and free), although you may need a pump (manual or electric) to bring it to the surface. However, if a property gets its water from a spring or well (possibly on a neighbour's land), make sure that there's no dispute over its ownership and your rights to use it, e.g. that it cannot be stopped or drained away by your neighbours.

You can create your own well if land has water. Dowsing (finding water by holding a piece of forked wood) is as accurate as anything devised by modern science and has an 80 per cent success rate, even though the 'science' behind it isn't understood. A good dowser or water diviner can estimate the amount and quality of water available to within 10 or 20 per cent accuracy. Before buying rural land without a water supply, engage an experienced dowser with a successful track record to check it.

Water Heaters

If you need to install a hot water boiler or immersion heater, ensure that it's large enough for the property, e.g. 100 litres for a studio apartment, 150 litres for a two-bedroom house, 200 litres for three to four rooms and 300 litres for five to seven rooms or two bathrooms. Many holiday homes have boilers that are inadequate for more than two people.

If you need to install a water heater or a larger water heater, you should consider the merits of both electric and bottled-gas heaters (if the latter is available). An electric water boiler with a capacity of 75 litres (barely sufficient for two people) usually takes between 75 and 125 minutes (in winter) to heat water to 40°C (104°F). A gas flow-through water heater is more expensive to purchase and install than an electric boiler, but you get unlimited hot water immediately whenever you want it and there are no standing charges. A gas heater should have a capacity of 10 to 16 litres per minute if it's to be used for a shower.

There's usually little difference in quality between different priced heaters, although a gas water heater with a permanent flame may use up to 50 per cent more gas than one without. A resident family with a constant consumption is usually better off with an electric heater, while non-residents using a property for short periods will find a self-igniting gas heater more economical. A solar power system can also be used to provide hot water (see page 257).

Security Measures

Before moving into a new home, you should check where the main stop-valve (stopcock) is located, so that you can turn off the water supply in an emergency. If the water supply stops for any reason, you should ensure that all the taps are turned off to prevent flooding when the supply starts again. In community properties (see page 143), the tap to turn the water on or off is usually located outside the building.

When leaving a property empty for an extended period, particularly during the winter in an area where there's the possibility of freezing, you should turn off the main stopcock, switch off the system's controls and drain the pipes as well as toilets (you can put salt in the toilet bowls to prevent freezing) and radiators. It's also recommended to have your cold water tank and the tank's ball valves checked periodically for corrosion, and to check the hoses on appliances such as washing machines and dishwashers. **It can be expensive if a pipe bursts and the leak goes undiscovered for a long time!**

WILLS

If you have assets (e.g. a home) in South Africa, you should make a South African will, which will specify how they're to be disposed of in the event of your death. **A will made in a foreign country won't be valid.** South Africa has a high rate of intestate deaths (people who die without leaving a will), which leads to a great deal of inconvenience and heartache for dependants. If you die without a will, your assets will be divided up as per the Intestate Succession Act, which might not be what you wanted. As well as this, your dependants might face delays in collecting their inheritance, tax penalties and administration charges.

South Africa has 'freedom of testation', meaning that you can name your own heirs. This, however, doesn't mean that you can put whatever you like in your will: it must comply with the terms of the Wills Act. To ensure that it does, it's important to have it drawn up by a professional, e.g. a lawyer or a trust company. It's recommended that you keep the will as simple as possible, identify your heirs clearly to avoid confusion, ensure that the terms are practical and divide the assets equitably to avoid disputes.

Don't use a will to leave instructions about organ donation or your funeral or cremation: by the time the will comes into operation, it will be too late. Also be careful about certain instructions that might be difficult or unwise for the executor to carry out. For example, an instruction to sell shares might oblige your heirs to do so when the stock price is low, thereby losing money.

An executor is appointed by the Master of the High Court to deal with your estate, although you can nominate your own executor and the Master will invariably agree to your choice. If you don't nominate an executor or he dies before you do, the Master will consider written nominations from your family. An executor's task is to collect your assets and debts, to settle the latter and divide the balance of your assets among your heirs. Normally, he will first put a notice in the *Government Gazette* and local newspaper inviting your creditors to notify him of any claims against your estate. The executor also collects details of your investments, values your assets and works out your tax liability. If there isn't enough money in your estate to pay your debts, your heirs might be asked to make up the difference or assets from your estate might be sold.

A 'Liquidation and Distribution Account' is submitted to the Master of the High Court, who must approve it and leave it open for inspection by anybody concerned for at least 21 days. This is done by putting a notice in the *Government Gazette* and local newspaper. If anybody has an objection, they approach the Master, who discusses it with the executor before reaching a decision, with which the executor must comply. When any objections have been dealt with, the executor can finalise the estate.

This process can take up to nine months: three to four weeks for the Master of the High Court to appoint an executor; 6 to 24 weeks to draw up a Liquidation and Distribution Account; two to four weeks for the Master to check the Account; three or four weeks for it to lie open for inspection; and two to six weeks to finalise the estate.

Your estate has to bear the following costs:

- Master's fees of between R42 (£3.65) and R600 (£52.17), depending on the value of the estate;
- Executor's fees, which by law cannot exceed 3.5 per cent of the gross assets (i.e. the amount before deducting debts or tax) of the estate, plus 6 per cent of any income (e.g. dividends, interest or rent) which the executor collects on behalf of the estate before it is finalised;
- Any valuations which the executor might have to arrange, e.g. of a property;
- Newspaper advertisements;
- Bank charges for the account that the executor must open in the name of your estate, in accordance with the Administration of Estates Act;
- Transfer costs of houses and other property, and fees for the cancellation of bonds;
- Estate duty (see page 216);
- Funeral expenses.

Your executor needs the following documents to finalise your will (you should ensure that your dependants know where to find them when you die): last signed original will, identity document, marriage certificate (if applicable), prenuptial agreement (if applicable), divorce order and degree of settlement (if applicable), copies of identity documents and marriage certificates of all heirs, names and addresses of your employer and pension fund, details of your medical aid fund, income tax details, vehicle registration details, any share or unit trust certificates, title deeds of any property owned, details of any other investments, mortgage bonds, cheque books and credit cards, details of all your debts and of any contracts that you have entered into, e.g. short-term or life insurance policies, and your death certificate.

APPENDICES

APPENDIX A: EMBASSIES

Selected foreign and South African embassies and high commissions are detailed below.

Foreign Embassies & High Commissions

Some countries have more than one ambassadorial office in South Africa and, before writing or visiting, you're recommended to confirm that you have the correct office. The addresses and telephone numbers for selected representative offices in South Africa are listed below:

Australia: Australian High Commission, PO Box 4749, Cape Town 8000 (☎ 021-419 5425).

Belgium: Belgian Consulate General, PO Box 2717, Cape Town 8000 (☎ 021-419 4690).

Botswana: Botswana Consulate, 4th Floor, Southern Life Building, Cape Town 8001 (☎ 021-421 1045).

Canada: Canadian High Commission, 19th Floor, Reserve Bank Building, St George's Mall, Cape Town (☎ 021-423 5240).

Chile: Chilean Embassy, PO Box 2067, Cape Town 8000 (☎ 021-421 2344).

China: Chinese Consulate, PO Box 1122, Cape Town 8000 (☎ 021-418 1187/9).

Denmark: Danish Embassy, PO Box 2942, Pretoria 0001 (☎ 012-322 0595).

European Union: Office of the European Union, PO Box 2515, Cape Town 8000 (☎ 021-423 0305).

France: French Consulate, PO Box 1702, Cape Town 8000 (☎ 021-423 1575).

Germany: German Embassy, 180 Blackwood Street, Pretoria (☎ 012-344 3854).

India: Indian High Commission, PO Box 3316, Cape Town 8000 (☎ 021-419 8110).

Ireland: Irish Embassy, Tulbagh Park, 1234 Church Street, Arcadia, Pretoria (☎ 012-342 5062).

Israel: Israeli Embassy, 3rd Floor, Dashing Centre, 339 Hilda Street, Hatfield, Pretoria (☎ 012-342 2693).

Italy: Italian Embassy, 796 George Avenue, 0083 Arcadi, Pretoria (☎ 012-430 5541).

Japan: Japanese Consulate, 2100 Standard Bank Building, Main Tower, Foreshore, Cape Town 8001 (☎ 021-425 1695).

Netherlands: Netherlands Consulate, PO Box 346, Cape Town 8000 (☎ 021-421 5660).

Norway: Norwegian Embassy, PO Box 4446, Cape Town 8000 (☎ 021-418 1276).

Portugal: Portuguese Consulate, PO Box 3433, Cape Town 8000 (☎ 021-418 0080).

Singapore: Singapore High Commission, 173 Beckett Street, Arcadia, Pretoria (☎ 012-343 4374).

Spain: Spanish Consulate, Southern Life Centre, Shortmarket Street 37, Cape Town (☎ 021-422 2415).

Sweden: Swedish Embassy, PO Box 3982, Cape Town 8000 (☎ 021-418 1276).

Switzerland: Swiss Embassy, PO Box 2289, Pretoria 0001 (☎ 012-436 707).

United Kingdom: British Consulate, PO Box 500, Cape Town 8000 (☎ 021-425 3670).

United States of America: American Embassy, PO Box 6773, Roggebaai, Cape Town (☎ 021-421 4280).

South African Embassies & High Commissions

The following is a selected list of South African embassies and high commissions in other countries.

Argentina: Embassy of South Africa, MT de Alvear 590, Piso 8, 1058 Capital Federal Buenos Aires (☎ 1-317 2900).

Australia: South African High Commission, Cnr Rhodes Place & State Circle, Yarralumla, Canberra, ACT 2600 (☎ 02-6273 2424).

Belgium: South African Embassy, Wetstraat 26, Box 7/8, 1000 Brussels (☎ 02-285 4400).

Canada: South African High Commission, 15 Sussex Drive, Ottawa, Ontario K1M 1MB (☎ 613-744 0330).

Chile: Embassy of South Africa, Avenida 11 de Septiembre 2353, Piso 17, Providencia, Santiago (☎ 231 2862).

China: South African Embassy, C801 Room, Yansha Centry, Liang Ma He Road, Chao Yang District, Beijing (☎ 10-6465 1941).

Denmark: South African Embassy, Gammel Vartov Vej 8, Box 128, 2900 Hellerup (☎ 3918-0155).

Finland: Embassy of South Africa, Rahapajankatu 1A5, 00160 Helsinki (☎ 9-6860 3100).

France: Embassy of South Africa, 59 Quai d'Orsay, 75343 Paris Cedex 07 (☎ 53-592 323).

Germany: Embassy of the Republic of South Africa, Tiergartenstrasse 18, 10785 Berlin (☎30-220730).

India: South African High Commission, B-18 Vasant Marg, Vasant Vihar, New Delhi 110057 (☎ 11-611 9411).

Netherlands: South African Embassy, Wassenaarseweg 40, 2596 CJ Den Hagg (☎ 070-392 4501).

Singapore: High Commission of South Africa, 15th Floor, Odeon Towers, 331 North Bridge Road (☎ 6-339 3319).

Spain: Embassy of South Africa, Claudio Coello 91, 28006 Madrid (☎ 91-436 3780).

Sweden: South African Embassy, Linnegatan 76, 11523 Stockholm (☎ 8-243 950).

Switzerland: South African Embassy, Alpenstrasse 29, 3006 Bern (☎ 31-350 1313).

United Kingdom: South African High Commission, South Africa House, Trafalgar Square, London WC2N 5DP (☎ 020-7451 7299, 💻 www.southafricahouse.com).

United States of America: South African Embassy, 3051 Massachusetts Avenue, NW Washington DC 20008 (☎ 202-232 4400, 💻 www.saembassy.org).

Appendix B: Further Reading

Property Magazines

The following English-language magazines contain articles about and advertisements for property in South Africa.

Homes Overseas Magazine (🖳 www.homesoverseas.co.uk). A monthly UK magazine which includes articles about buying property in South Africa and other countries.

Property Investor News (🖳 www.property-investor-news.com). A monthly UK magazine which includes articles about buying property in South Africa and other countries.

The Property Magazine (🖳 www.thepropertymag.co.za). A South African magazine distributed free to upmarket homes in South Africa and available from newsagents for around R30 (£2.60).

World Of Property, Outbound Publishing, 1 Commercial Road, Eastbourne, East Sussex BN21 3XQ, UK (☎ 01323-726040, ✉ outbounduk@aol.com). Quarterly magazine containing details of properties for sale in South Africa (and other countries).

Books

The books listed below are just a small selection of the many written for those planning to buy a home or work in South Africa. Note that some titles may be out of print but may still be obtainable from book shops and libraries. Books prefixed with an asterisk are recommended by the author.

Living & Working

The A to Z of Careers in South Africa (Don Nelson).

The A to Z of Work and Study Opportunities in South Africa (Don Nelson).

Business Blue Book of South Africa 2003 (National Publishing).

Doing Business in South Africa, editors Jonathan Reuvid and Ian Priestner (Kogan Page).

Everyman's Guide to the South African Economy, Andre Roux (Zebra).

The 50 Most Promising Companies in South Africa, Corporate Research Foundation (Zebra).

South Africa Business Guidebook: The Essential Guide to Doing Business in SA, (WriteStuff Publishing).

Starting Your Own Business in South Africa, Guy Macleod (Oxford University Press).

Successful Small Business Management in South Africa, Collin Wright (Struik).

Tourist Guides

Best Hikes in Southern Africa, David Bristow (Struik).

Birds of Southern Africa, Gordon Lindsay Maclean Roberts (New Holland).

Field Guide to the Mammals of Southern Africa, Chris and Tilde Stuart (New Holland).

Frommer's South Africa, (Frommer's).

Insight Guide South Africa, (Insight Guides).

LetsGo 2004 South Africa, (Let's Go Publications).

Safari Companion, Richard D Estes (Russell Friedman Books).

South Africa Eyewitness Travel Guides, (DK Publishing Inc).

***South Africa, Lesotho & Swaziland** (Lonely Planet).

***South Africa, Lesotho & Swaziland, The Rough Guide** (Rough Guides).

Top Birding Spots of Southern Africa, Hugh Chittenden (Southern).

Trees of Southern Africa, Keith Coates Palgrave (Struik).

Two Oceans, GM Branch (David Phillip).

Travel

The Electric Elephant, Dan Jacobson (Hamish Hamilton).

***The Lost World of the Kalahari**, Laurens van der Post (Penguin).

***Not Home Yet**, Justin Cartwright (HarperCollins).

Somewhere Over the Rainbow: Travels in South Africa, Gavin Bell (Trafalgar Square).

***South of the Limpopo: Travels through South Africa**, Dervla Murphy (Penguin).

Food & Wine

Simply South Africa: A Culinary Journey, Elaine Hurford (Struik).

South African Plonk Buyer's Guide, David Biggs (Ampersand).

***South African Wine Guide**, John Platter (Newsome McDowall).

Taste of South Africa (Human & Rousseau).

The Wines of South Africa, James Seely (Faber & Faber).

Fiction

***Age of Iron**, JM Coetzee (Penguin).

***Cry, The Beloved Country**, Alan Paton (Penguin).

***Disgrace**, JM Coetzee (Penguin).

A Dry White Season, Andre Brink (Penguin).

Fools and Other Stories, Njabulo Ndebele (Readers International).

July's People, Nadine Gordimer (Penguin).

The Heart of Redness, Zakes Mda (Farrar, Straus and Giroux).

Mafeking Road and Other Stories, Herman Charles Bosman (Human & Rousseau).

A Place Called Vatmaar, AHM Scholtz (Kwela Books).

***Selected Stories**, Nadine Gordimer (Bloomsbury).

The Smell of Apples, Mark Behr (Abacus).

***Unto Dust**, Herman Charles Bosman (Human & Rousseau).

***Welcome to Our Hillbrow**, Phaswane Mpe (International Specialized Book Service).

Miscellaneous

Anatomy of a Miracle: The End of Apartheid and the Birth of the New South Africa, Patti Waldmeir (Penguin).

The ANC and the Liberation Struggle: A Critical Political Biography, Dale McKinley (Pluto Press).

The Atlas of Apartheid, AJ Christopher (Witwatersrand University Press).

***The Boer War**, Thomas Pakenham (Abacus).

***Cape Town: The Making of a City**, Nigel Worden, Elizabeth van Heyningen and Vivian Bickford-Smith (David Phillip).

Cecil Rhodes, William Plomer (David Phillip).

***The Country of My Skull**, Antjie Krog (Three Rivers Press).

A Dictionary of South African English on Historical Principles: South African Words and their Origins (Oxford University Press).

Discovering Southern African Rock Art, JD Lewis-Williams (David Phillip).

A History of South Africa, Frank Welsh (HarperCollins).

***Illustrated History of South Africa**, edited by Dougie Oakes (Readers Digest).

***The Kruger National Park: A Social and Political History**, Jane Carruthers (University of Natal).

The Life and Times of Thabo Mbeki, Adrian Hadland and Jovial Rantao (Struik).

***Long Walk to Freedom**, Nelson Mandela (Abacus).

Mandela: The Authorised Biography, Anthony Sampson (Jonathan Ball/HarperCollins).

***My Traitor's Heart**, Rian Malan (Grove Press).

The New Century of South African Poetry, editor Michael Chapman (Jonathan Ball Publishers).

The Politics of Race, Class and Nationalism in 20th Century South Africa, editors Shula Marks and Stanley Trapido (Longman).

Robben Island - Symbol of Resistance, Barbara Hutton (Sacred Books).

Sing the Beloved Country: The Struggle for the New South Africa, Peter Hain (Pluto Press).

***Tomorrow is Another Country**, Allister Sparks (Univeristy of Chicago Press).

The Transfer of Power in South Africa, Rodney Davenport (Toronto University Press).

Trevor Huddleston, A Life, Robin Denniston (Macmillan).

Twentieth-Century South Africa, Willian Beinart (Oxford University Press).

The World that Made Mandela, Luli Callinicos (STE Publishers).

APPENDIX C: USEFUL WEBSITES

The ten chapters contain relevant website addresses. Those listed here are of general interest and not contained within the text.

General Information

AA Travel Guides (www.aatravel.co.za). Claimed to be the largest online travel database in South Africa.

Attorneys.co.za (www.attorneys.co.za). A directory of attorneys and law firms in South Africa.

Cape Town Tourism (www.cape-town.org). An extensive directory of information and links about all aspects of Cape Town.

City of Cape Town (www.capetown.gov.za). The site of the city's municipal authority, covering all aspects of the governance of Cape Town.

City of Johannesburg Official Website (www.joburg.org.za). A comprehensive site providing information about all aspects of the city, its history and entertainment.

Durban.co.za (www.durban.co.za). An extensive directory covering everything from business to lifestyle to travel in and around Durban.

Durban Official Website (www.durban.gov.za). A site covering Durban's business sector, council, community affairs, leisure, services and tourism.

Durban - South Africa's Playground (http://durban.kzn.org.za). The official provincial tourist site for Durban and the surrounding area.

EastLondonSA.com (www.eastlondonsa.com). Details about various aspects of life in East London, including accommodation, business, entertainment, history and transport.

Passport to the Best of Cape Town (http://capetown.gopassport.com). One of the best entertainment guides to Cape Town.

Port Elizabeth Omnibus Guide (www.pecc.gov.za). The official website for information about Port Elizabeth.

SA Everything (🖳 www.saeverything.co.za). A portal with links to sites covering a range of topics including business, computers, entertainment, home and garden, lifestyle, services, sport and travel.

SouthAfrica.info (🖳 www.safrica.info). Dubbed 'the official gateway to South Africa', this contains extensive, well presented information for tourists, investors, immigrants, citizens and South Africans abroad about public services, doing business, news, planning a trip, arts and entertainment, sport and much else.

South Africa Online (🖳 www.southafrica.co.za). A portal with links to sites covering the arts, business, computers, education, government, health, lifestyle, news, science, sport and travel.

South African Tourism (🖳 www.southafrica.net). The official tourist site and 'the most comprehensive online source of information on travel to and in South Africa'.

Statistics South Africa (🖳 www.statssa.gov.za). Lists of statistics about many aspects of South Africa, divided into categories.

Provincial Tourism Authorities

Eastern Cape Tourism (🖳 www.ectourism.co.za).

Free State Tourism (🖳 www.fstourism.co.za).

Gauteng Tourism Authority (🖳 www.gauteng.net).

Kwazulu-Natal Tourism Authority (🖳 www.tourism-kzn.org).

Limpopo (Northern Province) Tourism Authority (🖳 www.tourismboard.org.za).

Mpumalanga Tourism Authority (🖳 www.mpumalanga.com).

Northern Cape Tourism (🖳 www.northerncape.org.za).

Tourism North West (🖳 www.tourismnorthwest.co.za).

Western Cape Tourism (🖳 www.wcapetourism.org.za).

Expatriates

British Expatriates (🖳 www.britishexpat.com and www.ukworldwide.com). Two sites designed to keep British expatriates in touch with events in and information about the UK.

Direct Moving (🖳 www.directmoving.com). General expatriate information, tips and advice, and numerous links.

Escape Artist (🖳 www.escapeartist.com). One of the most comprehensive expatriate sites, including resources, links and directories covering most expatriate destinations. You can also subscribe to the free monthly online expatriate magazine, Escape from America.

ExpatAccess (🖳 www.expataccess.com). Aimed at those planning to move abroad, with free moving guides.

ExpatBoards (🖳 www.expatboards.com). A comprehensive site for expatriates, with popular discussion boards and special areas for Britons and Americans.

Expat Exchange (🖳 www.expatexchange.com). Reportedly the largest online 'community' for English-speaking expatriates, including articles on relocation and a question and answer facility.

Expat Forum (🖳 www.expatforum.com). Provides cost of living comparisons as well as over 20 country-specific forums.

Expat Mums (🖳 www.expat-moms.com). Information for expatriate mothers.

Expat Network (🖳 www.expatnetwork.com). The UK's leading expatriate website, which is essentially an employment network for expatriates, although it also includes numerous support services and a monthly online magazine, Nexus.

Expat Shopping (🖳 www.expatshopping.com). Order your favourite foods from home.

Expat World (🖳 www.expatworld.net). Information for American and British expatriates, including a subscription newsletter.

Expatriate Experts (🖳 www.expatexpert.com). Run by expatriate expert Robin Pascoe, providing advice and support.

Global People (🖳 www.peoplegoingglobal.com). Includes country-specific information with a particular emphasis on social and political issues.

Living Abroad (🖳 www.livingabroad.com). Includes an extensive list of country profiles, which are available only on payment.

Outpost Information Centre (🖳 www.outpostexpat.nl). Contains extensive country-specific information and links operated by the Shell Petroleum Company for its expatriate workers, but available to everyone.

Real Post Reports (🖳 www.realpostreports.com). Includes relocation services, recommended reading lists and 'real-life' stories written by expatriates in cities throughout the world.

Save Wealth Travel (🖳 www.savewealth.com/travel/warnings). Travel information and warnings.

Trade Partners (🖳 www.tradepartners.gov.uk). A UK government-sponsored site providing trade and investment (and general) information about most countries, including the US.

The Travel Doctor (🖳 www.tmvc.com.au/info10.html). Includes a country by country vaccination guide.

Travelfinder (🖳 www.travelfinder.com/twarn/travel_warnings.html). Travel information with warnings about danger areas.

World Health Organization (🖳 www.who.int). Health information.

The World Press (🖳 www.theworldpress.com). Links to media sites in practically every country in the world's media.

World Travel Guide (🖳 www.wtgonline.com). A general website for world travellers and expatriates.

Yankee Doodle (🖳 www.yankeedoodleiow.com). Import American products.

British Expatriates

British Expatriates (🖳 www.britishexpat.com and 🖳 www.ukworldwide.com). These websites keep British expatriates in touch with events and information in the United Kingdom.

Trade Partners (🖳 www.tradepartners.gov.uk). A government-sponsored website whose main aim is to provide trade and investment information for most countries. Even if you aren't intending to do business, the information is comprehensive and up to date.

American Expatriates

Americans Abroad (🖳 www.aca.ch). This website offers advice, information and services to Americans abroad.

US Government Trade (🖳 www.usatrade.gov). A huge website providing a wealth of information principally for Americans planning to trade and invest abroad, but useful for anyone planning a move abroad.

Australian & New Zealand Expatriates

Australians Abroad (🖳 www.australiansabroad.com). Information for Australians concerning relocating plus a forum to exchange information and advice.

Southern Cross Group (🖳 www.southern-cross-group.org). A website for Australians and New Zealanders providing information and the exchange of tips.

Women

Family Life Abroad (🖳 www.familylifeabroad.com). A wealth of information and articles on coping with family life abroad.

Foreign Wives Club (🖳 www.foreignwivesclub.com). An online community for women in bicultural marriages.

Third Culture Kids (🖳 www.tckworld.com). A website designed for expatriate children living abroad.

Travel For Kids (🖳 www.travelforkids.com). Advice on travelling with children around the world.

Women Of The World (🖳 www.wow-net.org). A website designed for female expats anywhere in the world.

Travel Information & Warnings

The websites listed below provide daily updated information about the political situation and natural disasters around the world, plus general travel and health advice and embassy addresses.

Australian Department of Foreign Affairs and Trade (🖳 www.dfat.gov.au/travel).

British Foreign and Commonwealth Office (🖳 www.fco.gov.uk).

Canadian Department of Foreign Affairs (💻 www.dfait-maeci.gc.ca). They also publish a useful series of free booklets for Canadians moving abroad.

New Zealand Ministry of Foreign Affairs and Trade (💻 www.mft.govt.nz).

SaveWealth Travel (💻 www.savewealth.com/travel/warnings).

The Travel Doctor (💻 www.tmvc.com.au). Contains a country by country vaccination guide.

US State Government (💻 www.state.gov/travel). US government website.

World Health Organization (💻 www.who.int).

Appendix D: Weights & Measures

South Africa uses the metric system of measurement. Those who are more familiar with the imperial system of measurement will find the tables on the following pages useful. Some comparisons shown are only approximate, but are close enough for most everyday uses. In addition to the variety of measurement systems used, clothes sizes often vary considerably with the manufacturer. The following websites allow you to make instant conversions between different measurement systems: www.omnis.demon.co.uk and www.unit-conversion.info.

Women's Clothes

Continental	34	36	38	40	42	44	46	48	50	52
UK	8	10	12	14	16	18	20	22	24	26
US	6	8	10	12	14	16	18	20	22	24

Pullovers	**Women's**						**Men's**					
Continental	40	42	44	46	48	50	44	46	48	50	52	54
UK	34	36	38	40	42	44	34	36	38	40	42	44
US	34	36	38	40	42	44	sm	med		lar	xl	

Men's Shirts

Continental	36	37	38	39	40	41	42	43	44	46
UK/US	14	14	15	15	16	16	17	17	18	-

Men's Underwear

Continental	5	6	7	8	9	10
UK	34	36	38	40	42	44
US	sm	med		lar		xl

Note: sm = small, med = medium, lar = large, xl = extra large

Children's Clothes

Continental	92	104	116	128	140	152
UK	16/18	20/22	24/26	28/30	32/34	36/38
US	2	4	6	8	10	12

Children's Shoes

Continental	18	19	20	21	22	23	24	25	26	27	28	29	30	31	32
UK/US	2	3	4	4	5	6	7	7	8	9	10	11	11	12	13
Continental	33	34	35	36	37	38									
UK/US	1	2	2	3	4	5									

Shoes (Women's and Men's)

Continental	35	36	37	37	38	39	40	41	42	42	43	44
UK	2	3	3	4	4	5	6	7	7	8	9	9
US	4	5	5	6	6	7	8	9	9	10	10	11

Weight

Imperial	Metric	Metric	Imperial
1oz	28.35g	1g	0.035oz
1lb*	454g	100g	3.5oz
1cwt	50.8kg	250g	9oz
1 ton	1,016kg	500g	18oz
2,205lb	1 tonne	1kg	2.2lb

Length

Imperial	Metric	Metric	Imperial
1in	2.54cm	1cm	0.39in
1ft	30.48cm	1m	3ft 3.25in
1yd	91.44cm	1km	0.62mi
1mi	1.6km	8km	5mi

Capacity

Imperial	Metric	Metric	Imperial
1 UK pint	0.57 litre	1 litre	1.75 UK pints
1 US pint	0.47 litre	1 litre	2.13 US pints
1 UK gallon	4.54 litres	1 litre	0.22 UK gallon
1 US gallon	3.78 litres	1 litre	0.26 US gallon

Note: An American 'cup' = around 250ml or 0.25 litre.

Area

Imperial	Metric	Metric	Imperial
1 sq. in	0.45 sq. cm	1 sq. cm	0.15 sq. in
1 sq. ft	0.09 sq. m	1 sq. m	10.76 sq. ft
1 sq. yd	0.84 sq. m	1 sq. m	1.2 sq. yds
1 acre	0.4 hectares	1 hectare	2.47 acres
1 sq. mile	2.56 sq. km	1 sq. km	0.39 sq. mile

Temperature

°Celsius	°Fahrenheit	
0	32	(freezing point of water)
5	41	
10	50	
15	59	
20	68	
25	77	
30	86	
35	95	
40	104	
50	122	

Notes: The boiling point of water is 100°C / 212°F.

Normal body temperature (if you're alive and well) is 37°C / 98.6°F.

Temperature Conversion

Celsius to Fahrenheit: multiply by 9, divide by 5 and add 32. (For a quick and approximate conversion, double the Celsius temperature and add 30.)

Fahrenheit to Celsius: subtract 32, multiply by 5 and divide by 9. (For a quick and approximate conversion, subtract 30 from the Fahrenheit temperature and divide by 2.)

Oven Temperatures

Gas	Electric	
	°F	°C
-	225–250	110–120
1	275	140
2	300	150
3	325	160
4	350	180
5	375	190
6	400	200
7	425	220
8	450	230
9	475	240

Air Pressure

PSI	Bar
10	0.5
20	1.4
30	2
40	2.8

Power

Kilowatts	Horsepower	Horsepower	Kilowatts
1	1.34	1	0.75

Appendix E: Maps

The map below shows the nine provinces of South Africa: Eastern Cape, Free State, Gauteng, Kwazulu-Natal, Limpopo (formerly Northern Province), Mpumalanga, North West, Northern Cape and Western Cape (sometimes called Western Province). The maps on the following pages show the country's major roads and principal climatic regions. A map showing geographical features can be found on page 6.

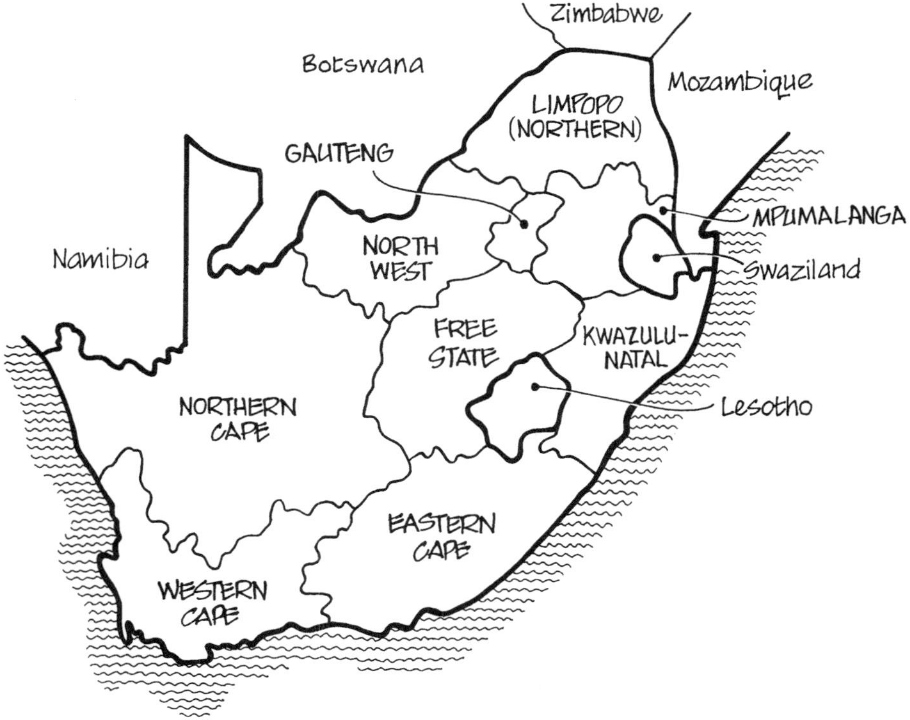

Major Roads

ZIMBABWE
MOZAMBIQUE
BOTSWANA
NAMIBIA
SWAZILAND
NDUMO
Pretoria
Nelspruit
Johannesburg
Upington
Kimberley
Bloemfontein
LESOTHO
Springbok
De Aar
Durban
Port Shepstone
Umtata
Beaufort West
East London
Cape Town
George
Mossel Bay
Knysna
Port Elizabeth
N1
N2
N3
N4
N7
N9
N10
N11
N12
N14

Climatic Regions

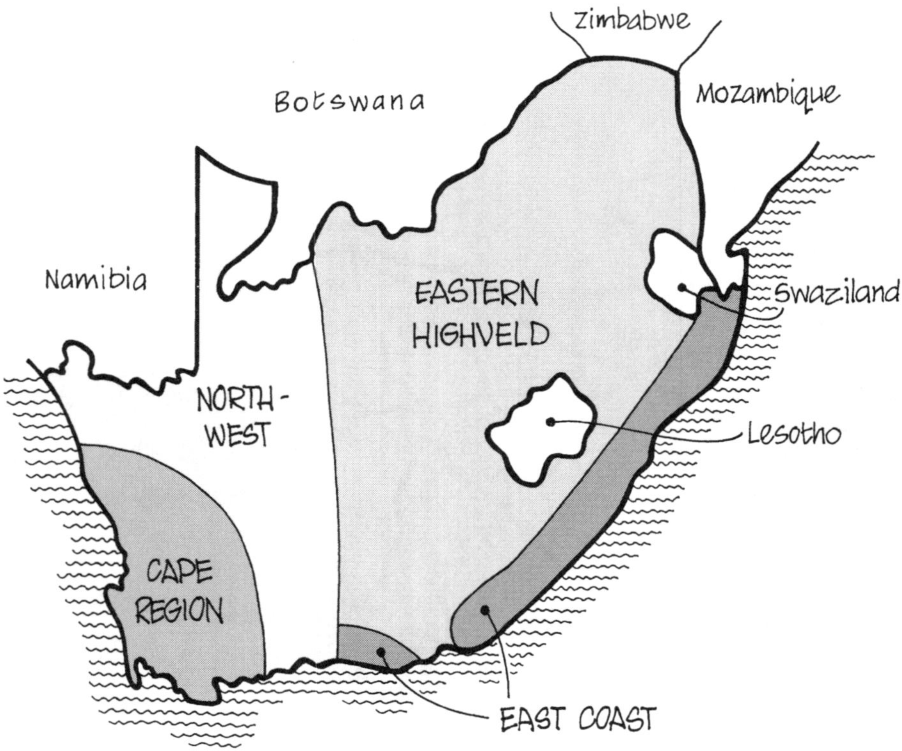

INDEX

A

B

C

D

E

F

G

H

I

K

L

M

N

O

P

R

S

T

U

V

W

Y

Menu
TABLE
MOUNTAIN

OTHER SURVIVAL BOOKS

The Alien's Guides: *The Alien's Guides to Britain* and *France* provide an 'alternative' look at life in these popular countries and will help you to appreciate the peculiarities (in both senses) of the British and French.

The Best Places to Buy a Home in France/Spain: The most comprehensive and up-to-date homebuying guides to France or Spain.

Buying, Selling and Letting Property: The most comprehensive and up-to-date source of information available for those intending to buy, sell or let a property in the UK and the only book on the subject updated annually.

Foreigners in France/Spain: Triumphs & Disasters: Real-life experiences of people who have emigrated to France and Spain.

How to Avoid Holiday and Travel Disasters: This book will help you to make the right decisions regarding every aspect of your travel arrangements and to avoid costly mistakes and disasters that can turn a trip into a nightmare.

Lifelines: Essential guides to specific regions of France and Spain, containing everything you need to know about local life. Titles in the series currently include the Costa del Sol, Dordogne/Lot, and Poitou-Charentes.

Renovating & Maintaining Your French Home: The ultimate guide to renovating and maintaining your dream home in France.

Retiring Abroad: The most comprehensive and up-to-date source of practical information available about retiring to a foreign country – contains profiles of the 20 most popular retirement destinations.

Wine Guides: *Rioja and its Wines* and *The Wines of Spain* are the most comprehensive and up-to-date sources of information available on the wines of Spain and of its most famous wine-producing region.

Broaden your horizons with Survival Books!

Order your copies today by phone, fax, post or email from: Survival Books, PO Box 146, Wetherby, West Yorks. LS23 6XZ, United Kingdom (☎/▤ +44 (0)1937-843523, ✉ orders@ survivalbooks.net, 💻 www.survivalbooks.net).

ORDER FORM

Qty.	Title	Price (incl. p&p)			Total
		UK	Europe	World	
	The Alien's Guide to Britain	£6.95	£8.95	£12.45	
	The Alien's Guide to France	£6.95	£8.95	£12.45	
	The Best Places to Buy a Home in France	£13.95	£15.95	£19.45	
	The Best Places to Buy a Home in Spain	£13.95	£15.95	£19.45	
	Buying a Home Abroad	£13.95	£15.95	£19.45	
	Buying a Home in Florida	£13.95	£15.95	£19.45	
	Buying a Home in France	£13.95	£15.95	£19.45	
	Buying a Home in Greece & Cyprus	£13.95	£15.95	£19.45	
	Buying a Home in Ireland	£11.95	£13.95	£17.45	
	Buying a Home in Italy	£13.95	£15.95	£19.45	
	Buying a Home in Portugal	£13.95	£15.95	£19.45	
	Buying a Home in South Africa	£13.95	£15.95	£19.45	
	Buying a Home in Spain	£13.95	£15.95	£19.45	
	Buying, Letting & Selling Property	£11.95	£13.95	£17.45	
	Foreigners in France: Triumphs & Disasters	£11.95	£13.95	£17.45	
	Foreigners in Spain: Triumphs & Disasters	£11.95	£13.95	£17.45	
	How to Avoid Holiday & Travel Disasters	£13.95	£15.95	£19.45	
	Costa del Sol Lifeline	£11.95	£13.95	£17.45	
	Dordogne/Lot Lifeline	£11.95	£13.95	£17.45	
	Poitou-Charentes Lifeline	£11.95	£13.95	£17.45	
	Living & Working Abroad	£14.95	£16.95	£20.45	
	Living & Working in America	£14.95	£16.95	£20.45	
	Living & Working in Australia	£14.95	£16.95	£20.45	
	Living & Working in Britain	£14.95	£16.95	£20.45	
	Living & Working in Canada	£16.95	£18.95	£22.45	
	Living & Working in the European Union	£16.95	£18.95	£22.45	
	Living & Working in the Far East	£16.95	£18.95	£22.45	
	Living & Working in France	£14.95	£16.95	£20.45	
	Living & Working in Germany	£16.95	£18.95	£22.45	
	Total carried forward (see over)				

ORDER FORM

Qty.	Title	Total brought forward			Total
		Price (incl. p&p)			
		UK	Europe	World	
	L&W in the Gulf States & Saudi Arabia	£16.95	£18.95	£22.45	
	L&W in Holland, Belgium & Luxembourg	£14.95	£16.95	£20.45	
	Living & Working in Ireland	£14.95	£16.95	£20.45	
	Living & Working in Italy	£16.95	£18.95	£22.45	
	Living & Working in London	£13.95	£15.95	£19.45	
	Living & Working in New Zealand	£14.95	£16.95	£20.45	
	Living & Working in Spain	£14.95	£16.95	£20.45	
	Living & Working in Switzerland	£16.95	£18.95	£22.45	
	Renovating & Maintaining Your French Home	£16.95	£18.95	£22.45	
	Retiring Abroad	£14.95	£16.95	£20.45	
	Rioja and its Wines	£11.95	£13.95	£17.45	
	The Wines of Spain	£13.95	£15.95	£19.45	
				Grand Total	

Order your copies today by phone, fax, post or email from: Survival Books, PO Box 146, Wetherby, West Yorks. LS23 6XZ, UK (☎/℻ +44 (0)1937-843523, ✉ orders@survivalbooks.net, 💻 www.survivalbooks.net). If you aren't entirely satisfied, simply return them to us within 14 days for a full and unconditional refund.

I enclose a cheque for the grand total/Please charge my Amex/Delta/Maestro (Switch)/MasterCard/Visa card as follows. (delete as applicable)

Card No. _ _ _ _ _ _ _ _ _ _ _ _ _ _ _ _ Security Code* _ _ _

Expiry date ____________ Issue number (Maestro/Switch only) ____________

Signature ____________ Tel. No. ____________

NAME ____________

ADDRESS ____________

____

____

* The security code is the last three digits on the signature strip.

NOTES

NOTES

NOTES

Notes

Notes

NOTES

Notes

www.solarbuzz.com

suntank.co.za

NOTES